D0323509

# Essentials

## of **Psychological Assessment** Series

Everything you need to know to administer, score, and interpret the major psychological tests.

I'd like to order the following *Essentials of Psychological Assessment*:

- ❑ WAIS®-III Assessment / 0471-28295-2
- ❑ WJ III™ Cognitive Abilities Assessment / 0471-34466-4
- ❑ Cross-Battery Assessment, Second Edition / 0471-75771-3
- ❑ Nonverbal Assessment / 0471-38318-X
- ❑ PAI® Assessment / 0471-08463-8
- ❑ CAS Assessment / 0471-29015-7
- ❑ MMPI-2™ Assessment / 0471-34533-4
- ❑ Myers-Briggs Type Indicator® Assessment / 0471-33239-9
- ❑ Rorschach® Assessment / 0471-33146-5
- ❑ Millon™ Inventories Assessment, Second Edition / 0471-21891-X
- ❑ TAT and Other Storytelling Techniques / 0471-39469-6
- ❑ MMPI-A™ Assessment / 0471-39815-2
- ❑ NEPSY® Assessment / 0471-32690-9
- ❑ Neuropsychological Assessment / 0471-40522-1
- ❑ WJ III™ Tests of Achievement Assessment / 0471-33059-0
- ❑ WMS®-III Assessment / 0471-38080-6
- ❑ Behavioral Assessment / 0471-35367-1
- ❑ Forensic Psychological Assessment / 0471-33186-4
- ❑ Bayley Scales of Infant Development II Assessment / 0471-32651-8
- ❑ Career Interest Assessment / 0471-35365-5
- ❑ WPPSI™-III Assessment / 0471-28895-0
- ❑ 16PF® Assessment / 0471-23424-9
- ❑ Assessment Report Writing / 0471-39487-4
- ❑ Stanford-Binet Intelligence Scales (SB5) Assessment / 0471-22404-9
- ❑ WISC®-IV Assessment / 0471-47691-9
- ❑ KABC-II Assessment / 0471-66733-1
- ❑ WIAT®-II and KTEA-II Assessment / 0471-70706-6
- ❑ Processing Assessment / 0471-71925-0
- ❑ School Neuropsychology / 0471-78372-2
- ❑ Cognitive Assessment with KAIT
  & Other Kaufman Measures / 0471-38317-1

**All titles are $34.95* each**

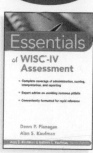

Essentials
of WISC®-IV
Assessment

- Complete coverage of administration, scoring, interpretation, and reporting
- Expert advice on avoiding common pitfalls
- Conveniently formatted for rapid reference

Dawn P. Flanagan
Alan S. Kaufman

Essentials
of School
Neuropsychology

- Complete coverage of administration, scoring, interpretation, and reporting
- Expert advice on avoiding common pitfalls
- Conveniently formatted for rapid reference

Daniel C. Miller

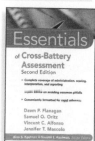

Essentials
of Cross-Battery
Assessment
Second Edition

- Complete coverage of administration, scoring, interpretation, and reporting
- Expert advice on avoiding common pitfalls
- Conveniently formatted for rapid reference

Dawn P. Flanagan
Samuel O. Ortiz
Vincent C. Alfonso
Jennifer T. Mascolo

**Please complete the order form on the back.**
**To order by phone, call toll free 1-877-762-2974**
**To order online: www.wiley.com/essentials**
**To order by mail: refer to order form on next page**

WILEY

# Essentials

## of **Psychological Assessment** Series

# ORDER FORM

Please send this order form with your payment (credit card or check) to:
John Wiley & Sons, Attn: J. Knott, 111 River Street, Hoboken, NJ 07030-5774

NAME _____

AFFILIATION _____

ADDRESS _____

CITY/STATE/ZIP _____

TELEPHONE _____

EMAIL _____

❏ Please add me to your e-mailing list

Quantity of Book(s) ordered _____ x \$34.95* each

| Shipping Charges: | Surface | 2-Day | 1-Day |
|---|---|---|---|
| First item | \$5.00 | \$10.50 | \$17.50 |
| Each additional item | \$3.00 | \$3.00 | \$4.00 |

For orders greater than 15 items, please contact Customer Care at 1-877-762-2974.

**PAYMENT METHOD:**
❏ Check/Money Order   ❏ Visa   ❏ Mastercard   ❏ AmEx

Card Number _____Exp. Date _____

Cardholder Name *(Please print)*_____

Signature _____
*Make checks payable to **John Wiley & Sons.** Credit card orders invalid if not signed.*
*All orders subject to credit approval. * Prices subject to change.*

**To order by phone, call toll free 1-877-762-2974**
**To order online: www.wiley.com/essentials**

# Essentials of
# Processing Assessment

# Essentials of Psychological Assessment Series
Series Editors, Alan S. Kaufman and Nadeen L. Kaufman

*Essentials of WAIS®-III Assessment*
by Alan S. Kaufman and Elizabeth O. Lichtenberger

*Essentials of CAS Assessment*
by Jack A. Naglieri

*Essentials of Forensic Psychological Assessment*
by Marc J. Ackerman

*Essentials of Bayley Scales of Infant Development–II Assessment*
by Maureen M. Black and Kathleen Matula

*Essentials of Myers-Briggs Type Indicator® Assessment*
by Naomi Quenk

*Essentials of WISC-III® and WPPSI-R® Assessment*
by Alan S. Kaufman and Elizabeth O. Lichtenberger

*Essentials of Rorschach® Assessment*
by Tara Rose, Nancy Kaser-Boyd, and Michael P. Maloney

*Essentials of Career Interest Assessment*
by Jeffrey P. Prince and Lisa J. Heiser

*Essentials of Cross-Battery Assessment*
by Dawn P. Flanagan and Samuel O. Ortiz

*Essentials of Cognitive Assessment with KAIT and Other Kaufman Measures*
by Elizabeth O. Lichtenberger, Debra Broadbooks, and Alan S. Kaufman

*Essentials of Nonverbal Assessment*
by Steve McCallum, Bruce Bracken, and John Wasserman

*Essentials of MMPI-2™ Assessment*
by David S. Nichols

*Essentials of NEPSY® Assessment*
by Sally L. Kemp, Ursula Kirk, and Marit Korkman

*Essentials of Individual Achievement Assessment*
by Douglas K. Smith

*Essentials of TAT and Other Storytelling Techniques Assessment*
by Hedwig Teglasi

*Essentials of WJ III® Tests of Achievement Assessment*
by Nancy Mather, Barbara J. Wendling, and Richard W. Woodcock

*Essentials of WJ III® Cognitive Abilities Assessment*
by Fredrick A. Schrank, Dawn P. Flanagan, Richard W. Woodcock, and Jennifer T. Mascolo

*Essentials of WMS®-III Assessment*
by Elizabeth O. Lichtenberger, Alan S. Kaufman, and Zona C. Lai

*Essentials of MMPI-A™ Assessment*
by Robert P. Archer and Radhika Krishnamurthy

*Essentials of Neuropsychological Assessment*
by Nancy Hebben and William Milberg

*Essentials of Behavioral Assessment*
by Michael C. Ramsay, Cecil R. Reynolds, and R. W. Kamphaus

*Essentials of Millon Inventories Assessment, Second Edition*
by Stephen N. Strack

*Essentials of PAI® Assessment*
by Leslie C. Morey

*Essentials of 16 PF® Assessment*
by Heather E. P. Cattell and James M. Schuerger

*Essentials of WPPSI™-III Assessment*
by Elizabeth O. Lichtenberger and Alan S. Kaufman

*Essentials of Assessment Report Writing*
by Elizabeth O. Lichtenberger, Nancy Mather, Nadeen L. Kaufman, and Alan S. Kaufman

*Essentials of Stanford-Binet Intelligence Scales (SB5) Assessment*
by Gale H. Roid and R. Andrew Barram

*Essentials of WISC-IV® Assessment*
by Dawn P. Flanagan and Alan S. Kaufman

*Essentials of KABC-II Assessment*
by Alan S. Kaufman, Elizabeth O. Lichtenberger, Elaine Fletcher-Janzen, and Nadeen L. Kaufman

*Essentials of WIAT®-II and KTEA-II Assessment*
by Elizabeth O. Lichtenberger and Donna R. Smith

*Essentials of Processing Assessment*
by Milton J. Dehn

# Essentials

## of Processing

## Assessment

Milton J. Dehn

John Wiley & Sons, Inc.

Copyright © 2006 by John Wiley & Sons, Inc. All rights reserved.

Published by John Wiley & Sons, Inc., Hoboken, New Jersey.
Published simultaneously in Canada.

No part of this publication may be reproduced, stored in a retrieval system, or transmitted in any form or by any means, electronic, mechanical, photocopying, recording, scanning, or otherwise, except as permitted under Sections 107 or 108 of the 1976 United States Copyright Act, without either the prior written permission of the Publisher, or authorization through payment of the appropriate per-copy fee to the Copyright Clearance Center, Inc., 222 Rosewood Drive, Danvers, MA 01923, (978) 750-8400, fax (978) 646-8600, or on the web at www.copyright.com. Requests to the Publisher for permission should be addressed to the Permissions Department, John Wiley & Sons, Inc., 111 River Street, Hoboken, NJ 07030, (201) 748-6011, fax (201) 748-6008, or online at http://www.wiley.com/go/permissions.

Limit of Liability/Disclaimer of Warranty: While the publisher and author have used their best efforts in preparing this book, they make no representations or warranties with respect to the accuracy or completeness of the contents of this book and specifically disclaim any implied warranties of merchantability or fitness for a particular purpose. No warranty may be created or extended by sales representatives or written sales materials. The advice and strategies contained herein may not be suitable for your situation. You should consult with a professional where appropriate. Neither the publisher nor author shall be liable for any loss of profit or any other commercial damages, including but not limited to special, incidental, consequential, or other damages.

This publication is designed to provide accurate and authoritative information in regard to the subject matter covered. It is sold with the understanding that the publisher is not engaged in rendering professional services. If legal, accounting, medical, psychological or any other expert assistance is required, the services of a competent professional person should be sought.

Designations used by companies to distinguish their products are often claimed as trademarks. In all instances where John Wiley & Sons, Inc. is aware of a claim, the product names appear in initial capital or all capital letters. Readers, however, should contact the appropriate companies for more complete information regarding trademarks and registration.

For general information on our other products and services please contact our Customer Care Department within the United States at (800) 762-2974, outside the United States at (317) 572-3993 or fax (317) 572-4002.

Wiley also publishes its books in a variety of electronic formats. Some content that appears in print may not be available in electronic books. For more information about Wiley products, visit our website at www.wiley.com.

**Library of Congress Cataloging-in-Publication Data:**

Dehn, Milton J.
    Essentials of processing assessment / Milton J. Dehn.
       p. cm. — (Essentials of psychological assessment series)
    Includes bibliographical references and index.
    ISBN-13: 978-0-471-71925-0 (paper)
    ISBN-10: 0-471-71925-0 (paper)
       1. Intelligence tests. 2. Cognition—Testing. I. Title. II. Series.

    BF431.D38 2005
    153.9'3—dc22

                                                    2005051361

Printed in the United States of America

10  9  8  7  6  5  4  3  2  1

*To my loving wife, Paula,*
*who for 36 years has fully*
*supported my endeavors.*
*She is a true psychologist,*
*one who effortlessly*
*understands human behavior.*

# CONTENTS

# SERIES PREFACE

I n the *Essentials of Psychological Assessment* series, we have attempted to provide the reader with books that will deliver key practical information in the most efficient and accessible style. The series features instruments in a variety of domains, such as cognition, personality, education, and neuropsychology. For the experienced clinician, books in the series will offer a concise yet thorough way to master utilization of the continuously evolving supply of new and revised instruments, as well as a convenient method for keeping up to date on the tried-and-true measures. The novice will find here a prioritized assembly of all the information and techniques that must be at one's fingertips to begin the complicated process of individual psychological diagnosis.

Wherever feasible, visual shortcuts to highlight key points are utilized alongside systematic, step-by-step guidelines. Chapters are focused and succinct. Topics are targeted for an easy understanding of the essentials of administration, scoring, interpretation, and clinical application. Theory and research are continually woven into the fabric of each book but always to enhance clinical inference, never to sidetrack or overwhelm. We have long been advocates of what has been called *intelligent testing*—the notion that a profile of test scores is meaningless unless it is brought to life by the clinical observations and astute detective work of knowledgeable examiners. Test profiles must be used to make a difference in the child's or adult's life, or why bother to test? We want this series to help our readers become the best intelligent testers they can be.

This volume provides practitioners with a framework for planning, conducting, and interpreting an assessment of cognitive processes. This systematic approach elucidates a challenging type of assessment that usually requires the compilation of an assessment battery from different tests. The author provides detailed information on which processes are measured by major contemporary intellectual scales, cognitive scales, memory scales, and scales purposely designed to assesses processing. After setting the stage by integrating theories of processing and examining relationships between processes and types of academic learning, the book applies a hypothesis-testing approach to processing assessment. Through step-by-step guidelines and worksheets, the author walks the reader through interpretation of intellectual and cognitive scales from a processing perspective and adds additional steps and insights to the interpretation of memory and processing scales. A *Processing Analysis Worksheet* that can be applied to any test or combination of tests is the heart of the interpretative model. It is our hope that the knowledge, insights, and practices gained from this volume will lead to more accurate diagnoses and more effective treatment for individuals who struggle with learning.

*Alan S. Kaufman, PhD, and Nadeen L. Kaufman, EdD, Series Editors*
Yale University School of Medicine

# One

## INTRODUCTION AND OVERVIEW

*All scientific theory is wrong. It is the job of science to improve theory. . . . In laying out the theory, we speak of what we think we know. We say that something is known if there is evidence to support the claim that it is known. Since such evidence is never fully adequate or complete, we do not imply that what we say "is known" is really (really) known to be true.*

—John Horn and Nayena Blankson, 2005, p. 41

In psychology, it is difficult to prove a theory because psychology is not a hard science. We deal with constructs that are difficult, if not impossible, to directly observe and measure. As Horn and Noll (1997) said, "No model of reality is reality" (p. 84). Consequently, we expect psychological theories and models to come and go. The historical path of the science of psychology is littered with theories that did not hold up under scientific investigation. For example, Galton (1883) believed that measures of sensory acuity and reaction time could provide an index of intelligence. In psychology, we have learned from the past. We are rightfully cautious of theories, and we demand extensive empirical evidence before we attempt to apply theoretical models.

The first premise of this book is that we need not wait until we have a proven theory of processing before we begin to routinely assess processing and apply processing models to diagnosis and treatment. The theoretical models of processing discussed in this book are at varying stages of development. These processing theories include a processing theory of learning, a cognitive theory of reading, a processing deficit theory of learning disabilities, information processing theory, neuropsychological theories, and theories of intelligence. Controversy surrounds these theories of processing and related assessment practices. Nonetheless, there is adequate evidence in support of cognitive processing constructs and the relationships various processes have with learning. Furthermore, we have the measurement technology in place to reliably and validly assess cognitive processes. Therefore, it is time to apply the existing knowledge and technology. Doing so will benefit those who struggle with processing and learning.

The second premise of this book is that psychological assessment helps us to better understand a struggling learner's cognitive processing strengths and weaknesses and provides us with credible hypotheses as to the cause of the learner's problems. Armed with such knowledge, we can more appropriately individualize interventions. However, this book is not about interventions or treatment for learning problems or processing problems. (The interested reader is referred to sources such as Mather and Wendling [2005].) Rather, it is about the cognitive processing assessment that should precede the design and implementation of interventions for learning problems and learning disabilities.

Psychologists and educators hold various beliefs about cognitive processes and the assessment of those processes. On one end of the continuum are those who believe that processing theories and models have limited merit and that processing can't really be assessed. On the other end are those who believe that processing constructs are sound and that processes can be measured directly with standardized instruments. In the middle are many psychologists and educators who are uncertain about processing constructs, such as working memory, and who are also unsure about how to assess processing and interpret the results. There are also those who accept processing constructs and the validity of assessment instruments designed to assess processing but consider the assessment a waste of time because of unclear aptitude-treatment interactions. Thus, it is not surprising that many school psychologists and related professionals conduct only a rudimentary assessment of processing or do none at all.

The main purpose of this book is to provide structure and guidance for using norm-referenced, standardized instruments to assess an individual's cognitive processes. The underlying goal of this book is to encourage psychologists and educators to effectively use what we currently know about processing and the assessment of processing to benefit individuals, especially those who struggle with learning or suffer from learning disabilities.

## COGNITIVE PROCESSES

The cognitive processes that underlie intellectual performance and learning are the focus of this book. Cognitive processing refers to all mental operations by which sensory input is perceived, transformed, stored, retrieved, and used. Carroll (1993, p. 10) defined a *cognitive process* as

[O]ne in which mental contents are operated on to produce some response. These mental contents may be representations or encodings either of external stimuli or of images, knowledges, rules, and similar materials from short-term or long-term memory. The response may be either covert (generally unobservable) or overt (observable).

**DON'T FORGET**

Cognitive processes are involved in perception, thinking, reasoning, problem solving, learning, and storing and retrieving information. As defined in this book, they do not include processes that are purely sensory or motoric.

Cognitive processes are at work whenever we think, reason, learn, problem solve, or store and retrieve information. Cognitive processing is only one aspect of brain functioning; there are many types of processing that go on in the brain. As used in this book, the term *processing* refers to *cognitive processing*. This book targets the higher level brain processes that are necessary for learning and successful daily functioning. Lower level processes, such as those that are purely sensory or motoric, are excluded from the definition of processing. Cognitive processing involves the complex integration and interaction of many interrelated processes that are spread throughout the brain. Most cognitive processing operates automatically, without directed effort or awareness, but at times, it enters our awareness and is controlled by decisions we make.

## ADVANCES IN PROCESSING ASSESSMENT

If information about an individual's processing capabilities is to be beneficial, then it must be information that is gathered through objective and valid methods. Those who challenge the validity and usefulness of current processing instruments may inadvertently be encouraging informal, subjective assessment that often results in misdiagnosis and misguided interventions. For instance, take the case of student who does not follow directions. This behavior has many possible causes, ranging from a hearing impairment to oppositional behavior. A common attribution for not following directions is that the student has a weakness in long-term memory storage and retrieval. To make such an inference based only on observations and other informal procedures is difficult to justify, given the abundance of highly reliable and valid measures of long-term storage and retrieval (see Chapter 7).

Part of the reluctance to assess processing may be due to the fact that valid as-

## DON'T FORGET

The most objective and valid assessment of processing is obtained through the use of standardized tests designed to assess processing.

sessment instruments for this purpose have been lacking until just recently. Psychological assessment of cognitive functioning has existed for a century, but only within the last generation have there been measurement tools designed for the direct assessment of processing. Prior to these recent developments, cognitive assessment instruments, namely IQ tests, focused mostly on the measurement of content (acquired knowledge) instead of processes. The number of assessment instruments that have developed to assess various aspects of processing has increased significantly within the last 15 years (see Appendix G). Most of these instruments are derived from empirically supported theories and have sufficient reliability and validity. Some focus on specific processes, such as phonemic awareness, while others sample a broader range of processes. Tests of memory, a critical cognitive process with many subtypes, have long been available but are underused when pupils are evaluated for learning disabilities. In addition to this new generation of processing instruments, many of the traditional scales have expanded into more direct assessment of cognitive processes. For instance, newer versions of traditional IQ tests have made the assessment of processing more explicit by including such factors as working memory and processing speed.

As processing assessment has been improving, research in the fields of reading, learning disabilities, cognitive psychology, psychometrics, and neuroscience has discovered much about the nature of cognitive processes and their relationships with learning (see Chapter 2 for a full discussion). For example, just a few years ago the construct of working memory was relatively unheard of outside of the field of cognitive psychology. Now there is a wealth of empirical evidence that clarifies and supports this new construct and its relationship with learning.

## PROCESSING AND LEARNING DISABILITIES

Since Public Law 94-142, federal legislation has defined a *learning disability* as "a disorder in one or more of the basic psychological processes" (Federal Register, December 29, 1977, p. 65083). This definition is consistent with the deficit model of learning disabilities and indicates that learning disabilities are due to deficiencies in one or more cognitive processes. Related definitions have defined a learning disability as a "perceptual processing deficit" (Cruickshank, 1977) and as "presumed to be due to central nervous system dysfunction" (Hammill, Leigh, McNutt, & Larsen, 1981, p. 336). Moreover, educational research, Torgesen,

Wagner, and Rashotte (1994), for example, has repeatedly found evidence of relationships between information processing deficits and learning disabilities. Whereas current federal law and regulations do not specifically require a processing assessment, an assessment of processing is certainly consistent with the law and currently accepted learning disability definitions.

With the elimination of the ability-achievement discrepancy requirement in the last round of federal special education legislation (Individuals with Disabilities Education Act [IDEA], 2004), many school systems across the nation are attempting to implement data-based interventions with students who are suspected of having a learning disability. How well a student responds to intervention is being used to determine eligibility for learning disability services instead of test scores. Moreover, advocates of the response-to-intervention model do not view processing weaknesses or deficits as relevant when designing individualized interventions. Consequently, intellectual, cognitive, and achievement testing has declined.

In fact, the current problem-solving intervention model minimizes the importance of etiology and aptitudes because it assumes that all students with low skills benefit from the delivery of similar interventions. While it is true that most low-skilled readers will benefit from basic evidence-based interventions, such as phonemic awareness training (National Reading Panel, 2000), not all learners benefit equally from the same interventions. The reason is that the same behaviors or learning problems can have different causes, causes that can often be identified prior to intervention by conducting an assessment. For example, a poor reader who has normal phonemic awareness but deficient long-term retrieval will not especially benefit from phonemic awareness training.

If learning depends on processing, information about a learner's processing strengths and weaknesses or deficits can only enhance the treatment design and increase the probability of success. While a global intellectual ability score is of little value in designing interventions, utilizing data about the individual's specific processes can lead to more effective interventions. Therefore, an assessment of processing should play a fundamental role in implementation of the new response-to-intervention model.

This book is predicated on a deficit model of learning disabilities in which a deficit in one or more cognitive processes accounts for academic learning difficulties or disabilities. In other words, it is presumed that a learning disability is related to,

## DON'T FORGET

The learning disability *deficit model* postulates that learning disabilities are associated with cognitive processing deficits that significantly impair learning.

if not caused by, some kind of processing deficiency within the individual. Of course, we all have cognitive processing strengths and weaknesses. For a processing weakness to be considered a deficit it must be severe enough to cause a significant impairment in some type of academic learning. To meet this criterion, the academic skill in question should be significantly delayed or subaverage, and the process of concern should be both subaverage and a significant intraindividual weakness. The implicit assumption of the processing deficit model is that a learning disability exists only when there is a processing deficit that can be associated with the specific academic learning deficiency.

Of course, all aspects of daily functioning throughout the life span depend on processing, not just academic learning, and processing deficits may be related to more than learning disorders. For instance, a deficit in executive processing has been linked to some behavioral disorders. Thus, processing assessment is conducted in several settings and for many reasons. Although the assessment practices covered in this text apply to any assessment of processing, the focus will be on psychological evaluations of individuals referred for learning problems.

## PROCESSING ASSESSMENT CHALLENGES

Given the many challenges inherent in processing assessment, it is understandable that many practitioners have avoided or minimized processing assessment. After the passage of Public Law 94-142 in the mid-1970s, states varied considerably in how they operationalized *basic psychological processes*. Their difficulty in operationalizing the construct and providing guidelines was understandable, given the dearth of research on processing and the paucity of processing tests at the time. In addition, processing is a very difficult construct to operationalize and measure because it is, by its very nature, difficult to observe directly. Consequently, cognitive processing has often been ill defined and mired in controversy. To add to this assessment challenge, processing consists of many domains, each of which are also arguable constructs that are difficult to separate and to measure directly. Finally, processes involve different levels of complexity and different depths of processing as well as similarities with what have usually been considered intellectual abilities.

### Intelligence and Abilities versus Cognitive Processes

The traditional approach to measuring cognitive abilities and learning potential has been to use IQ tests. While the construct of intelligence has many definitions, including some that are very similar to cognitive processing, the measurement of intelligence has primarily focused on just a few broad abilities. Some of the abilities measured by intelligence tests, such as fluid reasoning, can also be classified as processes, even though the common perception of such higher level processes has been that they are intelligence. Intelligence and cognitive processing are not necessarily dichotomous constructs. What is usually considered to be intelligence includes several types of cognitive processing.

The traditional measurement of intelligence has focused on the *products* or *content* of cognition, not the *processes* of cognition (Miller, 1999). For example, until recently about 50 percent of what intelligence tests measured was verbal ability or acquired knowledge, which is usually classified as crystallized intelligence. While the acquisition and retrieval of crystallized intelligence requires processing, it is mainly the content of crystallized intelligence that is being tapped by intellectual and cognitive tests. The level of crystallized intelligence is undeniably a strong indication of intellectual functioning and processing, but it is not a process per se. From crystallized intelligence scores we can only make inferences about what processing capabilities must be. Processing assessment attempts to measure cognition in a more direct manner than intellectual assessment does.

Another way in which intelligence, as it is typically measured, differs from processing assessment is how broad or narrow the focus is. Intellectual measurement has a broad focus, emphasizing general intelligence and a few broad abilities, while processing assessment tends toward a more narrow focus. Historically, processing assessment has attempted to decompose broad cognitive abilities and subtest performance into the narrow or specific processes they rely on (Kaplan, Fein, Kramer, Delis, & Morris, 1999). The disadvantage of this approach is that there are no norm-referenced scores for the disaggregated processes, forcing the practitioner to rely on clinical judgment. The alternative, as recommended in this book, is to interpret norm-referenced subtest and factor scores as representing cognitive processes. Such an approach is discouraged by Floyd (2005), who argues that cognitive subtest and composite scores reflect *abilities*, not the elementary *processes* utilized while completing the test items. However, all subtests and composites are multifactorial, even in regard to abilities. We agree on interpreting a given score as indicative of a particular ability because most of what that subtest or composite seems to be measuring is that particular ability. The same logic can be applied to processing. Some subtests and composites mainly measure one process, such as long-term retrieval. When this is the case, we should interpret the score as representing the primary process being measured.

Thus, processing and intelligence have an integral relationship, perhaps best conceptualized by Sternberg (1977). In Sternberg's theory, there are three basic kinds of processing components —metacomponents, performance components, and knowledge-acquisition components. Such processes underlie intellectual performance and are the essence of learning. Intelligence, processing, and learning are all interrelated; for example, the development of general intelligence, especially crystallized intelligence, depends on learning. Consequently, only processes that have moderate or higher correlations with general intelligence and learning are included in the processing assessment model promulgated in this book. For example, all types of memory have moderate relationships with general intelligence. Processes that have minimal relationships with intelligence and learning, such as reaction time and motoric processes, are excluded from consideration.

## PROCESSING ASSESSMENT BENEFITS

Despite the challenges of assessing processing, there are several benefits that may result from conducting a processing assessment (see Rapid Reference 1.1). An in-depth understanding of the individual's learning aptitudes should be the primary goal when evaluating individuals referred for learning difficulties. Processing assessment lends itself to this goal because it goes beyond the assessment of IQ, or general intellectual ability, and samples cognitive processes, providing a more complete picture of the individual. Processing assessment can also identify the likely cause of a learning problem, thereby helping us better understand *why* a learner may be experiencing learning problems. Not only does it help us better understand what may be impairing learning, but processing assessment may also actually be a better way of identifying and diagnosing learning disabilities than the long-standing ability-achievement discrepancy method. Finally, processing assessment provides information that can be utilized to design more effective and individualized treatment.

## *Rapid Reference 1.1*

### Processing Assessment Benefits

1. It provides a more comprehensive, in-depth assessment of learning aptitudes.
2. It helps to identify potential causes of learning problems.
3. It can be used to diagnose learning disabilities.
4. The results can be used to design effective interventions.

## SUMMARY

Given the advancements in measurement technology and the established research base, it is time for every practitioner to conduct an assessment of processing when evaluating individuals referred for cognitive or learning problems. Although there is still much art involved (this is where clinical skills apply), the technology of processing assessment is far enough along to justify its regular use. If we are knowledgeable about cognitive processes and duly exercise the appropriate restraints when interpreting results, processing assessment can be used to benefit the children, adolescents, and adults we evaluate. As with any psychological assessment, the goal of processing assessment is to gain a more in-depth understanding of the individual and that individual's strengths and weaknesses. Such knowledge can be utilized not only to more accurately diagnose but also to design more individualized and potentially more effective interventions.

## GENERAL LEARNING OUTCOMES

From reading, studying, and applying the practices advocated in this book, the reader will

1. know the components of several processing models and how these models can be integrated into a single model for assessment purposes.
2. know how various processes are related to specific types of learning.
3. know how to plan and organize a processing assessment, based on a hypothesis testing and a selective testing approach.
4. know how to apply cross-battery assessment methods to processing assessment.
5. know how to interpret processing assessment results from different types of assessment instruments.
6. know which processes are measured by contemporary intellectual, cognitive, and memory scales.
7. know how to apply a general method of analyzing and interpreting processing strengths and weaknesses to results from any standardized test or combination of tests.
8. be aware of scales designed to screen for processing difficulties, scales designed to assess processing in a comprehensive fashion, and scales designed to assess specific processes.

## PREVIEW OF THE CHAPTERS

Chapter 2, "Processing and Learning," proposes an integrated model of processing for assessment purposes, after reviewing contemporary processing theories—information processing theory, Luria's theory, and Cattell-Horn-Carroll

(CHC) theory. The chapter also identifies the specific processes that are most important for specific types of academic learning.

Chapter 3, "Strategies for Assessing Processing," provides a structure for planning and organizing a comprehensive, yet time-efficient, evaluation of processing. A processing assessment emanates from the hypotheses that are selected after referral concerns are clarified through preliminary interviews and observations. The applications of a selective testing and cross-battery approach are discussed in detail.

Chapter 4, "How to Interpret Processing Assessment Results," focuses on how psychometric and clinical interpretative guidelines uniquely apply to the interpretation of processing assessment results. After responding to concerns about profile analysis, this chapter introduces an interpretative model and a processing analysis worksheet that apply to the results of any test or combination of tests. The chapter concludes with recommendations for explaining results to parents, teachers, and students.

Chapter 5, "Assessing Processing with Traditional Intelligence Scales," reviews the three Wechsler scales and the Stanford-Binet from a processing assessment perspective. The focus is on the step-by-step analysis and interpretation of the processing factors from each scale, with additional procedures for calculating clinical factors.

Chapter 6, "Assessing Processing with Cognitive Scales," reviews prominent cognitive scales—the Kaufman Assessment Battery for Children, second edition; the Cognitive Assessment System; the Woodcock-Johnson III Tests of Cognitive Abilities; and the Wechsler Intelligence Scale for Children, fourth edition (WISC-IV) Integrated.

Chapter 7, "Assessing Memory," begins with an in-depth discussion of the Children's Memory Scale and the Wechsler Memory Scale, third edition and concludes with a listing of other memory scales. The interpretative advice includes an explanation of how to integrate memory scores with results from other scales.

Chapter 8, "Using Scales Designed to Assess Processing," overviews scales that are specifically designed to assess processing. Information is provided on neuropsychological assessment, the NEPSY Developmental Neuropsychological Assessment, executive processing scales, a rating scale that screens for processing problems, and scales that assess several other processes.

Chapter 9, "Illustrative Case Reports," illustrates the applications of this book's interpretative guidelines, including guidelines for writing a report that emphasizes a processing assessment.

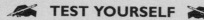 **TEST YOURSELF**

1. **In the last decade there has been a rapid expansion in the number of assessment instruments designed to assess processing.** True or False?

2. **As defined here, which of the following is *not* a cognitive process?**
   (a) Storing information
   (b) Perception
   (c) Sensation
   (d) Problem solving

3. **Processes underlie performance on an intellectual abilities scale.** True or False?

4. **List three potential benefits of assessing processing.**

5. **Current federal legislation defines a learning disability as "a disorder in one or more of the basic psychological processes."** True or False?

6. **Typically, processing assessment has a broader focus than intellectual assessment.** True or False?

7. **Traditional intellectual scales have emphasized the measurement of cognitive processes over the measurement of cognitive content and products.** True or False?

*Answers:* 1. True; 2. c; 3. True; 4. See Rapid Reference 1.1; 5. True; 6. False; 7. False

# Two

# PROCESSING AND LEARNING

everal theories of processing have emerged over the past half-century. To date, there is not a single unified theory of processing, but all of the theories involve a transformation of sensory input into neural code, which is stored and later retrieved. Cognitive psychologists introduced a theory of human information processing and cognitive learning in the 1960s (Neisser, 1967). Since then, cognitive research has found extensive support for the construct of information processing (Anderson, 1990; Gagne, 1993). The broadening knowledge base has increased our understanding of how humans learn, and it has led to the development of processing assessment scales and the inclusion of processing measures in existing cognitive tests. Currently, the research on processing is being led by neuroscientists who utilize the latest brain-scanning technology to study how cognitive processing occurs (Berninger & Richards, 2002).

Learning, the acquisition of knowledge and procedures, depends on the integration of many cognitive processes in the human brain. Although processing is required for all types of learning, *learning* in this book will be used to refer to the learning of reading, mathematics, language, and writing skills as well as academic knowledge such as science and social studies. The general learning cycle involves taking in selected information through one or more senses, manipulating that information in short-term or working memory, encoding the information into long-term storage, and retrieving the information to produce an expression or response. The most effective learners are those who actively control the necessary cognitive processes. Although most processing does not enter our awareness or require directed efforts to control it, active, conscious control of learning processes seems to be necessary for most academic learning. For instance, one must consciously manipulate information in order to study effectively for a classroom test. The importance of different types of processing varies, depending on the type of learning. For example, the processes that correlate the highest with learning mathematics are different from those that correlate the highest with learning to read.

Research on students with learning disabilities (LDs) has often found that these students have deficits in one or more types of processing. A deficit in one or more types of memory is the most common finding. Studies have also found (Naglieri & Das, 1997c) that students with an LD often have attentional deficits, similar to the attentional deficits of children with Attention-Deficit/Hyperactivity

**DON'T FORGET**

The following are common processing difficulties of students with a learning disability:

Memory
Attention
Executive processing
Complex processing

Disorder (ADHD). As indicated by their poor use of learning strategies, students with LDs also tend to have difficulties with executive processing; for example, executive processing is involved when a learner selects a mnemonic technique for memorizing a list of words. Another general finding has been that individuals with an LD struggle more when the required processing increases in complexity; for example, they tend to have more difficulty repeating digits backward than simply repeating digits as spoken.

## PROCESSING MODELS

### Information Processing

Cognitive psychologists seek to understand mental events or processes. They go beyond the behavioral model of learning, which focuses on identifying relationships between externally observable stimuli and responses. The cognitive model of processing attempts to explain learning and behavior in terms of mental constructs. In the 1960s a cognitive model of mental processing known as *information processing* emerged.

The information processing model used the computer as a metaphor for human mental processing (Gagne, 1993). Just as with the computer, the model described how information flowed and was processed from input from the environment to output back into the environment. The general model included the main components of receptors (the senses), immediate memory, working memory, long-term memory, effectors (glands and muscles that produce a response), and control processes (see Figure 2.1). The main processes were selective perception, encoding and storage, retrieval, response organization, and control.

In response to criticism that the information processing model was too linear

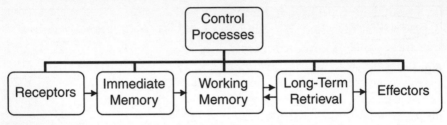

**Figure 2.1 Components and Flow of Information in the Information Processing Model**

and static, cognitive psychologists also proposed a neural network model that allowed for parallel processing (Gagne, 1993). The neural network model assumes that there are interconnected processing units in the brain that allow different cognitive processes to take place simultaneously.

The cognitive model of information processing classifies knowledge into two main types—declarative and procedural (Gagne, 1993). Declarative knowledge is factual knowledge, such as knowing that something is the case. Procedural knowledge is knowing how to do something. The two types of knowledge are stored in long-term memory differently. The facts and ideas of declarative knowledge are typically stored in organized, hierarchical networks in which related ideas are interconnected and stored together. Declarative knowledge can also be stored in the form of visual images and linear orderings. An integrated unit of declarative memory storage that incorporates facts, images, and linear orderings is referred to as a *schema*. Procedural knowledge, on the other hand, is thought to be stored in a series of *if-then* contingencies referred to as *production systems*. The *if* part contains the rules that apply, and the *then* part contains the actions to be carried out. With practice, the procedures become automated and require little conscious processing or control to implement.

## DON'T FORGET

There are two types of knowledge in the information processing model:

Declarative knowledge is factual knowledge.

Procedural knowledge is knowing how to do something.

### Neuroscience

With the advancement of brain-imaging technology, neuroscientists are now able to study brain functions as people perform specific cognitive tasks (Berninger & Richards, 2002). As a result, neuroscientists have been able to provide new insights into

**Figure 2.2   Communication between Neurons**

mental processing. The recent findings of neuroscientists have increased our knowledge of how the brain functions and have also provided general support for the information processing model.

At the basic brain level, processing occurs when physically separated neurons communicate with each other. Neurons have three components: a cell body, an axon, and a dendrite. The axons carry information away from the cell body to other neurons, and the dendrites carry information from other neurons into the cell body (see Figure 2.2). The dendrites have a branchlike structure that collects information from other neurons. The small space that separates the axon terminals from the dendrites is known as a *synapse*. With an estimated 180 billion neurons, there are trillions of possible connections in the brain. From a brain-based perspective, learning results from specific changes in the neuronal connections, and these changes involve how neurons communicate with each other (Berninger & Richards, 2002).

The brain is organized into structural units that vary in shape and size across individuals. There are also many individual differences in the precise location of these structures. There is not a one-to-one relationship between a brain structure and a function; structures may participate in many different functions. Some brain structures and functions, such as sensory and motor functions, have a specific location in the brain. However, the more complex higher order cognitive functions are distributed throughout the brain in neural networks. Functional systems may also reorganize over the course of development.

The neuronal connections, or pathways, in the brain are not only numerous but also redundant. Alternative pathways may also be developed as learning occurs. The result is that the brain may activate more than one pathway when trying to accomplish a specific task. For example, when a reader attempts to decode a word, the brain is using both visual and auditory pathways in parallel.

## Luria's Theory and PASS Theory

Luria (1970) proposed a theory of brain organization and processing that divides the brain into three functional units (see Rapid Reference 2.1). The first

*≡Rapid Reference 2.1*

**Luria Brain Units, *Processes*, and Brain Locations**

| First functional unit | Second functional unit | Third functional unit |
|---|---|---|
| Process: *attention*<br>Location: brain stem | Processes: *successive and simultaneous*<br>Location: occipital, parietal, and temporal lobes | Process: *planning*<br>Location: frontal lobes |

functional unit is responsible for arousal and attention and is located in the brain stem. The second functional unit serves as the primary intake of information, the processing of that information, and the association of that information with acquired knowledge (Kemp, Kirk, & Korkman, 2001). The second functional unit, located in the occipital, parietal, and temporal lobes, receives and processes visual, auditory, and other sensory information. The main types of processing in the second unit consist of simultaneous processing and successive processing. Simultaneous processing is a mental process by which the individual integrates separate stimuli into a single whole or group (Luria, 1970). Successive processing is a mental process by which the individual integrates stimuli into a specific serial order that forms a chainlike progression (Naglieri & Das, 1997c). The third functional unit, located in the frontal region of the brain, regulates the executive functions of planning, monitoring and strategizing performance needed for efficient problem solving. Luria viewed these units and processes as part of an interdependent system. For example, the third functional unit is affected by the attentional/arousal function in the first unit while regulating processing in the second unit. Given the proper state of arousal/attention, the planning, simultaneous, and successive processes interact to acquire knowledge.

The original Kaufman Assessment Battery for Children (K-ABC) was based in part on Luria's theory (also on Sperry's cerebral specialization theory), but only included measures of Sequential and Simultaneous processing (Kaufman & Kaufman, 1983). The 2004 revision of the K-ABC (Kaufman & Kaufman, 2004a) added two more processing scales—Planning and Learning. The authors of KABC-II built the test on a dual theoretical framework, basing the scales on both Luria's neuropsychological theory and on the psychometric CHC theory (discussed in the next section). The Kaufmans equated the Luria processing scales with broad cognitive processes from the CHC theory as follows: sequential processing with short-term memory; simultaneous processing with visual processing; planning with fluid reasoning; and learning with long-term retrieval (see Chapter 6 for a full discussion of the KABC-II).

Das and his colleagues (Das, Naglieri, & Kirby, 1994) based another cognitive assessment scale on Luria's processing theory. From the work of Luria and the influences of cognitive psychology and neuropsychology, the planning, attention, simultaneous, and successive theory emerged and became known as PASS theory (see Rapid Reference 2.2). Naglieri and Das (1997a) operationalized PASS theory in the form of the Cognitive Assessment System (CAS), a test of cognitive processes (see Chapter 6 for a full discussion of the CAS).

### Cattell-Horn-Carroll (CHC) Theory of Intelligence

Cattell-Horn-Carroll (CHC) theory is a contemporary theory of intelligence and human cognitive abilities, not a processing theory per se. CHC theory posits a trilevel hierarchical model, with $g$, or general intelligence, at the top; 10 broad abilities at the middle level, or stratum; and approximately 70 narrow abilities at the lowest level (McGrew & Woodcock, 2001). The model is applicable to processing assessment because most of the broad abilities identified by the theory can also be considered cognitive processes (see Rapid Reference 2.3). The cognitive processing abilities include visual processing, auditory processing, short-term memory, long-term storage and retrieval, fluid intelligence, and processing speed.

> ### ≡Rapid Reference 2.2
>
> ## Components of the PASS Theory
>
> Planning
> Attention
> Simultaneous processing
> Successive processing

> ### ≡Rapid Reference 2.3
>
> ## CHC Theory Broad Abilities
>
> Fluid Intelligence* (*Gf*)
> Quantitative Intelligence (*Gq*)
> Crystallized Intelligence (*Gc*)
> Reading and Writing (*Grw*)
> Short-Term Memory* (*Gsm*)
> Visual Processing* (*Gv*)
> Auditory Processing* (*Ga*)
> Long-Term Storage and Retrieval* (*Glr*)
> Processing Speed* (*Gs*)
> Decision/Reaction Time/Speed (*Gt*)
>
> *Processes incorporated into this text's integrated processing model
> Source: McGrew and Woodcock (2001).

Crystallized intelligence, quantitative knowledge, and reading and writing ability are also broad cognitive abilities but are not considered types of processing for the purposes of this book. Decision/Reaction Time/Speed is also a type of processing but will not be included in this book's proposed assessment model because psychometric scales seldom measure it.

CHC theory is the consolidation of two theories of intelligence—Carroll's and Horn-Cattell's. Raymond Cattell identified the theory's first two types of intelligence—fluid and crystallized—in the 1940s. Fluid intelligence is the ability to reason, form concepts, and solve problems that often include novel content or procedures. Crystallized intelligence is the breadth and depth of knowledge, including verbal ability. John Horn and others went on to find support for several more types of intelligence, expanding the theory to eight or nine broad factors (Horn & Blankson, 2005). In the late 1980s, John B. Carroll (1993) completed a meta-analysis of more than 400 well-designed studies of intelligence conducted in the twentieth century. Carroll's factor analytic model turned out to be a close match with Horn-Cattell theory. Thus, in the late 1990s Horn and Cattell agreed to integrate their theories. Since then, the theory has gained acceptance and influence.

The Woodcock-Johnson III Tests of Cognitive Abilities (WJ III COG; Woodcock, McGrew, & Mather, 2001b) is based on CHC theory (see Chapter 6 for a full discussion of the WJ III COG), as is the recent revision of the Stanford-Binet (Roid, 2003a). As noted in the previous section, the KABC-II (Kaufman & Kaufman, 2004a) is based on *both* the CHC and Luria theories. The cross-battery assessment model (Flanagan & Ortiz, 2001) also uses CHC theory as a framework for classifying the subtests and factors from all existing intellectual and cognitive scales.

In addition to extensive factor analytic evidence in support of CHC theory (McGrew, 2005), there is developmental evidence from studies of the WJ III COG. The divergent growth curves displayed in Figure 2.3 provide evidence for the existence of unique cognitive processes that grow and decline across the life span. The curves are based on cross-sectional (not longitudinal) changes in median performance on WJ III COG test factors. Not only does this norming data provide support for unique cognitive processes but they also illustrate the developmental growth and decline for each ability or process. For example, the *Glr* (long-term retrieval) curve reveals less developmental change than the other factors, whereas the *Gs* (processing speed) curve indicates that processing speed rises sharply, followed by a steady progressive decline (McGrew & Woodcock, 2001).

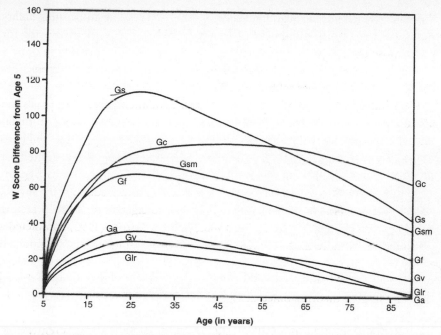

**Figure 2.3    Plot of Seven WJ III COG Factor Growth Curves by Age**

*Source:* From *Woodcock-Johnson® III Technical Manual* (Figure 4-1), by K. S. McGrew and R. W. Woodcock, 2001, Itasca, IL: Riverside Publishing. Copyright 2001 by The Riverside Publishing Company. Reproduced with permission of the publisher. All rights reserved.

## AN INTEGRATED PROCESSING MODEL

The theoretical constructs that have been developed to explain processing in the human brain are varied yet have many similarities. Although the theories come from different sources—cognitive science, neuropsychology, neuroscience, education, and psychometrics—there is a good deal of consensus about the components and functions of the processing system. Each theory has been supported by research in the field from which it evolved and by research in related fields. The expanding research base has led to a number of new processing assessment instruments in the past 10 years. In fact, there is more variability in how to measure different processes than there is in the constructs themselves. The variety of measures attests to the difficulties of operationalizing the constructs and measuring processes.

In order to plan, conduct, and interpret a valid assessment that increases our understanding of an individual learner's processing capabilities, it is necessary to have a framework from which to work. What is being proposed here is not a new theory or model of processing but rather a synthesis of existing models that will result in a practical schema that can be used for assessment purposes and for understanding learning.

The human information processing model originally proposed in the 1960s has withstood the test of time. It has been validated by research in cognitive psychology, educational psychology, neuropsychology, and neuroscience. Although the original model now looks too simple and too static, it did incorporate all of the core components and processes. Thus, the cognitive model is the basis of the model proposed here. This integrated model emphasizes learning and integrates processes identified by other fields of research.

In this integrated model (see Figure 2.4) working memory is the core. It is considered the core because all conscious, and much automated, processing passes through it and because most academic learning depends on it. Working memory integrates and manipulates information as it processes input from the environment that has entered through the senses and perceptual parts of the brain and as it processes information retrieved from long-term stores of knowledge. Output that is not automatically generated also passes through working memory. Many of the processes identified as separate components by various theories are thought to mainly function within working memory; these include visual and auditory processing, successive and simultaneous processing, and fluid reasoning. Working memory is also linked with and directed by executive processes.

Of course there is constant interaction among all the components and different types of processes. The brain does not process information in an isolated one-piece-at-a-time or linear fashion. It is a very complex organism with multiple, integrated parallel processes occurring simultaneously. Parallel processes may be working to accomplish the same task, such as visual and auditory processes working to decode a word, or they may be working on different tasks at the same time. Thus, it is difficult to represent the complexity of processing in a single graphic, and it is just as difficult to assess just one type of processing at a time. Figure 2.4 attempts to illustrate the main components and processes that have been identified, but many more arrows would be needed to indicate all the interactions that are typically involved.

One of the theories included in this integrated model that has not been generally regarded as a processing theory is CHC theory. Nevertheless, most of the CHC broad abilities clearly involve types of cognitive processing. The first assessment instrument based on CHC theory, the WJ III COG (Woodcock et al., 2001b), is also based on a theory of information processing (Woodcock, 1998). Some experts in the field of cognitive assessment have recently begun to merge processing with CHC. For example, the authors of the KABC-II, Kaufman and Kaufman (2004a), have linked Luria's processing theory with CHC theory when

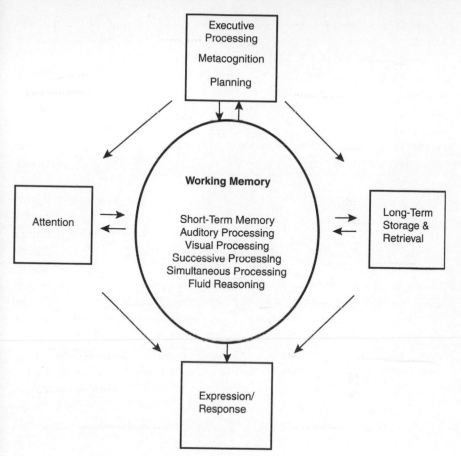

**Figure 2.4  An Integrated Processing Model**

they equated successive processing with short-term memory, simultaneous processing with visual processing, and planning with fluid reasoning. Woodcock (Schrank, Flanagan, Woodcock, & Mascolo, 2002) also proposed an information processing model for the cognitive abilities measured by the WJ III COG.

## PROCESSING COMPONENTS

### Attention

Without attention, much information available to the individual would never be processed. Although we all know what attention is, the processes involved are complex; there are qualitatively different aspects of attention. Attention begins with arousal, either because stimuli are inherently interesting or because we initiate the arousal in our minds. The primary aspect of attention is focusing on and responding to certain stimuli in the environment. The ability to stay focused on relevant stimuli when distracting stimuli are present is known as selective attention. Sustained attention is the ability to persist—to stay on task—especially when the task is not inherently stimulating. Attention, like other components of processing, is controlled by executive functioning. There is no doubt that attention is necessary for learning and successful functioning in the environment.

## Short-Term Memory

Short-term memory is the ability to apprehend and hold information in immediate awareness and then use it within a few seconds. According to the research of cognitive psychologists, information can be held in short-term memory for about 7 seconds. Rehearsal, or repeating information, is one way of extending the interval, but information that is not acted upon will certainly be lost from short-term memory within 15 to 20 seconds. It is common for people to refer to short-term memory as if it lasted for several minutes when, in fact, information recalled after 7 to 20 seconds is usually being retrieved from long-term memory. The other limitation of short-term memory is the number of units (referred to as the span) that can be held at a time. In the typical individual the span is around seven units. What changes developmentally is the size of the units. For example, for a beginning reader each phoneme is a unit, later, words become the units, and, finally, ideas become the units.

## Working Memory

Working memory plays a critical role in cognitive processing and learning. Individuals who have problems in working memory have difficulties thinking and acquiring skills. Whenever we are thinking about something, we are using our working memory. Problem solving or trying to comprehend text is working memory in action. Working memory is the interface between input and output. It is where learning takes place. Working memory uses information that is available in short-term memory or retrieves information from long-term memory, or both; performs some action on these two stores of information; and then stores the new product in long-term memory or uses it to construct an expression or response.

The construct of working memory evolved from the work of cognitive psychologists such as Neisser (1967) and Anderson (1990). Neuroscientists, such as

Berninger and Richards (2002), have found validation for the construct in brain imaging studies, but it is mainly educational research that has firmly established working memory's existence, functions, characteristics, and role in learning. H. Lee Swanson (1999) and others (Seigneuric, Ehrlich, Oakhill, & Nicola, 2000; Swanson & Berninger, 1996) have extensively researched the topic and repeatedly linked working memory limitations to learning problems in reading, mathematics, and writing.

Short-term memory and working memory are closely interrelated. Sometimes, working memory is described as a subtype of short-term memory. The main distinction between the two is that working memory is conscious processing, and it involves manipulation of information, whereas short-term memory is more static in nature, requiring only storage of information for a brief period of time. Consequently, the processing demands of working memory are higher than those of short-term memory. Whenever we are actively processing information in short-term memory, we are utilizing working memory. The classic Wechsler Digit Span subtest illustrates the difference between short-term and working memory. Whereas Digits Forward may only require basic short-term memory, Digits Backward clearly requires working memory because of the need to manipulate the digits.

Just as with short-term memory, the capacity of working memory is limited. The typical individual can manipulate five to nine units, or chunks, of information at a time. As long as specific information is being acted upon, it remains in working memory. Once we are finished manipulating a piece of information, it will only remain in working memory for an additional 5 to 15 seconds. Thus, someone who has less working memory capacity than average will not be able to process as much information. The result will be less information encoded into long-term memory and, ultimately, less learning. Clearly, working memory limitations or deficits have profound implications for classroom instruction and learning.

When it comes to academic learning, the level of automaticity is the main variable that determines how much working memory is available for a given task. The fundamental idea of automaticity is that information can be processed with little effort or attention; it is the extent to which processing occurs subconsciously or automatically. However, automaticity is not like a built-in reflex. Rather, it involves the processing of complex information that ordinarily requires long periods of training and practice before the behavior or skill can be executed with little effort or attention. Once a skill is automated, more working memory is available for processing other information; for example, a reader who has developed decoding automaticity has more working memory resources to devote to reading

# DON'T FORGET

The more a skill is automatized, the less working memory it requires.

# CAUTION

What appears to be a limitation in working memory is sometimes due to a lack of automaticity in basic skills, such as reading.

comprehension. Thus, automaticity is an indication of expertise, and novices lack it.

Automaticity also depends on the degree of mastery of basic academic skills; for example, a fluent reader who has acquired a large reading vocabulary and does not need to consciously decode words is a reader who has reached a high level of automaticity in reading. When assessing working memory, it is important to know the level of development and mastery for each of the basic academic skills. A learner with a normal working memory may appear to have a deficient working memory because basic skills that are not mastered or automated require all or most of working memory to perform them.

Working memory processes information that is both visual and aural. Visual working memory is thought to be more wholistic and usually involves manipulating visual imagery. Auditory working memory often involves the manipulation of sequences, such as when phonemes are blended into a word. Within individuals, the capacity of visual working memory may vary from that of auditory working memory. Thus, it is important to assess both types.

Information that is encoded into long-term semantic memory arrives there after being manipulated and organized by working memory. When we strive to understand and organize incoming information, we are using our working memory. Through working memory we retrieve relevant prior knowledge from long-term memory and make connections between the new and existing information. Whenever we add to our knowledge, or schema, of something, it occurs through the encoding function of working memory. The encoding of each new piece of information may require up to a minute or more.

How much information can be processed in working memory may also be related to processing speed. An overloaded working memory may slow down processing speed, and slow processing speed may limit the

# DON'T FORGET

Working memory involves the following:

Auditory/Verbal working memory

Visual working memory

Successive processing

Simultaneous processing

functioning of working memory. The WJ III COG (Woodcock et al., 2001b) has combined these two processes into one construct (composite score) referred to as Cognitive Efficiency. The idea is that the combination of processing speed and short-term or working memory determines just how much information an individual can process and how quickly he or she can process it.

## Long-Term Storage and Retrieval

Long-term storage and retrieval is the ability to store information in long-term memory and fluently retrieve it later. From a processing perspective, storage and retrieval is not the acquired knowledge that is stored in long-term memory but rather the *process* of storing (encoding) and retrieving information. The focus is on the efficiency of the long-term storage and retrieval processes. Long-term memory depends on short-term and working memory because storage, or encoding, processes transfer new information from working memory into long-term memory. Retrieval from long-term memory can be automatic or controlled, but both routes put stored information into a form that can be used for current processing and generating a response.

There are many different types of long-term memory, such as episodic memory, associative memory, and meaningful or semantic memory. CHC theory distinguishes between several *narrow* long-term memory abilities (see Rapid Reference 2.4), which were first identified by Carroll (1993) and later used for test classification purposes by Flanagan, McGrew, and Ortiz (2000). One of these types, naming facility, is the speed of direct recall of information from acquired knowledge. Naming facility, which is often referred to as rapid automatic naming, is critical for the development of reading (Manis et al., 1999). The types of long-term memory that are perhaps most important for academic learning are associative memory and semantic memory (memory for concepts and meaning). In both associative and semantic memory, information that is related is linked together.

## Processing Speed

The popular concept of processing speed is that it is how quickly we can think or how quickly we can mentally process information in general. Although such a construct may ultimately prove to have validity, it is too difficult to measure at this time. A more pragmatic definition of processing speed is that it is the speed at which an individual automatically performs relatively easy or overlearned cognitive tasks, such as a clerical type of task that requires simple decisions. Current

---

## ≡Rapid Reference 2.4

### Narrow Abilities of the CHC Long-Term Storage and Retrieval Factor

*Associative memory:* Recall one part of a previously learned pair of items when the other part is presented

*Meaningful/semantic memory:* Recall information when there is meaningful relation between the bits of information

*Free-recall memory:* Recall (without associations) of unrelated items

*Ideational fluency:* Rapidly produce a series of words, phrases related to a specific condition or object

*Associational fluency:* Rapidly produce words or phrases similar in meaning to a given word or concept

*Expressional fluency:* Rapidly produce different ways of saying much the same thing

*Originality:* Produce clever expressions or interpretations

*Naming facility:* Rapidly produce names for concepts or things when presented with objects or pictures

*Word fluency:* Rapidly produce isolated words that have specific phonemic, structural, or orthographic characteristics

*Figural fluency:* Rapidly draw as many things as possible when presented with a nonmeaningful visual stimulus

*Figural flexibility:* Rapidly change set and try a variety of approaches to solutions for figural problems

*Sensitivity to problems:* Rapidly think of a number of alternative solutions to practical problems

*Originality/creativity:* Rapidly produce unusual, original, divergent, or uncommon responses to a given topic, situation, or task

*Learning abilities:* General learning ability rate

*Source:* From "The Cattell-Horn-Carroll Theory of Cognitive Abilities," by K. S. McGrew, 2005, in D. P. Flanagan and P. L. Harrison (Eds.), *Contemporary Intellectual Assessment: Theories, Tests, and Issues, 2nd Ed.,* p. 154. Copyright 2005 by Guilford Press. Adapted and reprinted with permission.

---

measures of processing speed, such as the WISC-IV Coding and Symbol Search subtests (Wechsler, 2003a), are consistent with this definition. The types of processing speed measured by most cognitive scales include perceptual speed, rate of test taking, and number facility (see Rapid Reference 2.5). It is important to remember that fine motor skills can influence performance on these types of tasks and thus confound processing speed test results. The development of automaticity in skills such as reading and mathematics depends on adequate processing speed.

≡*Rapid Reference 2.5*

### Types of Processing Speed

*Perceptual speed:* Rapidly search for and compare known visual symbols

*Rate of test taking:* Rapidly perform tests that are relatively easy

*Number facility:* Rapidly and accurately manipulate and deal with numbers

*Speed of reasoning:* Speed or fluency in performing reasoning tasks

*Reading speed:* Silently read and comprehend connected text rapidly and automatically

*Writing speed:* Copying words and sentences or writing words and sentences as quickly as possible

*Source:* From "The Cattell-Horn-Carroll Theory of Cognitive Abilities," by K. S. McGrew, 2005, in D. P. Flanagan and P. L. Harrison (Eds.), *Contemporary Intellectual Assessment: Theories, Tests, and Issues, 2nd Ed.*, p. 155. Copyright 2005 by Guilford Press. Adapted and reprinted with permission.

## Phonemic Awareness and Phonological Processing

Phonemic awareness is knowledge of the sound structure of spoken words. It is the understanding that spoken language is composed of different sounds called *phonemes*. Phonemes, the smallest units of sound in a word, are combined in a variety of ways to form syllables and words. For example, the word *tree* has three phonemes: /t/ /r/ /i/. The English language consists of about 41 phonemes (25 consonants and 16 vowels) that are represented by hundreds of different graphemes. *Graphemes* are the letters or units of written language that represent phonemes in the spelling of words. The learning of grapheme-phoneme associations is known as *phonics*.

The first indication that young children have developed phonemic awareness is that they are able to rhyme. Being able to alliterate, or say words that start with the same sound, is another indication that phonemic awareness is developing. Other abilities indicative of well-developed phonemic awareness include phoneme detection, phoneme matching, phoneme isolation, phoneme completion, phoneme deletion, phoneme reversal, phoneme segmentation, and phoneme blending.

Not only must children be aware of phonemes and the graphemes that represent phonemes, but they also must learn how to manipulate phonemes. Decoding words involves both segmenting the syllables and words into sounds and then blending these sounds into a smoothly pronounced word. This type of processing is known as *phonological processing*. Phonological processing requires phonemic awareness, and it involves the coding of phonological information in working memory and the retrieval of phonological information from long-term memory. As the process becomes more automatic, it takes less working memory to do it. Phonological processing generally refers to the use of phonological information in processing spoken or written language (Gillon, 2004). Phonological processing encompasses *phonemic awareness* and *phonological awareness* (the awareness of the sound structure of spoken language). The three terms are often used interchangeably even though the constructs are somewhat distinct. *As used in this text, phonemic awareness includes phonological awareness and phonological processing.*

Phonemic awareness is the single best predictor of early literacy development and reading performance. It enables the child to decode, or sound out, printed words by breaking down words into sound units. Extensive research in the 1990s clearly established the importance of phonemic awareness and its relationship with reading and spelling (Gillon, 2004; Metsala, 1999; National Reading Panel, 2000). Most children who become proficient readers have strong phonemic awareness prior to formal reading instruction. Those who don't will struggle with decoding and have a difficult time becoming fluent readers. Without automaticity they will need more of their working memory capacity for decoding and be able to devote less working memory to reading comprehension. Early intervention can make a difference; phonemic awareness training has proven to be very effective. The National Reading Panel (2000) found such training to have a large effect size on phonemic awareness and moderate effect sizes for reading and spelling outcomes. There have also been several measures of phonemic awareness and phonological processing developed in the past decade (see Chapter 8 for details on these measures). Rapid automatic naming, or naming facility, tasks can also be used to measure the efficiency of retrieving phonological information from long-term memory.

## DON'T FORGET

Phonological processing includes manipulating phonemes by doing the following:

    Rhyming

    Blending

    Segmenting

    Reversing

    Deleting

## Visual Processing

Visual processing is the ability to perceive, analyze, synthesize, and think with visual patterns, including the ability to store and recall visual representations. Mental manipulation and transformation of visual patterns and stimuli are usually involved. Visual processing also involves the ability to visualize stimuli (in the mind's eye)

≡ *Rapid Reference 2.6*

## Types of Visual Processing

*Visualization:* Mentally imagine, manipulate, match, or transform objects or visual patterns

*Spatial relations:* Rapidly perceive and manipulate visual patterns

*Closure speed:* Quickly identify a familiar object from incomplete visual stimuli

*Length estimation:* Accurately estimate or compare visual lengths or distances without measurement instruments

*Visual memory:* Form and briefly store a mental representation or image of a visual shape or configuration and then recognize or recall it later

*Spatial scanning:* Quickly survey a wide or complicated spatial field or pattern and identify a particular configuration

*Serial perceptual integration:* Identify a pictorial or visual pattern when parts of the pattern are presented rapidly in serial order

*Imagery:* Mentally depict and/or manipulate an object that is not present

Other narrow visual processing abilities are *flexibility of closure, perceptual illusions,* and *perceptual alterations.*

Source: From "The Cattell-Horn-Carroll Theory of Cognitive Abilities," by K. S. McGrew, 2005, in D. P. Flanagan and P. L. Harrison (Eds.), *Contemporary Intellectual Assessment: Theories, Tests, and Issues, 2nd Ed.,* p. 152. Copyright 2005 by Guilford Press. Adapted and reprinted with permission.

that are not present. Visual processing is also referred to as *visual-spatial thinking* or *processing*. See Rapid Reference 2.6 for different subtypes of visual processing and their definitions.

Research results do not indicate a strong relationship between visual processing and academic learning. For example, the correlations between the WJ III Visual-Spatial cluster and the WJ III academic skills clusters are among the lowest cited in the WJ III Technical Manual (McGrew & Woodcock, 2001). Nevertheless, visual processing is involved in learning and appears to be most related to mathematics (Mather & Wendling, 2005).

### Auditory Processing

Auditory processing is the ability to perceive, analyze, synthesize, and discriminate auditory stimuli, including the ability to process and discriminate speech sounds. Phonemic and phonological awareness, or processing, is closely related to auditory processing and may be considered a subtype of auditory processing. See Rapid Reference 2.7 for the subtypes of auditory processing.

*≡Rapid Reference 2.7*

### Types of Auditory Processing

*Phonetic coding:* Code and process phonemic information

*Speech sound discrimination:* Detect and discriminate differences in phonemes or speech sounds

*Resistance to auditory stimulus distortion:* Overcome distortion or distraction when listening to speech/language

*Memory for sound patterns:* Short-term retention of tones, patterns, and voices

*Musical discrimination and judgment:* Discriminate and judge tonal patterns in music

Other narrow auditory processing abilities are *general sound discrimination, temporal tracking, maintaining and judging rhythm, sound intensity/duration discrimination, sound frequency discrimination, hearing and speech threshold factors, absolute pitch,* and *sound localization.*

*Source:* From "The Cattell-Horn-Carroll Theory of Cognitive Abilities," by K. S. McGrew, 2005, in D. P. Flanagan and P. L. Harrison (Eds.), *Contemporary Intellectual Assessment: Theories, Tests, and Issues, 2nd Ed.,* p. 153. Copyright 2005 by Guilford Press. Adapted and reprinted with permission.

## Successive/Sequential Processing

Successive processing, sometimes referred to as *sequential processing,* was originally described by Luria (1970). Successive processing involves the perception of stimuli in sequence or the arrangement of stimuli sequentially, and then the coding and storage of sequential stimuli. During successive processing, stimuli are arranged in a specific serial order that forms a chainlike progression in which each stimulus is only related to the one it follows (Naglieri, 1999). Much of sequential processing is automatized, but the conscious manipulation of sequential stimuli requires working memory resources. Spoken speech and reading decoding are tasks that involve successive processing. Auditory short-term memory also depends on successive processing.

## Simultaneous Processing

Simultaneous processing is the other primary mode of coding and problem solving in Luria's model. Simultaneous processing involves the integration of separate stimuli into a conceptual whole in which all of the elements of the stimuli are interrelated. Although this type of processing also deals with verbal or aural content, simultaneous processing usually involves visual-spatial processing as the individual perceives stimuli as a whole. Understanding how the separate stimuli are related to each other is necessary for organizing them. Manipulation and organization of the stimuli take place in working memory. Constructing an object from a drawing is an example of a task that involves simultaneous processing.

## Executive Processing

Executive processes are processes that self-direct or control our cognitive resources and processing; executive processing oversees and manages all other types of cognitive processing. Executive processing includes setting goals, planning, self-monitoring, self-regulating, solving problems, self-evaluating, and adjusting (see Rapid Reference 2.8). For example, *using* rehearsal to retain information in short-term memory is a processing strategy; *deciding* to use rehearsal is executive processing. In the brain, executive processes are mainly located in the prefrontal lobes. There isn't just one executive function controlling all types of processing; it is more like a board of directors, not just one administrator managing the processing systems (Berninger and Richards, 2002).

Many executive processes are automatic and are embedded in processing events or skills. Without executive processing it would be difficult for us to make effective use of our processing capabilities. Well-developed executive processes are critical for daily functioning and for successful independent learning. Research (Singer & Bashir, 1999) has found that students with learning problems are often deficient in executive processing. Executive processes also play a role in behavioral inhibition. According to Barkley (1997), an expert in ADHD, individuals with ADHD have deficiencies in executive processing that account for the behaviors associated with ADHD.

The prefrontal lobes and executive processes are not fully developed until late adolescence, but executive processes begin to develop in early childhood. Internalization of speech is one way that executive skills develop. Initially, the language of other people controls the behavior of a

*≡Rapid Reference 2.8*

### Executive Processing

Goal setting

Planning

Problem solving

Self-monitoring

Self-regulating

Self-evaluating

Adjusting

young child. Over time the adult commands are internalized and lead to the development of such executive skills as self-monitoring and inhibition (Dawson & Guare, 2004). Even older individuals will sometimes exhibit their internal executive processing by thinking aloud when they encounter a novel or challenging task.

### Metacognition

When an individual consciously uses executive control processes, it is referred to as *metacognition* (Livingston, 2003). Making a decision to write down a list of items to purchase at the grocery store is an example of a metacognition. Metacognition begins with self-awareness of one's skills and one's cognitive processing strengths and weaknesses. It also involves knowing which processing strategies are effective and understanding how one's processes can be utilized to accomplish the task at hand. Knowing how the levels of one's skills and processes match up with the requirements of a given task is also important to successful goal attainment. The outcome of this understanding is the selection of an appropriate cognitive process or strategy that engages the processes that are most likely to effectively accomplish an objective. For example, a person may know that it will be impossible to retrieve a list of names unless he or she reviews the list and associates each name with a face. Knowing when, how, where, and why to apply a particular processing strategy is the essence of metacognition and leads to the selection and use of effective processing strategies.

Monitoring one's progress toward goal attainment is the next phase of metacognition. Much of monitoring is on automatic pilot and becomes conscious only when a problem is detected. For example, the reader who is monitoring comprehension will become aware that a word or idea is not understood, and the flow of reading will be interrupted. Studies (Dehn, 1997) have found that poor readers often do not detect errors in text and are often unaware that they are lacking comprehension as they read.

The final stage of the executive processing cycle is adjusting or revising. Some revision procedures are fairly automatic; for example, the reader may simply reread an incomprehensible sentence. Others involve analyzing the problem, thinking about the possible solutions, considering the strengths of one's processing resources, and selecting a strategy that is most likely to succeed.

> **DON'T FORGET**
> ....................................................................
> Metacognitive knowledge includes knowing when, how, where, and why to apply a particular cognitive strategy.

## Planning

Planning is a critical executive or metacognitive process necessary for learning and successful everyday functioning. For example, effective problem solving necessitates planning or determining how to go about solving the problem. Planning usually begins with goal setting and the selection of strategies to obtain that goal. Monitoring is engaged as the plan is put into action and the problem-solving approach is modified or another one selected if necessary. We all know what planning is; however, it is difficult to measure real-life planning with a formal test.

## Fluid Reasoning

Fluid reasoning is the ability to reason, form concepts, and solve problems, particularly when confronted with a novel task or unfamiliar situation. It involves both deductive and inductive reasoning. Fluid reasoning is a higher level process that is one of the last cognitive abilities/processes to fully develop. Full development of fluid reasoning cannot be expected until early adolescence. Fluid reasoning is highly correlated with general intelligence. Fluid reasoning is also related to quantitative reasoning and is predictive of performance in higher level mathematics. Measures of fluid reasoning usually involve nonverbal tasks, although fluid reasoning is also involved in verbal tasks such as reading comprehension. See Rapid Reference 2.9 for subtypes of fluid reasoning.

*≡Rapid Reference 2.9*

### Types of Fluid Reasoning

*Deductive reasoning:* Reason and draw conclusions from given general conditions or premises to the specific

*Induction:* Reasoning from specific cases or observations to general rules

*Quantitative reasoning:* Reason with concepts involving mathematical relations and properties

*Piagetian reasoning:* Demonstrate the acquisition and application of *seriation, conservation,* and *classification*

*Speed of reasoning:* Speed or fluency in performing reasoning tasks

*Source:* From "The Cattell-Horn-Carroll Theory of Cognitive Abilities," by K. S. McGrew, 2005, in D. P. Flanagan and P. L. Harrison (Eds.), *Contemporary Intellectual Assessment: Theories, Tests, and Issues, 2nd Ed.,* p. 154. Copyright 2005 by Guilford Press. Adapted and reprinted with permission.

# DON'T FORGET

## The Main Processing Components (for Assessment Purposes)

Attention

Auditory processing

Executive processing

Fluid reasoning

Long-term retrieval

Phonemic awareness

Planning

Processing speed

Short-term memory

Simultaneous processing

Successive processing

Visual processing

Working memory

## The Integration of Processing

None of the previously described processes functions in isolation. Not only is there parallel processing, but the processes are also integrated into functional systems that are necessary for complex behavior. Multiple brain structures and processes are involved in any one function, and the same structures and processes participate in more than one functional system (Berninger & Richards, 2002). The result is that overall mental processing is greater than the sum of its parts and that attempting to measure cognitive processes in isolation is extremely challenging.

## HOW PROCESSING RELATES TO ACADEMIC LEARNING

It is the premise of this book that learning depends on effective processing and that some processes are more closely related to, or more predictive of, specific types of academic learning. Thus, a learner with a significant learning difficulty or learning disability that cannot be attributed to exclusionary causes, such as poor school attendance or an emotional disorder, is most likely experiencing the learning difficulty or disability because of a significant processing weakness or processing deficit. In other words, in most cases a processing problem is accounting for the learning problem. That is, the processing problem is the main reason *why* the learner is having significant difficulty acquiring one or more of the basic academic skills of reading, mathematics, or written language.

There are many individual differences in mental processing, and there are ipsative, or individual, processing strengths and weaknesses within each of us. The plasticity of the brain and the fact that multiple processes are engaged in functional systems generally allow us to learn and function adequately, even when one or more of our processes are deficient. However, a deficit in even one type of processing may disrupt learning in a way in which other normal or strong processes cannot compensate. This is especially true when the process that is deficient plays a critical role in a specific type of learning, for example, the role of phonemic processing in reading. Thus, to gain a more complete understanding of a struggling learner's strengths and weaknesses, assessment of processing is very important.

## Processes Related to All Types of Academic Achievement

Cognitive processing is not easily separated into discrete components and processes. As cognition occurs, most of the processing system is at work in an integrated manner. Thus, any type of learning depends on all types of processing to varying degrees. Processes that are critical for all types of learning are working memory, processing speed, executive processing, and long-term storage and retrieval (McGrew & Woodcock, 2001).

## Processes Important to Reading

For many children, learning to read is a significant challenge. Reading difficulties and disorders have been the subject of numerous investigations. After reviewing the scientific literature on reading, the National Reading Panel (2000) concluded that phonemic awareness and letter knowledge are the two best school-entry predictors of how well children will learn to read. Numerous studies of reading have confirmed that phonemic awareness—the ability to focus on and manipulate phonemes in spoken words—is a process that is necessary for reading decoding, or basic reading skills (Hoskyn & Swanson, 2000). The National Reading Panel also reviewed phonemic awareness interventions and found further evidence of the relationship between phonemic awareness and reading. Phonemic awareness interventions not only improved phonemic awareness but also led to significant improvements in basic reading skills. As indicated by the overall effect size of .53, basic reading skills improved by slightly more than half a standard deviation when phonemic awareness instruction was provided (National Reading Panel, 2000).

Basic rapid processing of symbols and words is necessary for developing fluent reading skills. This rapid processing depends on working memory, processing speed, and long-term retrieval. Rapid automatic naming, or naming facility, is a specific type of long-term retrieval that involves associations between print (graphemes) and sound (phonemes). Rapid automatic naming is strongly associated with reading acquisition (Manis, Seidenberg, & Doi, 1999).

The essential role that working memory plays in the development of reading is well documented by numerous studies (Swanson, 2000). In general, students with LDs have significant normative and individual deficits in working memory. For example, a WISC-IV standardization study of children with a reading disorder (Wechsler, 2003b) found their Working Memory Index mean of 87 to be their lowest index score and significantly lower than the mean of a matched control group. The decoding of words in working memory is a linear, sequential process. Thus, successive processing is another process involved in reading decoding and often deficient in children with reading disabilities (Steele & Dehn, 2003).

Reading comprehension takes place in working memory and thus requires sufficient working memory resources. The amount of working memory that can be devoted to reading comprehension depends on the degree of automaticity of basic reading skills. A reader who is struggling to decode words and lacks fluency usually does not have enough working memory resources left over to devote to comprehension. Thus, a child with a basic reading skills disability has a high risk of reading comprehension problems, especially as comprehension demands increase in later school years.

Another process that is highly related with reading comprehension is fluid reasoning. A reader who is low in fluid reasoning may do well with literal reading comprehension but may be challenged when it comes to inferential comprehension, such as drawing conclusions from text. While important for reading comprehension, fluid reasoning is largely unrelated to basic reading skills.

Executive processing also plays a critical role in reading comprehension (Dehn, 1997). From selecting effective reading strategies and monitoring comprehension to resolving comprehension roadblocks, executive processing is absolutely necessary for successful reading comprehension. A reader may have good reading fluency and possess adequate fluid reasoning abilities but lack comprehension if executive processing is not engaged while reading.

Studies examining the relationship between CHC cognitive abilities and reading (Evans, Floyd, McGrew, & Leforgee, 2002) have found support for the strong relations between some cognitive processes and reading. The CHC processes that demonstrate significant relations with basic reading

# DON'T FORGET

The following are the processes most important for basic reading skills:

Phonemic awareness/Auditory processing

Working memory/Short-term memory

Long-term retrieval/Rapid automatic naming

Successive processing

# DON'T FORGET

The following are the processes most important for reading comprehension:

Working memory

Fluid reasoning

Executive processing

Long-term retrieval

skills are short-term memory, long-term retrieval, processing speed, and auditory processing. The Evans et al. study also found consistent moderate relations between basic reading skills and working memory and phonemic awareness.

## Processes Important to Mathematics

Reading and written language disorders are often comorbid, whereas mathematics disorders often stand alone. This difference may be because some of the processes that have high correlations with math skills are different from the processes that have high correlations with reading and written language. As with reading and writing, math depends on adequate working memory resources (Wilson & Swanson, 2001), adequate processing speed, and the ability to store and retrieve information. In contrast to reading and writing, math skills depend more heavily on visual processing and fluid reasoning. Visual processing is important for the early acquisition of basic math skills, but it is also important to advanced mathematics, such as geometry. Fluid reasoning is necessary for problem solving; it is especially related to math reasoning, such as what is required in algebra. Students with reading and writing disabilities but not a math disability often have strengths in visual processing and fluid reasoning. In contrast, those with a math disability often have deficits in one or both of these areas. For example, a WISC-IV standardization study of students with a math disorder found their mean Perceptual Reasoning Index of 87.7 (a scale that measures both visual processing and fluid reasoning) to be their lowest index score and significantly lower than the mean of a matched control group.

## Processes Important to Written Language

Writing skills are highly correlated with reading skills and require many similar processes, namely auditory/ phonemic processing, working memory, processing speed, and long-term

> **DON'T FORGET**
>
> The following are the processes most important for mathematics:
> - Visual processing
> - Fluid reasoning
> - Working memory
> - Processing speed

> **DON'T FORGET**
>
> The following are the processes most important for writing:
> - Auditory processing/Phonemic awareness
> - Executive processing/Planning
> - Working memory
> - Processing speed

storage and retrieval. Writing clearly places high demands on working memory as the writer must hold information while structuring it into sentences. Thus, automaticity of basic writing skills, such as spelling, lays the groundwork for higher level skills such as composition and written expression. Written expression also requires executive processing, in particular planning and organization.

## AN EXAMPLE OF PROCESSING DURING LEARNING

The integration of processes and their roles in learning can be illustrated by the functioning of a learner during a typical classroom lesson in mathematics. To begin with, the learner employs executive processing to set goals and to make plans to accomplish those goals. Deciding to pay attention to the lesson and to selectively screen out background noise is also an executive decision. As the learner listens to the teacher's instruction, auditory processing is engaged. When the teacher writes a story problem on the board, the learner, who is a fluent reader, utilizes visual processing and briefly uses phonological processing to decode an unfamiliar word. During problem solving, short-term memory and working memory are critical as the learner holds and manipulates information. The problem-solving procedures also require the engagement of fluid reasoning to apply acquired math facts and algorithms and the engagement of executive processes, once again, to monitor progress toward a solution. Of course, the learner will also be retrieving math facts and procedures from long-term memory during problem solving. When a learning task is analyzed, it is obvious that even the most basic and automated tasks require the involvement of multiple processes efficiently working together.

 **TEST YOURSELF**

1. **Which of the following processing theories originally used the computer as a metaphor for processing?**
   (a) Neuroscience
   (b) Luria's
   (c) Information processing
   (d) CHC
2. **CHC theory is usually considered a theory of** _____.
   (a) behavior
   (b) intelligence
   (c) processing speed
   (d) brain functioning

3. **Which of the following processes has the weakest relationship with basic reading skills?**

    (a) Fluid reasoning

    (b) Working memory

    (c) Phonemic awareness

    (d) Long-term retrieval

4. **Which of the following types of processing plays a role in directing how the other processes function?**

    (a) Working memory

    (b) Attention

    (c) Simultaneous processing

    (d) Executive processing

5. **Automacity increases the capacity of which type of processing?**

    (a) Working memory

    (b) Attention

    (c) Executive processing

    (d) Visual processing

6. **Knowing when, how, where, and why to apply a particular processing strategy is known as _____.**

    (a) successive processing

    (b) fluid reasoning

    (c) working memory

    (d) metacognition

7. **Research has found that students with learning disabilities typically have deficits in one or more types of processing.** True or False?

8. **How does knowing something about a child's processing strengths and weaknesses help us to better understand a child's learning difficulties?**

9. **Describe the interaction between working memory and long-term memory.**

10. **Think about your own processing skills, and list your individual processing strengths and weaknesses.**

*Answers:* 1. c; 2. b; 3. a; 4. d; 5. a; 6. d; 7. True; 8. Knowing a child's processing strengths and weaknesses helps us to better understand the child's learning difficulties mainly because learning depends on processing. Identifying processing weaknesses or deficits will help us to understand *why* the child is having a particular learning difficulty and understand which processes are helping or hindering a specific type of academic learning. 9. There is a constant two-way interaction between working memory and long-term memory. Working memory takes in new information, manipulates and organizes it, links it with related information that has been retrieved from long-term memory, and then stores it in long-term memory. Working memory also retrieves information from long-term memory and uses this information to construct a response. 10. Answers will vary.

# Three

## STRATEGIES FOR ASSESSING PROCESSING

**B**asic knowledge of human cognitive processing is a prerequisite for those who assess processing in individuals referred for learning difficulties. A theoretical basis (provided in Chapter 2) enhances and facilitates the planning, implementation, and interpretation of an individualized processing assessment. The goal of any psychoeducational assessment should be to gain a better understanding of the learner, with an eye toward designing effective interventions for that individual. Devoid of theoretical context, the meaning of assessment results is often unclear or misconstrued. Processing weaknesses and deficits may even go undetected when evaluations of processing are driven by atheoretical diagnostic or educational criteria instead of a hypothesis testing approach based on theory. Assessment procedures should be individualized for each referral; there isn't a standard battery for assessing processing. Assessments procedures should be determined by the hypotheses selected to address the referral concerns. The generation and selection of processing hypotheses is discerning when the practitioner has an informed theoretical orientation.

Systematic planning before conducting a processing assessment is likely to increase the efficiency of the assessment and the usefulness of the results. In addition to providing a structure for planning and organizing an assessment, this chapter outlines a multidimensional approach to assessment that includes interviewing, observations, and records review, in addition to standardized testing. Guidelines for selecting tests, factors, and subtests are offered, along with a selective testing table for a variety of tests. The chapter concludes with an introduction to a cross-battery method that will ensure efficiency and facilitate the interpretation that is discussed in Chapter 4.

When it comes to assessing processing, the goal is to gain a better understanding of the examinee's processing strengths and weaknesses and to determine whether a processing weakness or deficit may be related to an academic learning deficiency. Assessment of processing should be part of the evaluation whenever a pupil is referred for learning problems or a possible LD. Because processing problems are thought to underlie many learning problems or LDs, an understanding of the referred individual's learning problems would be incomplete without a processing assessment. In an educational setting, the extent to which processing is assessed should not be determined by the need to establish educational or diagnostic criteria but rather by the need to gain a better understanding of why the pupil is having learning difficulties.

Once a learner's processing strengths and weaknesses have been identified, this knowledge can be used to document LDs and design individualized interventions and appropriate educational programming. Educational interventions are likely to be more effective when they take into account the processing weaknesses associated with a given learning problem. For example, there are many potential processing problems that can account for a delay in reading development. An intervention for a student who has a phonemic awareness deficit should be distinct from an intervention designed for a student whose phonemic awareness is fine but has difficulty with long-term retrieval. Thus, assessment of processing should be conducted with treatment in mind.

## MULTIDIMENSIONAL ASSESSMENT

As with other types of psychological and educational assessment, the assessment of processing should be multidimensional. A single method of assessment or a single source of data is not enough when assessing psychological constructs. Generally, the interpretation and validity of assessment results improves as the number of data collection methods increases. When assessment results converge, such as when observations support test scores, evaluators can be more confident in the meaning of the results. When assessment results are divergent or contradictory, explanatory hypotheses should be generated and tested through further assessment. Placement, diagnostic, and programming decisions should never be based on one source of data alone. Best practices in assessment of processing require multidimensional assessment.

Assessment methods can be divided into formal and informal methods. Standardized, norm-referenced tests are the main type of formal assessment. Informal methods consist of observations, interviews, reviews of records, and other unstandardized procedures, such as an unstandardized rating scale. Informal methods may be structured, semistructured, or unstructured. Some informal methods may be supported by research, but informal methods are less objective than formal methods and more subject to influences such as examiner bias. The reliability and validity of most informal procedures is unknown. Thus, a standardized test or procedure, because of its increased objectivity, reliability, and va-

> ## DON'T FORGET
>
> Processing assessment should be multidimensional and should include standardized testing as well as one or more informal methods, such as a review of records, interviews, and observations.

lidity, should always be part of a processing assessment. However, an assessment of processing should never be limited to a formal procedure alone; other evaluation methods, including informal methods, should always be included. For example, interviews and observations should be part of every processing assessment and usually should precede formal testing.

Although it is common practice in some educational settings to assess processing with only informal methods, a valid assessment of processing requires standardized testing. Besides reliability concerns, a primary reason for including standardized testing is the nature of processing itself. As discussed earlier, the development of processing constructs and our knowledge of processing are still evolving. In addition, many types of processing do not lend themselves well to observation because of their complexity and internalization. The other main reason for conducting standardized testing is the lack of one-to-one correspondence between an observable behavior and a type of processing. For example, it may be observed that a student has difficulty following directions. Determining the specific processing difficulty that accounts for not following directions is challenging because several processes, including attention, working memory, and retrieval, are involved in following directions.

## PRELIMINARY DATA COLLECTION

Prior to selecting and administering standardized tests, evaluators should develop hypotheses that account for the referral concerns. The generation and selection of logical hypotheses begins with a careful examination of the presenting problems or reasons for referral. Especially when it comes to assessing processing, the referral concerns need to be fleshed out in detail before an appropriate processing assessment can be planned and conducted. Simply relying on the concerns stated on a referral form is likely to be ineffective because the individual making the referral often does not identify potential processing difficulties even when he or she has observed them.

> ## CAUTION
>
> Do not rely solely on the initially stated referral concerns when assessing processing. To fully identify processing concerns, interview the individual who made the referral.

## Interviewing

In an educational setting, clarification and identification of the referral concerns typically involves an initial interview with the teacher or parent who referred the student. The traditional referral forms, developmental histories, and structured and semistructured interview formats seldom include items related to processing. Thus, the interviewer must make a special effort to develop questions that directly inquire about the learner's processing. One strategy for selecting interview items is to inquire about each of the main processing components. (See Chapter 2 for a discussion of the components and Rapid Reference 3.1 for suggested interview items.) Another strategy is to begin with questions about the processing weaknesses, such as memory, that are most frequently associated with LDs. Per-

## ≣Rapid Reference 3.1

### Examples of Teacher and Parent Interview Items for Each Process

*Note: For each process, the first item is more of an open-ended question, while the second item is a more focused question.*

*Attention:*
1. How well does the student stay on task or sustain attention?
2. How well does the student sustain attention and stay on task while working on a typical assignment?

*Auditory Processing:*
1. How well does the student discriminate between different sounds?
2. Does the student mistake words he or she hears, such as *cat* for *can?*

*Executive Processing:*
1. How well does the student apply learning strategies that you have taught?
2. How well does the student detect his or her mistakes on a writing assignment?

*Fluid Reasoning:*
1. How well does the student problem solve when confronted with an unfamiliar task?
2. When given a problem to solve, does the student apply a logical strategy?

*Long-Term Retrieval:*
1. How quickly and how well does the student retrieve information on demand?
2. Does the student have difficulty recognizing letters, numbers, and shapes?

*Phonemic Awareness:*
1. Does the student have difficulty with rhyming or recognizing words that sound the same?
2. How well does the student segment the speech sounds in a word?

(continued)

*Planning:*
1. How well does the student plan and organize?
2. How well does the student plan a schedule for completing a long-term project?

*Processing Speed:*
1. How quickly and fluently does the student perform simple mental tasks?
2. How quickly does the student typically complete a simple worksheet when under pressure to complete it quickly?

*Short-Term Memory:*
1. How well does the student remember information, such as directions, for several seconds?
2. Does the student frequently ask you to repeat directions just seconds after you stated them?

*Simultaneous Processing:*
1. How well does the student understand the whole idea when presented with different elements of an idea?
2. How well does the student integrate objects into a whole, such as putting a puzzle together?

*Successive Processing:*
1. How well does the student arrange items or information sequentially?
2. Does the student have difficulty saying the alphabet in order?

*Visual Processing:*
1. How well does the student acquire and manipulate information presented visually?
2. Does the student have difficulty recognizing letters or words in different forms?

*Working Memory:*
1. How well does the student mentally manipulate information, such as doing mental arithmetic?
2. How much repetition does the student need before he or she is able to retain information?

haps the most efficient and focused strategy is to first identify the areas of academic learning difficulty, then inquire specifically about the processes that are highly correlated with these learning deficits, such as asking questions about phonemic awareness when there is a basic reading skills weakness (see Rapid Reference 3.2). With all three strategies, begin with open questions and proceed with more focused or closed questions to obtain the most specific and complete information. When the interviewee is unsure of a question or a response, the interviewer should provide behavioral examples.

Besides asking the teacher or parent what she or he has observed, it is important to elicit hypotheses regarding the student's learning problems, especially during the initial interview when clarifying referral concerns. The expression of these hypotheses may elucidate possible processing difficulties. For example, it may be the teacher's hypothesis that a student is struggling because of retrieval problems. One

## ≡Rapid Reference 3.2

### Examples of Processing Interview Items by Academic Skill Area

*Reading:*
1. How well does the student manipulate phonemes, such as blending and segmenting the phonemes in words?
2. How quickly does the student name objects?
3. How well does the student remember new letters or words?
4. How well does the student use context clues when trying to comprehend?

*Mathematics:*
1. How well does the student keep track of numbers when asked to do mental arithmetic?
2. How quickly does the student complete simple calculations?
3. How well does the student categorize and group information?

*Written Language:*
1. How well does the student plan and organize a writing assignment?
2. How well does the student keep track of his or her ideas when trying to express those ideas in writing?

way to encourage the expression of processing hypotheses is to ask the teacher *why* she or he thinks the student is experiencing each specific learning problem. When teachers do not explicitly state processing hypotheses, the interviewer may need to provide more structure by asking questions such as "Do you think the student is having difficulty with basic reading skills because he can't remember new words or because he has difficulty sounding them out?" Effective interviewing will not only clarify the referral concerns and hypotheses but will also allow the interviewer to identify the concerns and hypotheses that need to be assessed.

After an assessment plan, including processing hypotheses, has been developed, in-depth interviews should be conducted with the learner and the learner's parents and teachers. The interviewer can most effectively gather more information about processing concerns, as well as data for testing processing hypotheses, by asking questions directly about processing. Interviewees will have varying levels of understanding processing or may even have misconceptions about processing. Consequently, the interviewer will need to operationalize processing by providing concrete examples. When interviewing children and adolescents, it will be necessary to bring the items down to their level. The interviewer should focus on observable behaviors and on behaviors that occur when the learner is engaged in the academic area(s) of difficulty. Except for eliciting the interviewees' hypotheses about the learning difficulty, the interviewer should avoid items that ask for inferences. The interviewer also needs to be cognizant of attempts by some interviewees to portray the learner as having significant learning and processing problems, with the hopes of having the learner placed in special education. Thus, information from interviewees should never be used alone to confirm processing hypotheses or reach diagnostic decisions. Rather, interview responses should be viewed as information that needs to be corroborated through other assessment sources and methods before it can be accepted as valid.

Some structured interviews and questionnaires provide sections or individual items that address processing concerns. One example of a standardized questionnaire is the Aggregate Neurobehavioral Student Health and Educational Review (ANSER) System (Levine, 1997), which contains items that tap attention, memory, organization, and sequencing. An advantage of the ANSER System is that it is a multiinformant—parent, teacher, and student—scale. Practitioners who are interested in a thorough review of effective interviewing techniques and a comprehensive list of suggested interview items should consult other sources, such as Sattler (2002).

## Screening

In addition to or in lieu of an interview, a standardized or unstandardized screener may be useful for gathering more information about referral concerns and potential processing problems. One example of a standardized and normed screener is the Psychological Processing Checklist (PPC; Swerdlik, Swerdlik, Kahn, & Thomas, 2003a). This 35-item teacher rating scale (see Chapter 8 for details) produces a Total Score, as well as scores in Auditory Processing, Visual Processing, Organization, Attention, Visual-Motor Processing, and Social Perception. Another standardized teacher rating scale that contains processing items is the Learning Disabilities Diagnostic Inventory (Hammill & Bryant, 1998), which divides the items by listening, speaking, reading, writing, mathematics, and reasoning. Unstandardized, informal checklists or rating scales can also be an efficient method of gathering information for the purposes of clarifying referral concerns and developing hypotheses.

## Reviewing Records

Before or after an initial interview, an evaluator will usually review the pupil's records or history. Since educational records, such as report cards, do not usually contain explicit data and comments on processing, finding evidence of previous processing difficulties may involve some detective work, for example, reviewing teachers' anecdotal reports for clues that point toward potential processing problems. The reviewer will usually need to look for behaviors that are associated with different types of processing. For example, a teacher's comment that the child has difficulty retaining information from one day to the next is indicative of a long-term storage and retrieval problem. Comments on report cards and other teacher reports should be scrutinized carefully (see Rapid Reference 3.3 for additional tips). In addition to educational records, a review of medical or neurological records is pertinent when there are processing concerns.

When searching for evidence of processing weaknesses in records, the evaluator should pay particular attention to the onset of the processing deficit and how frequently it has been reported. Unless there has been a brain injury or an illness that affected the brain, it can be assumed that processing strengths and weaknesses have

## ⩶ Rapid Reference 3.3

### Difficulties That Are Indicative of Possible Processing Problems

*Attention:* Staying on task; paying attention; ignoring distractions; completing boring tasks; following written instructions

*Auditory Processing:* Adequately understanding language; differentiating between different sounds; pronouncing words clearly; coping with noise in the classroom

*Executive Processing:* Detecting errors; inhibiting behaviors; using strategies that have been taught

*Fluid Reasoning:* Applying computational skills; developing hypotheses; synthesizing related material; inferring meaning; matching; sorting; classifying; applying concepts

*Long-Term Retrieval:* Recognizing whole words; naming letters; accessing desired information; remembering directions; retrieving needed words; responding in an acceptable amount of time; remembering in general

*Phonemic Awareness:* Decoding words in isolation; associating sounds with letters; blending sounds

*Planning:* Completing projects on time; maintaining an assignment calendar; using time wisely

*Processing Speed:* Reading with fluency; completing tests on time

*Short-Term Memory:* Remembering directions; restating information

*Simultaneous Processing:* Recognizing the main idea; mapping

*Successive Processing:* Arranging things in order; following all of the steps in directions; organizing facts sequentially; sequencing numbers; writing from left to right; sequencing meaningful sentences

*Visual Processing:* Reproducing correct letter forms; estimating distance; spacing problems on a page

*Working Memory:* Organizing written expression; paraphrasing information; taking meaningful notes; integrating current information with past experience

## DON'T FORGET

When reviewing records, existing intellectual or cognitive test scores should be reanalyzed, using the Processing Analysis Worksheet in Appendix C.

been with the learner all along. Deficits in basic processes such as auditory and visual processing and short-term and long-term memory should be evident as soon as a child enters school. However, deficits in the higher level processes, such as fluid reasoning and executive processing, may not become apparent until the later childhood years when the frontal lobes become fully developed. Difficulties in basic processes, such as attention, that are first reported in later school years are not likely to be actual ongoing deficiencies and should be carefully investigated. For example, attentional problems that originate in middle school may not be due to a processing deficiency in attention. Such behavior might be related to diminished interest in academic learning, or it may also be related to mental health concerns, such as depression. In reviewing records, the evaluator should also track how frequently and consistently the processing concern has been recorded. Isolated reports should not be accepted as adequate documentation but rather as red flags that need to be investigated further. Some reported difficulties may be situation-specific behaviors that serve a function in a particular environment but are not actual processing deficiencies.

Another major aspect of reviewing records is collecting and interpreting data from previous psychological or educational testing. When doing so, it is important that the original test scores be analyzed instead of relying solely on the interpretation found in the existing report(s). The examiner or team that completed previous assessments may not have been aware of processing measures embedded in scales that were used, or they may have interpreted processing assessment results incorrectly. For example, a child may have obtained an extremely low WISC-III Digit Span subtest, but it was never interpreted as a possible deficit in working or short-term memory. To analyze existing test scores from a processing perspective, follow the procedures on the Processing Analysis Worksheet found in Appendix C. By the end of this book, the reader will be familiar with the analytical procedures and processing implications of test scores from a variety of cognitive batteries and processing scales.

### Observations

In addition to a review of the records and a preliminary interview, an initial observation should be conducted. It is most productive to observe the referred pupil when the student is engaged in academic areas of difficulty. An observation for processing problems is similar to a functional behavioral assessment (FBA) observation (Watson & Steege, 2003). During an FBA observation, the observer is trying to discover the relationships between behaviors, that is, trying to determine why the targeted behavior is occurring. It is much the same when observing for processing deficits. The observer should be alert for indicators of processing problems that may be related to the acade-

## CAUTION

Without test results and data from other methods, observations of processing should only be used to develop and support hypotheses, not draw conclusions.

mic learning problems. To accomplish this goal, the observer needs to be familiar with the relationships between types of academic learning and types of processing (see Chapter 2) as well as behaviors that may be indicative of types of processing (see Rapid Reference 3.3). Even an observer with expertise in assessing processing needs to be cautious about making inferences from observed behaviors, mainly due to the lack of one-to-one correspondence between behaviors and processes. To really understand behavior-processing relationships, you must analyze the processing demands of the task being observed (Hale & Fiorello, 2004). Furthermore, without convergent data from other sources, observations alone should never be used to draw conclusions about processing strengths and weaknesses. Rather, observations should mainly be used to generate hypotheses and to support other sources of data.

Similar to structured interview formats, structured observations that itemize behaviors to observe may also contain processing behaviors to varying degrees. Such formats are typically based on expert opinion, such as the one found in Volpiansky, Chiang, Dehn, Frankenburger, and Griffin (2003), and seldom have norms or reliability and validity evidence.

### Observations during Testing

Observations conducted during the administration of standardized tests can provide valuable clinical insights and data about the examinee's processing strengths and weaknesses. Because performance on factors and subtests involves more than one process, careful observation may identify the process having the most impact on performance. For example, an observation that the examinee had difficulty with word retrieval supports a long-term retrieval deficit hypothesis. At other times, observations can identify noncognitive influences on performance, such as when a child expresses a negative attitude toward the testing situation. Some batteries provide structure for recording or rating test-taking behaviors, such as persistence, cooperation, and attention, that are known to affect test performance. Other batteries require the examiner to record observations of processes, such as planning. There are even standardized rating scales for test session behavior, such as a scale designed for the Wechsler Intelligence Scale for Children, third edition (WISC-III; Glutting & Oakland, 1993). Detailed advice on behaviors to observe and how to interpret them is provided by Sattler (2001). In general, observations gathered during testing are informal data that should be considered, along with test scores, when weighing the evidence for and against hypotheses.

## A HYPOTHESIS TESTING APPROACH TO ASSESSMENT

Once the referral concerns have been identified and clarified, the next phase in planning a comprehensive and efficient processing assessment is to generate hypotheses that account for each of the referral concerns. Some of these hypotheses may have already been put forward by the student's teachers or parents. It is the responsibility of the examiner and other members of the multidisciplinary evaluation team to determine the remaining hypotheses. Hypothesis generation is best facilitated by a team brainstorming process that results in at least one credible hypothesis for each referral concern. After hypotheses have been generated, those that are worthy of assessment are chosen. Hypotheses that seem to lack relevance or merit, regardless of the source of these hypotheses, need not be included. When determining whether a hypothesis is worthy of investigation, the examiner or team should consider the extent to which the hypothesized processing problem is related to the specific academic learning concern. There should be a logical, if not empirically based, connection between the hypotheses generated and the referral concerns. This is where theories of processing and empirical evidence of processing-learning relationships play a role. For example, a phonemic awareness deficit has very little to do with math learning problems, and weaknesses in fluid reasoning would be unlikely to impact basic reading skills (see Rapid Reference 3.4 for examples of processing hypothesis). Of course, not all hypotheses that account for learning problems may relate to cognitive processing. Instructional, behavioral, or environmental variables may also be impacting the student's learning.

Basing processing evaluations on hypothesis testing serves several functions and has several advantages. First, explicitly generating and selecting hypotheses forces the examiner and multidisciplinary evaluation team to carefully think about and consider the referral concerns and how best to assess them. Each hypothesis should be one possible explanation for *why* the learner is experiencing a specific learning problem. Hypotheses should flow from the referral questions. Evaluators who initially have difficulty generating hypotheses should first state the referral questions. For example, when the referral concern is difficulty with basic reading skills, a logical referral question would be "Does the learner have a deficit in phonemic awareness?" and the corresponding hypothesis would be

## ≡Rapid Reference 3.4

### Examples of Processing Hypotheses by Academic Area of Difficulty

*Basic Reading Skills:*
The learner has a weakness in phonemic awareness.
The learner has a weakness in long-term retrieval, especially rapid automatic naming.
The learner has a weakness in working memory.
The learner has a weakness in successive processing.

*Reading Comprehension:*
The learner has a weakness in executive processing.
The learner has a weakness in fluid reasoning.

*Math Calculation:*
The learner has a weakness in visual processing.
The learner has a weakness in processing speed.

*Math Reasoning:*
The learner has a weakness in fluid reasoning.
The learner has a weakness in planning.

*Written Expression:*
The learner has weaknesses in executive processing, especially organization.

"The learner has a deficit in phonemic awareness." Thus, hypothesis generation and selection can increase our understanding of the learner even before testing is conducted. Second, an explicit, structured, and recorded hypothesis testing approach allows those who are novices to conduct a thorough and individualized processing assessment. Those with expertise in processing assessment have usually chunked and automatized the steps and may not need to verbalize and record each step. Third, following a hypotheses testing approach truly individualizes the assessment, forcing the evaluator to abandon a standard battery approach and adapt to the unique concerns of each case. Finally, following the hypothesis testing method results in an efficient, time-saving assessment that avoids redundancies while measuring all of the processes that need to be assessed.

After the processing hypotheses have been selected, the next step is to determine the best assessment procedure for testing each hypothesis. In many cases, an informal procedure, such as an observation, will provide enough data to test one or more hypotheses. For other hypotheses, standardized testing will be necessary. In most situations, one instrument, such as a comprehensive memory scale, can be used to test several hypotheses. While selecting the assessment methods, it may also be a good time for the multidisciplinary team to assign specific assessment tasks to team members.

## CAUTION

Avoid hypothesis confirmation bias by assuming that an a prior hypothesis is false unless there is considerable convergent evidence to the contrary.

Effective use of the hypothesis testing model depends on delaying the selection of standardized measures until after the hypotheses have been identified. In other words, processing assessment should be hypothesis-driven, not battery-driven. Selecting the instrument(s) in advance of choosing hypotheses, or using the same instruments with every assessment, is not only inefficient but also poor practice.

When hypotheses are selected prior to assessment, they are known as *a priori hypotheses*. From a scientific perspective, the main purpose of generating hypotheses before acquiring and analyzing data is to increase the objectivity of the investigation and the interpretation of results. As data is collected and analyzed, new insights often arise, and more hypotheses may be added. When the results are confusing and inconsistent or are not what would be predicted from the hypotheses, it is often necessary to generate new hypotheses that account for the findings. These hypotheses are referred to as *a posteriori hypotheses*. When additional assessment data needs to be generated to test these hypotheses, the examiner cycles back to an earlier step. Thus, the hypothesis testing method is an iterative approach.

When using a hypothesis testing approach to assessment, it is critical that evaluators keep an open mind and avoid hypothesis confirmation bias (Hale & Fiorello, 2004). That is, we must not fall into the trap of looking only for confirming evidence and ignoring data that does not support our a priori hypothesis. The best safeguard is to look for other explanations and to assume that the hypothesis is false (or that the null hypothesis is true) unless there is considerable convergent evidence to the contrary.

## USING THE PROCESSING ASSESSMENT ORGANIZER

Many practitioners already have expertise in assessing processing and have automatized their planning and assessment procedures. For those who have not, an organizational scheme such as the Processing Assessment Organizer displayed in Appendix B may be helpful. To use this form, fill in the columns as each of the steps discussed previously is completed (see Rapid Reference 3.5). The first three columns provide the plan to follow during the assessment. The fourth and fifth columns are completed as results become available and ideas for programming are generated. The form can either be used by an individual examiner or by a multidisciplinary evaluation team. Following the assessment plan that has been explicitly formulated ensures that all concerns are assessed and each hypothesis investigated. Having a plan and following it also increases efficiency by avoiding redundancies and the need for follow-up assessment of omitted areas. When the assessment is finished, a completed form is also useful for writing reports and reviewing the entire assessment process at meetings. Thus, the form can be used to plan and organize an assessment from beginning to end. The format is applicable to all types of assessment, but the suggestions provided here are limited to processing assessment.

The first three columns of the Processing Assessment Organizer (see Rapid Reference 3.5) should be completed during the planning and initial phases of the evaluation. As discussed previously, the referral concerns should include all those academic learning concerns and processing concerns identified after a review of records, initial interviews, and initial observations; the concerns should not be limited to those stated on a referral form. Then for each concern, enter the hypotheses that have been selected for testing. There should be at least one hypothesis for each concern. In the third column, enter an assessment method for each hypothesis. If only a portion of a test is necessary, enter the specific factors or subtests that will be administered (see later sections in this chapter for more explanation). The remaining two columns are to be completed when the assessment is finished (see Chapter 4 for more details). A numbering system should be used to organize all of the entries so that it is clear which information applies to which concern and hypothesis; for example, begin by numbering the first referral concern as 1, proceed by numbering the hypotheses selected for that concern as 1.1, 1.2, and so on, and numbering the information in the remaining columns in the same way (see Rapid Reference 3.6 for a partially completed case study).

## ≡ Rapid Reference 3.5

### Completing the Processing Assessment Organizer

1. *List referral concerns in column 1.* Determine the referral concerns after preliminary data collection.

2. *Enter selected processing hypotheses in column 2.* After considering all reasonable hypotheses, select at least one processing hypothesis for each referral concern.

3. *Enter the selected testing methods in column 3.* For each hypothesis, list the assessment method(s) selected to test it. When conducting standardized testing, list the specific factors or subtests that will be used to test each hypothesis.

4. *Enter assessment results in column 4.* After data collection is complete and results have been analyzed, enter the findings that specifically relate to each hypothesis (see Rapid Reference 4.10). Identify the level of functioning and any processes that are strengths/assets or weaknesses/deficits (entering test scores is optional).

5. *Enter conclusions about the hypotheses in column 5.* After weighing the evidence for and against each hypothesis, enter a concluding statement. Educational implications and suggestions for programming may also be entered in this column.

# ≋ Rapid Reference 3.6

## Processing Assessment Organizer

Student: _____ Form Completed By: _____ Case Study #1 _____ DOB: _____ Date: _____ Age: 11 Grade: 5

| Referral Concerns | Processing Hypotheses | Assessment Methods | Assessment Results | Conclusions |
|---|---|---|---|---|
| I. Struggles in math | I.A. Has a weakness/deficit in fluid reasoning | I.A.1. WISC-IV Fluid Reasoning subtests | | |
| | I.B. Has a weakness/deficit in visual processing | I.B.1. WJ III Visual Processing Cluster I.B.2. WISC-IV Block Design subtest | | |

| | | | | | | | |
|---|---|---|---|---|---|---|---|
| 2. Is slow to complete homework | 2.A. Has a weakness/deficit in planning | 2.A.1. Interview parent<br>2.A.2. Interview student<br>2.A.3. Observe student | | | | | |
| | 2.B. Has a weakness/deficit in processing speed | 2.B.1. WISC-IV Processing Speed Index | | | | | |
| 3. Does poorly on classroom exams | 3.A. Has a weakness/deficit in long-term retrieval | 3.A.1. WJ III Long-Term Retrieval Cluster | | | | | |
| 4. Has difficulty learning new concepts | 4.A. Has a weakness/deficit in long-term retrieval | 4.A.1. WJ III Long-Term Retrieval Cluster | | | | | |
| | 4.B Has a weakness/deficit in fluid reasoning | 4.B.1. WISC-IV Fluid Reasoning subtests | | | | | |
| 5. Has weak reading comprehension | 5.A. Has a weakness/deficit in working memory | 5.A.1. WISC-IV Working Memory Index | | | | | |
| | 5.B. Has a weakness/deficit in executive processing | 5.B.1. Interview parent<br>5.B.2. Interview student<br>5.B.3. Observe student | | | | | |

## GENERAL GUIDELINES FOR SELECTING PROCESSING MEASURES

One of the major goals of this book is to provide guidance in selecting measures of specific processes. The intent of this section is to review some general psychometric principles that apply when selecting tests and components of tests, such as subtests and factors.

### Reliability and Validity

As with other types of assessment, documentation of a processing instrument's reliability and validity is very important. Reliability coefficients, which are derived from test-retest studies or internal consistency analysis, indicate the stability and precision of a test score. The higher the reliability estimate, the less measurement error associated with the score. When reliability coefficients are .90 or above, reliability is considered adequate, and test scores can be used to make diagnostic decisions. Practitioners need to be cautious when making decisions, or even when identifying functioning levels and individual strengths and weaknesses, based on scores that have coefficients of less than .90. In such instances, strong corroborative evidence needs to support the score before it is given much credibility. Scores that have reliability coefficients of less than .80 should not be used alone but may be combined with other test scores to produce a useable composite with higher reliability. Composite scores have higher reliability than individual subtest scores, mainly because composite scores are based on more items and, thus, will fluctuate less than subtest scores. Consequently, interpretation and decisions should be based primarily on composite scores, not on subtest scores. Reliability coefficients for several recommended processing measures will be provided in later chapters.

Validity can be demonstrated through a variety of studies that address content, criterion (predictive and concurrent), and construct validity. Validity evidence is crucial because it documents the extent to which a test and its subscales measure the constructs they are intended to measure. At the very least, a test manual should

> **CAUTION**
>
> In selecting portions of tests to administer, factors should be chosen over subtests when possible. This is because factor scores are more reliable and because factors usually have better construct validity. Also, interpretation and decisions should be based primarily on factor scores, not subtest scores. Factor scores with reliability coefficients of less than .90 should be interpreted cautiously and require corroboration from other sources of data.

provide concurrent validity data that demonstrates a significant relationship between the test's scales and similar scales in established test batteries. Ideally, for a test that is used to assess processing, there should be empirical evidence demonstrating the test's ability to discriminate between populations that are known to have processing differences; for example, a study finding a lower working memory mean in a reading disabled sample would provide evidence of construct validity. Validity information on specific scales is provided in subsequent chapters.

## Other Selection Criteria

If reliability and validity evidence is adequate, the practitioner should carefully review the test's purpose and structure as well as definitions of factors and subtests. Professional practice standards emphasize that tests should only be used for intended purposes; for example, a test of short-term memory should not be used to measure general intelligence. In most instances, validity studies support a test's purported structure. However, the abilities, skills, and processes that underlie performance on most tests, scales, or subtests are complex, as many factor analytic studies of scales and subtests reveal. There are also many processing commonalities across subtests that have not been explicitly grouped for processing assessment. For example, on the WISC-IV, fluid reasoning is measured by both Verbal Comprehension and Perceptual Reasoning subtests (Keith, Fine, Taub, Reynolds, & Kranzler, 2004). Thus, the expert examiner may select a combination of subtests to assess fluid reasoning even though the WISC-IV does not provide a fluid reasoning factor score. There are also times when research finds that tests, factors, or subtests may not be measuring what the test's manual claims they are measuring. For example, factor analytic studies of the CAS (Naglieri & Das, 1997a) Planning and Attention scales by Keith, Kranzler, and Flanagan (2001) found that these two CAS processing scales may be primarily measuring processing speed instead of planning and attention. Thus, in some instances it is acceptable to use factors or subtests to assess processes other than those explicitly identified by the test.

Once the examiner has knowledge of the available scales and what they measure, selection of the standardized tests should be guided by the referral concerns and hypotheses that account for these concerns. The priority is to assess processes that have strong relationships with the area(s) of academic deficiency. One strategy for efficient processing assessment is to focus mainly on the hypothesized processing weaknesses or deficits. However, there are instances when the assessment should go beyond the testing of hypothesized weaknesses, especially when the pupil is being referred for the first time or when the pupil is experiencing academic learning difficulties in all areas. Also, a comprehensive processing assessment should include testing for potential strengths; identifying strengths puts relative weaknesses in perspective.

Because hypotheses may change during the course of an evaluation, more testing and other informal procedures may be added after the initial plan is developed. There may also be situations where it is difficult to select the most plausible hypotheses or it cannot be determined just how in-depth the testing should be. In such instances, it may be best to using a screening approach, beginning with a broad-based but short scale. After the screening reveals potential weaknesses, these can be tested in more depth.

## SELECTING SPECIFIC TESTS, FACTORS, AND SUBTESTS

Many standardized tests designed to primarily assess constructs other than processing actually contain direct measures of specific processes. For example, some achievement tests include long-term retrieval and phonemic awareness factors, while IQ tests typically measure several processes. Thus, a practitioner who is administering an intellectual scale with the goal of obtaining the examinee's Full Scale IQ is also (sometimes unwittingly) obtaining data on several processes. In other words, administration of a general cognitive abilities scale may accomplish two goals simultaneously if the examiner utilizes the embedded processing data. Consequently, assessment of processing must begin with knowledge of which instruments assess processes and which processes are measured by each test. Appendix G provides a comprehensive list of standardized tests that measure each of the 13 processes identified in Chapter 2. All types of standardized tests are included, ranging from tests that measure only one process, such as phonemic awareness, to batteries that include several processes.

Regarding contemporary intellectual and cognitive tests, the Selective Testing Table for Processes Measured by Cognitive Tests (see Appendix A) identifies the processes that are measured by each test's factors and subtests. Only the 13 processes from the Integrated Processing Model (discussed in Chapter 2) are listed; nonprocessing factors, such as crystallized abilities or achievement, are excluded. Because the typical instrument measures only a few processes, there are many blank cells in the table. When an instrument has an identified factor that measures a specific process, the factor's name is listed in uppercase letters. When only subtests measure a process but are not officially grouped together as a factor, their names are listed in lowercase letters. Factors are better choices than individual subtests because of the increased reliability and validity associated with factors. For example, if one test has a fluid reasoning factor, it is a better choice than using a combination of subtests that measure fluid reasoning but do not produce a standardized fluid reasoning factor score. In cases where you must rely on individual subtests, administration of at least two subtests is recommended.

The Selective Testing Table for Processes Measured by Cognitive Tests can be used in several ways. The first option is to examine the scale or battery that you typically administer to determine which processes it actually measures. The second option is to select the scale or battery that measures as many of the chosen processes as possible. Practitioners who faithfully implement a hypothesis-driven processing assessment will need to employ the third option. Under the third option, all of the processes selected for assessment need to be assessed. Except in cases where one of the instruments addresses all of the processing hypotheses, the practitioner will need to use a combination of scales or batteries to complete the desired processing assessment (see Rapid Reference 3.7 for the steps involved). Finally, a clinician can use the table to investigate differences between two global scores. For instance, an examinee who has a deficit in processing speed might have obtained a lower Full Scale score on the WISC-IV than she did on the Stanford-Binet Intelligence Scales, fifth edition (SB5) because the SB5 does not include a processing speed factor.

## ≡Rapid Reference 3.7

### Steps for Conducting a Cross-Battery Processing Assessment

1. From the hypotheses, select processes that need to be assessed through standardized testing.

2. Use the tables in Appendixes A and G to determine the primary test or battery. The primary test should measure as many of the selected processes as possible.

3. Using the tables in Appendixes A and G, select a test that measures as many of the remaining processes as possible.

4. Using the tables in Appendixes A and G, select tests that measure the last remaining processes. Limit the number of tests utilized to as few as possible.

5. To ensure efficient and manageable assessment, avoid redundant testing; measure each process only once. This means that only portions of some scales will be administered.

6. Preference should be given to those tests that measure processing with factors instead of isolated subtests. In cases where subtests must be used, administer at least two subtests for each process.

7. Administer and score the selected tests, factors, and subtests. Within tests, do not administer nonprocessing factors or subtests (unless needed for another purpose), and do not administer processing factors and subtests that were not selected.

A comprehensive assessment of processing can be especially challenging because there are few, if any, standardized scales that measure more than a few select processes. For some evaluations and reevaluations, a comprehensive assessment of processing is unnecessary, or the practitioner decides to limit the processing areas that will be assessed. However, when a comprehensive and in-depth evaluation of processing is desired, the use of more than one scale will usually be necessary. Even when only a few areas of processing are selected for assessment, a cross-battery approach may be indispensable because not all of the selected processes might be found in one test. In both of these instances, evaluators will be able to complete assessments more efficiently if they adhere to a cross-battery approach.

The cross-battery method involves administering a compilation of factors and subtests from different tests in order to measure all of the areas selected for assessment. Informal cross-battery assessment is not new; many practitioners have mixed tests and batteries when evaluating individuals. However, a systematic method of cross-battery assessment was only recently developed by Flanagan, McGrew, and Ortiz (Flanagan et al., 2000; Flanagan & Ortiz, 2001; McGrew & Flanagan, 1998). Their cross-battery approach is linked with the CHC theory of human cognitive abilities. After analyzing and classifying all major intellectual and cognitive scales according to the CHC factors they measure, Flanagan, McGrew, and Ortiz developed procedures for combining scales in a cross-battery fashion in order to assess a broader range of cognitive abilities. For example, the Wechsler scales do not have a measure of auditory processing; thus, the auditory processing cluster from the WJ III COG might be administered in conjunction with a Wechsler scale when data on auditory processing is sought.

The cross-battery approach to processing assessment recommended in this book is an adaptation of the model proposed by Flanagan et al. (2000). The processing cross-battery model proposed here is not limited to CHC cognitive factors. Rather, the model includes all of the main processes identified in the integrated processing model discussed in Chapter 2 (see Rapid Reference 2.10). Thus, the Selective Testing Table for Processes Measured by Cognitive Tests found in Appendix A includes recommended factors and subtests for non-CHC processes, as well as six CHC cognitive processes. Including 13 processes in the integrated model makes it necessary to broaden the scope of recommended processing measures. In addition to intellectual and cognitive scales, other types of tests that measure various processes (see Rapid Reference 3.8) may need to be included in a cross-battery processing assessment. Among these are achievement tests, memory scales, processing tests, and tests designed to measure specific types of processing, such as phonemic awareness and attention (also see Chapters 7 and 8 and Appendix G). For example, subtests or factors selected from different types of tests, such as cognitive and achievement, can be combined into one cross-battery assessment plan, and later the results from both types of tests can be analyzed together.

The processing cross-battery approach also differs from the CHC approach in other ways. First, the placement of the factors and subtests in the Selective Testing Table for Processes Measured by Cognitive Tests (Appendix A) is derived from several sources. The classification of factors and subtests for the CHC processes

===Rapid Reference 3.8

**Categories of Standardized Measures That Can Be Used to Assess Processing**

Intellectual scales
Cognitive scales
Achievement tests
Memory scales
Neuropsychological tests
Tests of executive functioning
Tests of phonemic awareness
Processing scales
Behavior scales

are mostly based on empirical evidence reported by Flanagan and others (Flanagan & Kaufman, 2004; Flanagan et al., 2000; Flanagan & Ortiz, 2001; McGrew & Flanagan, 1998). Suggested factors and subtests for measuring the other processes are mostly based on a test's factor structure, as reported in the test's technical manual and supported by factor analytic studies of the standardization data. The suggestions for tests, factors, and subtests in the Processes Measured by Standardized Tests table (Appendix G) are based on construct validity information reported in test manuals, the definitions of the factors and subtests, and an analysis of the processes involved in the factors and subtests.

Second, in the CHC model, only subtests are categorized, not factors. A *factor,* as the term implies, is usually derived from factor analysis and is thought to represent an underlying trait or ability. On psychological tests, factors consist of items or subtests that seem to be measuring the same broad trait or ability. The term *factor,* as used in this text, applies to any grouping of subtests and the score associated with that grouping. On tests, factors go by a variety of names, including *composites, clusters, indexes,* and *scales.* Because factors are preferable to subtests, factors are listed in the selective testing cells whenever factors that measure a specific process are available. When selecting that factor, one should administer the subtests (two or more) that comprise that factor and use the factor score for interpretation. In the selective testing table cells that list subtests, not all possible subtests are listed; generally, the stronger measures of the process are displayed when there are several from which to pick. For processes where measures are limited, the subtests displayed may be relatively weak. (For detailed information on each factor or subtest in the Selective Testing Table for Processes Measured by Cognitive Tests, see Chapters 5 and 6.)

A systematic cross-battery approach to assessment is actually a time-saving, efficient approach even though more than one test is utilized. Evaluators should not give entire tests; rather, they should administer only those subtests and factors that measure the selected areas. For example, only the working memory and processing speed subtests of the WISC-IV might be administered in conjunction with only the long-term retrieval and auditory processing subtests from the WJ III COG. Administering only selected factors and subtests is acceptable, unless a test's authors specifically state that the entire scale or a certain subset must be administered in order for any of the factor or subtest results to be valid. A test's subtests and factors always have their own norm-derived scores that can be used independently of a full-scale score that depends on administration of the entire test. Administering an entire test in order to obtain a full composite score is of limited value in processing assessment unless the full scale comprises a broad sampling of processes and the full scale represents overall cognitive processing.

Another way in which the cross-battery approach is efficient is that it avoids redundant testing. For instance, if processing speed has already been assessed by administration of the WISC-IV, it should not be tested again when using another scale in conjunction with the WISC-IV. This guideline also applies to the administration of factors that tap more than one process. For example, the WISC-IV's Perceptual Reasoning Index measures both visual processing and fluid reasoning. Thus, there is no need to conduct additional testing of visual processing and fluid reasoning. If adhered to, the cross-battery method is actually very efficient, and being aware of the processing classifications of a test's components can reduce unnecessary testing.

Selection of the tests, factors, and subtests for a cross-battery assessment begins after the evaluators have determined the processing hypotheses that need to be investigated. For example, given the referral concern of difficulty decoding words, two hypotheses might be generated: (1) a phonemic awareness weakness or deficit accounts for the difficulty and (2) a long-term retrieval weakness or deficit accounts for the difficulty. Phonemic awareness and long-term retrieval might not be found on the same test, at least not any one instrument in the evaluator's possession. Thus, administration of factors and subtests from two or more tests may be necessary. Long-term memory subtests might be selected from a memory scale, such as the Children's Memory Scale (Cohen, 1997a), while phonemic awareness might be assessed with a separate scale designed specifically for that purpose. In using both tests, only subtests that specifically assess these two areas should be administered. A selective testing approach does not mean that evaluators should mix and match factors and subtests from several measures. To keep the interpretation of results manageable and valid, examiners should limit the tests involved to two or three whenever possible.

---

 **TEST YOURSELF**

1. **What should determine the processes selected for assessment?**
   (a) The amount of time allocated for assessment
   (b) The processes contained in your most frequently used battery
   (c) The processing hypotheses derived from the referral concerns
   (d) The severity of the processing concerns

2. **Processing assessment should be primarily at the subtest level instead of the factor level.** True or False?

3. **When generating processing hypotheses, it is most important to consider**
   (a) the relationship between processes and the academic area of concern.
   (b) the original hypotheses of the person who made the referral.
   (c) the availability of a battery for testing certain processes.
   (d) one hypothesis that can account for the majority of the concerns.

4. **Which is the best reason for using standardized tests to assess processing?**
   (a) There are now many to choose from.
   (b) The typically administered scales contain measures of processing.
   (c) Informal methods lack validity and are time consuming.
   (d) There's no one-to-one correspondence between a behavior and a process.

5. **When organizing a cross-battery assessment, it is important to avoid**
   (a) using more than one test or scale.
   (b) testing the same process twice.
   (c) using a noncognitive test or scale.
   (d) using factors as measures of the processes.

6. **A comment found in the examinee's records about difficulties inhibiting behavior may be indicative of a processing deficiency in**
   (a) working memory.
   (b) fluid reasoning.
   (c) simultaneous processing.
   (d) executive processing.

(continued)

**7. According to the Selective Testing Table for Processes Measured by Cognitive Tests, which process is most frequently measured by cognitive tests?**

(a) Working memory

(b) Auditory processing

(c) Visual processing

(d) Successive processing

*Answers:* 1. c; 2. False; 3. a; 4. d; 5. b; 6. d; 7. c

Four

# HOW TO INTERPRET PROCESSING ASSESSMENT RESULTS

Administering tests and collecting data is the easy part of assessment. With most evaluations, the foremost challenge is a proper interpretation of the assessment data, especially test results. The meaning of assessment data must be determined by the evaluator. Even with a faithful application of statistical procedures and diagnostic criteria, in the final analysis, the meaning ascribed to test scores and other data comes down to clinical judgment. The meaning of test results also depends on the characteristics and the cognitive profile of the examinee. Because the goal of assessment and the subsequent interpretation is to better understand the individual and why that individual is encountering learning problems, simply reporting scores, reviewing data, and documenting symptoms is not enough.

It is assumed that the evaluator has expertise in assessment of processing and an in-depth knowledge of processing itself. Practitioners need to stay current with the latest empirical evidence on processes and their relationships with learning. The adage "A little knowledge is a dangerous thing" applies here. A little knowledge can result in misdiagnosis, incorrect attributions, and misunderstanding of the learner, as well as lost opportunities for effective interventions. Given the controversies and misconceptions surrounding processing, it is incumbent on those who conduct LD evaluations, and processing evaluations in particular, to stay current with research and assessment developments in the field. Good clinical judgment is informed judgment.

In each case, the meaning of assessment data is dependent upon the individual who has been evaluated. Each person is unique, and that uniqueness should result in a different interpretation of assessment results for each individual. Even identical test scores do not have the same meaning and implications across individuals. Test scores take on meaning that is dependent on the characteristics of the examinee. For example, an average processing speed score of 91 might be an individual strength for one person but an individual weakness for another. The implications of a given processing speed score will change depending on the individual's processing profile and other related variables, especially variables related to learning. There are many variables to take into account when interpreting processing assessment results. Thus, the evaluator should follow an organized, systematic approach to interpretation.

The centerpiece of this chapter is a step-by-step method of analyzing processing test scores that applies to any test or battery administered, even when a cross-battery evaluation has been conducted. The reader will learn how to calculate clinical factor scores and how to focus the normative and ipsative interpretation on processing factors, minimizing subtest interpretation. There will also be discussion about the controversies and concerns that surround profile analysis, clinical interpretation, cross-battery analysis, and diagnosing LDs.

## PROFILE ANALYSIS

A traditional interpretative approach that examines subtest scores for patterns of strengths and weaknesses within an individual is known as profile analysis. There is a long-standing controversy surrounding profile analysis, with many contemporary researchers, such as Glutting, McDermott, and Konold (1997) condemning the practice. Psychometric profile analysis, which uses statistical procedures and actuarial methods to analyze test scores, was initially viewed as an improvement over open-ended clinical profile analysis. The main application of psychometric profile analysis is the interpretation of Wechsler subtest scores and was advocated by Alan Kaufman in *Intelligent Testing with the WISC-R* (1979). Concerns about the method arose from the low reliability and poor stability of subtest scores, the lack of subtest specificity (subtests measuring more than one ability), and empirical evidence demonstrating that profiles are not diagnostic. In general, using profile analysis to differentiate various diagnostic groups has not been supported (Mueller, Dennis, & Short, 1986; Smith & Watkins, 2004).

Psychometric profile analysis is conducted by computing the mean of the scores involved, usually subtest scaled scores, and then comparing each subtest score to that mean to determine whether there is a significant discrepancy. Generally, the .05 or .01 level of significance is used. When statistical tables are unavailable for making this determination, a difference of one standard deviation will, in most cases, amount to a significant difference. Subtests with significantly lower scores are interpreted as individual, or relative, weaknesses, while significantly higher scores are interpreted as individual strengths. Thus, profile analysis is an intra-individual, or ipsative, type of analysis.

Critics contend that profile analysis should not be conducted and that only global test scores should be used. However, interpretation of only a full-scale or full-composite score provides no information about intra-individual strengths and weaknesses. A global score is basically the average of the abilities and processes measured by the test. A global score may be useful for predicting general learning aptitude or as an average for determining strengths and weaknesses, but it provides only limited information about the individual. Using only a global cognitive or processing composite score is similar to reporting a general achievement score; such a score tells nothing about the learner's specific skills in reading, mathematics, or writing.

To completely avoid profile analysis because of the concerns that have been raised is to discard potentially valuable information about the examinee's strengths and weaknesses. In fact, there is little point in administering a comprehensive cognitive scale if only the composite score is going to be used. When assessing processing, an ipsative, or profile analysis, is particularly necessary because there are only a few comprehensive scales that even provide a composite score that is representative of overall processing. In addition, global processing is poorly defined and understood; the constructs for individual processes are better developed. Consequently, with processing assessment, it is necessary to focus interpretation on individual processes. In doing so, it is most informative to compare individual processes with each other. Profile analysis also allows the testing of the hypotheses that were generated during assessment planning. Thus, despite the concerns, intra-individual profile analysis of processing assessment results should be conducted, but not necessarily with subtest scores.

A more defensible approach to profile analysis is to examine and compare factor scores instead of subtest scores. This author recommends that the primary interpretation of test scores be at the factor level, an approach that has been advocated by Sattler (2001) and Flanagan and Kaufman (2004). A factor is a broad ability (or a broad processing domain, such as executive functioning) that is comprised of more specific, or narrow, abilities (or subprocesses) that are measured by subtests. Exploratory and confirmatory factor analyses of tests identify and confirm the factors that are being measured and the subtest loadings on each. Because most processing tests are theoretically derived, factor analytic results usually support or conform to the theoretical factor structure. Subtests that are the best measures of each factor are used to compute that factor's score. On tests, factor scores go by various names—*composites, scales, indexes,* and *clusters;* in this book, they are all referred to as *factor scores.* Even when a test does not provide processing factor scores, practitioners should avoid subtest profile analysis. In such instances, *clinical factor scores* may be calculated and used for analysis (procedures for computing clinical factor scores are discussed later in this chapter).

**DON'T FORGET**

......................................................

A factor represents a theoretical construct, such as working memory, and is comprised of two or more subtests. On tests, factors may be labeled as *composites, scales, indexes,* or *clusters.* Intra-individual analysis of processing test results should focus on *factor scores,* not on subtest scores or global scores.

Profile analysis at the factor level reduces some of the concerns that are associated with subtest profile analysis. Compared to subtests, factors more broadly sample the processing domain being measured, especially when each subtest involved samples a different narrow process, or subprocess, within that factor. There are also several statistical advantages to interpreting factor scores instead of subtest scores. The main advantage is an increase in reliability and stability; factor scores are based on more items and do not fluctuate as much over time. There is also an increase in predictive validity and diagnostic utility. However, the most important reason for using factor scores as the primary indicators of processing strengths and weaknesses has to do with construct validity. Based on our current understanding of human cognitive and processing abilities, factor scores are better representations of the core processes, such as visual processing and working memory.

Profile analysis of factors is also more defensible when profile interpretation is grounded in theory and when the test results are corroborated by other data (Flanagan & Kaufman, 2004). Pure psychometric (statistical) interpretation without a theoretical basis or without linking the interpretation with learning lacks validity and usefulness. When theory and research support the conclusions drawn from profile analysis, those interpretations have increased validity. Also, the results of profile analysis always need to be corroborated by other data that are consistent with the test scores. For example, when a significantly low test score indicates a weakness in working memory, that finding needs to be supported by data from other sources or methods before any conclusions are drawn.

Profile analysis is also more credible and informative when it is conducted

**DON'T FORGET**

......................................................

Profile analysis at the factor level is more defensible than subtest profile analysis because factor scores are more reliable, have better predictive validity, and more broadly sample processing constructs.

hand in hand with normative analysis. This is because ipsative, or intra-individual, analysis alone can be misleading. For example, an examinee's visual processing score of 84 may be a relative individual strength even though it is a below-average score compared to the population mean. Before completing an ipsative analysis, the evaluator should always compare the examinee's scores to the population mean and classify the scores as average, below average (a weakness), or above average (a strength).

Using a factor profile analysis approach to identify ipsative processing strengths and weaknesses is also supported by data from recent standardization studies. For example, a WISC-IV standardization study (Wechsler, 2003b) of children with a reading disability found that they obtained a significantly lower mean on the working memory factor, just as would be predicted from reading research. A standardization study of the CAS (Naglieri & Das, 1997a) found a reading disability profile where the successive processing mean was lowest, again just as predicted.

However, this author is not advocating using profile analysis to diagnose individuals or even to differentiate diagnostic groups. Research on established profiles, such as the Bannatyne LD profile for Wechsler subtests (Bannatyne, 1974) has concluded that the Bannatyne profile has low diagnostic utility because it correctly recognizes only about a third of children with a learning disability and incorrectly identifies about 14 percent of normal children (Smith & Watkins, 2004). Instead of making a diagnosis, the main purpose of profile analysis is to gain an in-depth understanding of the individual's processing strengths and weaknesses, to test hypotheses, and to inform treatment planning.

## GENERAL INTERPRETIVE GUIDELINES

### Normative and Ipsative Interpretation

The main purpose of profile analysis at the factor level is to identify the learner's intra-individual strengths and weaknesses. This task is usually accomplished by comparing each factor score with the mean of the scores involved or by comparing factor scores with one another in a pairwise fashion. Most standardized tests provide tables for determining when differences between the mean and the factor scores are statistically significant. Strengths and weaknesses discovered through this procedure are usually referred to as *relative* strengths and weaknesses because they are relative to the individual's average functioning level in the domain under consideration. In this book, intra-individual strengths and weaknesses are referred to as *ipsative* strengths and weaknesses, and scores outside the average range in the normal distribution are referred to as *normative* strengths or weaknesses.

Although the primary identification of strengths and weaknesses is accomplished through ipsative, or intra-individual, profile analysis at the factor level, evaluators also need to consider where the examinee's factor score ranks in the normal distribution or the actual distribution established during test standardization. Normative classification of a score puts strengths and weaknesses into context. For example, a child may have a high average processing mean of 109. When an average working memory score of 91 is compared to this mean, it is found to be significantly lower and is identified as an ipsative weakness. However, it would be misleading to report that working memory is a weakness without also stating that it is average compared to the normal distribution. The implication is that the learner's working memory may still be adequate, given that it is average, even though it is a weakness compared to that learner's other processing capabilities. The same holds true for the low end of the distribution. A working memory score of 84 may be a strength for a learner with a mean processing level of 71, but it is important that working memory still be identified as below average compared to the standardization sample mean.

The suggested labels for these normative ranges will vary by test, and the range of scores described as average may also vary. For the purposes of interpreting processing results, it is recommended that the average range be restricted to the middle 50 percent of the distribution as opposed to describing any score within one standard deviation of the mean (the middle 68 percent of the distribution) as average. Thus, when the mean is 100 and the standard deviation is 15, any score from 90 through 109 should be considered average.

On the other hand, identification of strengths and weaknesses should not occur without an ipsative analysis. To describe a learner as having processing weaknesses based only on a normative analysis is also misleading. For example, you might describe a score of 83 as indicative of a weakness in working memory. However, if all of the learner's cognitive abilities and processing levels are below average, then the meaning of the low working memory score, or weakness, is different. In such instances, it is more likely that the learner has generally low cognitive ability or Mental Retardation than a true processing deficit.

# DON'T FORGET

To facilitate analysis of processing scores, reserve the descriptive label of *average* for the middle 50 percent of the distribution, even for tests that label the middle 68 percent as average. When the mean is 100 and the standard deviation is 15, only scores from 90 through 109 should be considered average.

## Statistical Significance

Psychometric ipsative analysis of test scores depends on actuarial tables that provide critical values at the .01, .05 and, sometimes, .15 levels of significance. Because of inherent measurement error, any difference between test scores that is not significant is likely due to chance and should not be interpreted or even mentioned. To say that "his long-term retrieval score is lower than his short-term memory score" is to imply that the difference is significant (real). As a result, naïve recipients of such information may reach an incorrect conclusion. In the absence of statistical tables for specific test score comparisons, it is possible to determine statistical significance by using confidence intervals. For example, compute the 95 percent confidence interval about each score and compare the bands. When the 95 percent bands do not overlap, the scores are significantly discrepant at the .05 level.

### Weakness versus Deficit

Whenever we analyze test results, we must check for weaknesses (and strengths) from both a normative and ipsative viewpoint and then clearly communicate which type of weakness the examinee displays. A weakness from both perspectives is a more serious problem because it represents poor performance relative to peers, as well as in comparison to the learner's own abilities. A weakness from both perspectives is also a strong indication of a possible LD. Naglieri (1999) described a score that is below average (below 90) *and* an intraindividual weakness as a *cognitive weakness*. Another way to describe it is to use the term *deficit*. In this book, the term *deficit*, or *processing deficit*, refers to a score that is both a normative *and* an ipsative weakness. (See Rapid Reference 4.1.)

Although deficits are indicative of LDs and likely causing an impairment in learning or daily functioning, an ipsative weakness alone may also severely interfere with the acquisition of academic skills. Thus, all ipsative weaknesses should be examined closely, with pertinent informal assessment data taken into account. On the other hand, we all have individual strengths and weaknesses, or at least will obtain variable scores when tested. The existence of a weakness does not necessarily mean that we have a learning impairment or LD. For example, an individual with a high fluid reasoning ability may be able to compensate for an ipsative weakness in long-term retrieval. Other factors, such as acade-

### ≡Rapid Reference 4.1

#### Deficits and Assets

- A *deficit* is defined as the occurrence of both a normative *and* ipsative weakness. A deficit is a more serious problem than just one type of weakness, and a deficit is indicative of a possible LD.

- An *asset* is defined as the occurrence of both a normative *and* ipsative strength. Assets can be utilized when designing interventions.

mic skills, need to be considered when assessing the impact of a specific processing weakness.

## Unitary versus Nonunitary Factors

Another general test interpretation guideline that applies to interpretation of processing assessment results is whether the individual's factor score represents a unitary ability or construct. A factor is unitary when the difference between the highest and lowest subtest scores is not unusually large. When extreme differences exist between the subtest scores that comprise a factor, the factor should be considered nonunitary. A high degree of scatter indicates that the subtests may not be sampling the same construct for that individual or that the underlying narrow abilities measured by the subtests are not equivalent for that individual. When a factor is nonunitary, the factor score may not represent a unitary ability. In these instances, it may be inappropriate to interpret the factor score as representative of the underlying processing ability the factor is intended to measure. This is similar to interpreting a WISC-IV Full Scale IQ of 85 as representative of general intelligence when the Verbal Comprehension Index is 70 and the Perceptual Reasoning Index is 100. According to Flanagan and Kaufman (2004), an unusually large difference exists when the difference between the highest and lowest subtest scores is greater than 1.5 standard deviations. For example, for subtest scores with a mean of 100 and a standard deviation of 15, a difference of more than 22 points would indicate that the factor is nonunitary.

Nonunitary factors should still be included in the analysis, such as using them to compute a mean processing score. Nonunitary factors that are either a normative or ipsative weakness alone should be interpreted cautiously, if at all, and should not be used in pairwise comparisons. However, nonunitary factors that are deficits should still be investigated and interpreted (albeit cautiously) because the occurrence of a deficit is uncommon. Therefore, not all of an individual's significant factor strengths and weaknesses may be interpretable. Factor scores, even when significantly discrepant from the individual's mean must represent unitary abilities if they are to be interpreted without caveats (Flanagan & Kaufman, 2004).

When a nonunitary factor occurs, the clinician should examine the subtests involved and generate hypotheses that account for the subtest scatter, taking testing behaviors and other evaluation data into account. For instance, an examinee may perform poorly on one short-term memory subtest but not on the other. Examining the content of the two subtests and the narrow abilities that they measure may reveal an explanation. For example, the low-score subtest might have

## ≣Rapid Reference 4.2

### Nonunitary Factors

- A factor should be considered nonunitary when the difference between the factor's highest and lowest subtest scores exceeds 1.5 standard deviations.
- A factor may be nonunitary because the underlying processing subtypes may not be equivalent.
- Nonunitary factors should be used to compute a mean for ipsative analysis but should not be included in pairwise comparisons.
- Nonunitary factors should be interpreted cautiously, if at all.
- Clinicians should investigate and interpret nonunitary factors that are categorized as deficits because the occurrence of a deficit is uncommon.

involved the repetition of numbers while the other involved the repetition of words. One hypothesis might be that the examinee lacks number facility. Such hypotheses should be investigated through further testing and assessment. Another approach to dealing with nonunitary factors is to administer an additional subtest that taps another narrow ability within the broad factor. This approach will provide a broader sampling of the processing construct involved. The recommendation to examine subtest scores in an effort to understand nonunitary factor scores does not mean that clinicians should conduct a subtest profile analysis of the entire test; subtest interpretation should still be avoided. That is why additional, broader sampling of the processing construct is advised (see Rapid Reference 4.2).

### Base Rates of Occurrence

Another psychometric statistic to consider when conducting profile analysis and interpreting test scores is the base rate (see Rapid Reference 4.3). Test manuals that provide tables for significance testing also usually provide base-rate tables that report

## ≣Rapid Reference 4.3

### Application of Base-Rate Rules

- Consider a discrepancy to be uncommon or infrequent when the base rate is 15 percent or lower.
- Treat a statistically significant weakness that is relatively common as a hypothesis that needs to be investigated.
- Do not strictly apply base-rate rules because a relatively common significant weakness or deficit may still be an impairment for some individuals. When other sources of assessment data corroborate the weakness or impairment, interpret the weakness.

the frequency of intra-individual differences in the standardization sample. The idea of using base-rate information is to determine just how common, infrequent, or rare a given discrepancy is. For example, a difference of 12 points between working memory and the mean processing score might be statistically significant but yet occur in approximately 25 percent of the population. Given that this discrepancy or profile is not that uncommon, the importance of the finding is questionable.

Many test authors and experts in interpretation recommend interpreting or stressing the importance of significant strengths and weaknesses only when the base rate is as low as 15 percent or 10 percent. However, strictly following such an actuarial rule and not using clinical judgment may result in not identifying actual strengths and weakness as well as missed opportunities to support and treat a struggling learner. When a test score is significantly discrepant but is not that infrequent (has a base rate higher than 15 percent), clinicians need to consider several variables before deciding whether to interpret the score as indicative of a strength or weakness. The primary consideration is whether there is corroborating information or data that supports the seriousness of the weakness. For instance, the difference or discrepancy may not be very infrequent, but the weakness is clearly problematic, based on other sources of data. In other words, a difference that is statistically significant but not that infrequent should be treated as a hypothesis to be verified with other data. Just because a given weakness occurs in 25 percent or more of the population does not mean that the weakness is not causing a serious processing or learning dysfunction in a particular student. In cases where an actual *deficit* (both a normative and ipsative weakness) has been identified, base rates can usually be ignored. This is because all deficits can be considered unusual and infrequent (Naglieri, 1999). Each case needs to be carefully examined and all of the variables taken into account; rules regarding base-rate use should not take precedence.

## HYPOTHESIS TESTING

Interpretation is facilitated by a well-thought-out, planned, and organized assessment that addresses all of the referral concerns and the hypotheses that might account for those concerns (see A Hypothesis Testing Approach To Assessment section in Chapter 3). Trying to make sense of data when the purpose for collecting that data is uncertain can be frustrating, at the very least. Individual psychological assessment and interpretation of the results should adhere to the same principles as scientific research. For example, results from research investigations would be given little credibility if the researchers did not follow the scientific method and develop hypotheses before collecting data. The same principle applies to individual psychoeducational evaluations.

Given a list of a priori hypotheses, the evaluator(s) should begin by weighing the evidence for and against each hypothesis. The evidence consists of test scores and relevant data collected through other methods. The Processing Assessment Organizer (see Appendix B) provides a structure for doing this (see Rapid Reference 3.5 for complete instructions). The specific data and test scores that apply to each hypothesis should be written in the Assessment Results column and numbered by the hypothesis with which they are associated. After weighing the evidence, a decision about each hypothesis should be made and recorded in the Conclusions column as either *supported, not supported,* or *inconclusive.* Later in this chapter, see Rapid Reference 4.7 for a completed Processing Assessment Organizer, and note how the results from the Processing Analysis Worksheet (Rapid Reference 4.6) are incorporated.

Even when the data clearly support a hypothesis, oral and written conclusions and generalizations should be stated cautiously. In many cases, the data will be inconclusive, and the evaluator(s) will not be able to reach a decision about the hypothesis. Inconclusive findings need to be honestly communicated to the student, parents, teachers, and other members of the multidisciplinary team. In instances where results are inconclusive and answers are still sought, the evaluator(s) should generate additional hypotheses and investigate these through further assessment. New, a posteriori hypotheses (hypotheses generated after the assessment has been completed) may also be necessary when there are unexpected findings or the data do not support the original hypotheses. Remember, there are often no firm conclusions that can be drawn about an individual's specific processing capabilities.

When testing a hypothesis, do not assume the hypothesis is true. Presuming the hypothesis is true, such as presuming that a learner has a specific processing deficit, is likely to bias analysis of the assessment data. It is just as likely, if not more so, that a weakness or deficit hypothesis is untrue. Even when the data are convergent and supportive of a hypothesis, alternative hypotheses, or explanations, should be considered. We should also give nonsupporting data as much credence as the supporting data. If we only attend to data that supports our hypotheses, we will arrive at erroneous conclusions and diagnoses.

## DON'T FORGET

Hypothesis testing should guide interpretation of assessment data. Objectively weigh the evidence for and against a priori hypotheses. Develop and investigate a posteriori hypotheses when unexpected results occur.

## Clinical Interpretation

Making full use of assessment results requires clinical analysis and interpretation, in addition to psychometric, actuarial-based, analysis. Clinical interpretation includes an examination of all the data, including observations of behavior during testing, observations of the examinee in a learning environment, information gathered through interviews, and data collected through other informal methods. For instance, the clinician will take into account an examinee's extreme nervousness or anxiety while completing speeded tests. The clinician must also integrate all of the data, looking for a convergence of data that lends support or nonsupport for the hypotheses on which the assessment was based.

Clinical analysis also involves scrutinizing the test scores in search of meaningful profiles, or patterns. First, the practitioner should examine processing scores that tend to be closely related or cluster together, such as working memory and processing speed. In the cognitive abilities literature, these are referred to as *shared abilities*. When a significant weakness or deficit exists in one process, it is important to consider the impact of the deficiency on related processes, such as the affect of a short-term memory deficit on long-term storage and retrieval. Finally, a clinician with expertise in LDs should look for specific patterns of symptoms (processing weaknesses or deficits) that are characteristic of a specific disorder. For example, weaknesses or deficits in phonemic awareness, long-term retrieval (especially rapid automatic naming), and successive processing are characteristic of a Reading Disorder. Cautious application of this diagnostic process is critical because patterns are not diagnostic in and of themselves.

An expert in processing assessment must also be well versed in the structure of psychological tests. Tests and subtests that purport to measure the same construct may produce divergent scores. For example, a visual processing score from one test may be significantly different from the visual processing score on another scale. A clinician with expertise in cognitive assessment will be able to discern why. Perhaps the different scores result from the fact that each visual processing subtest or factor is measuring a different narrow ability (subtype) of visual processing or a different combination of narrow abilities.

## CAUTION

Test scores don't diagnose; clinicians do. A test score alone should never be used to make a diagnosis or even a determination of a processing strength, weakness, or deficit. A clinician should weigh all of the data when making diagnostic decisions.

## Include Processing Strengths

Because assessments originate with referral concerns, we tend to ignore

individual strengths or assets, even
when they clearly emerge from assessment results. In a comprehensive
assessment, suspected strengths
should also be pursued. Identifying
strengths or assets is beneficial because incorporating them into interventions may increase the probability

> # CAUTION
>
> ...................................................
>
> If only suspected areas of weakness
> are tested, an ipsative analysis is un-
> likely to reveal any strengths or weak-
> nesses because the individual's mean is
> based only on weaknesses.

of success. For example, a learner may have an asset in long-term storage and retrieval that may be utilized to offset a deficit in phonemic awareness.

There is another concern with limiting an evaluation to an assessment of potential weaknesses. When only potential processing weaknesses are included, the
individual's mean (based on the obtained factor scores) may not provide a valid
estimate of overall processing ability. That is, the mean will be lower than the actual overall processing level because only deficient processes were included in the
computation. The result is that actual weaknesses will not be identified.

## ANALYSIS OF PROCESSING ASSESSMENT RESULTS

A general interpretative model can be applied to the analysis and interpretation
of all processing assessment results, regardless of the test or combination of tests
administered. The number of steps necessary will vary somewhat, depending on
which test was administered, but the guidelines and the Processing Analysis
Worksheet found in Appendix C apply to results from any test or combination of
tests. Each guideline or step is explained in the following, stated briefly on the
Processing Analysis Worksheet in Appendix C, and also summarized in Rapid
Reference 4.4. Also, see the Illustration of Processing Analysis Steps section in
this chapter and the completed worksheet in Rapid Reference 4.6.

1. *Calculate subtest, factor, and composite scores.* Using age norms provided by
   the test's publisher, calculate the usual standard scores for all of the
   subtests, factors, and composites that were administered.
2. *Exclude nonprocessing scores from the analysis.* When a test that is not restricted to the measurement of processing is utilized (such as an intellectual, cognitive, or achievement test), the clinician must first determine whether to administer the entire battery or just the factors or
   subtests that measure specific processes. If the entire battery or some
   nonprocessing factors or subtests were administered, then exclude
   the nonprocessing factors or subtests from the processing analysis.

$\equiv$*Rapid Reference 4.4*

## Processing Analysis Steps

1. Calculate subtest, factor, and composite scores using age norms from the test's manual.

2. Exclude nonprocessing scores from the analysis.

3. When factor scores are unavailable, compute clinical factor scores by averaging the scores of the subtests involved and rounding to the nearest whole number. It may be necessary to first convert subtest scores to a metric with a mean of 100 and a standard deviation of 15.

4. Complete columns 1–4 of the worksheet by entering the appropriate names in Columns 1, 2, and 3 and the corresponding factor score in the fourth column.

5. Compute the examinee's processing factor mean, using all available processing factor scores and rounding to the nearest whole number.

6. Calculate the difference score for each processing factor by subtracting the processing factor mean from each processing factor score. Enter the difference with a + or – in the sixth column.

7. Determine normative strengths and weaknesses, with scores from 90–109 being considered average, scores below 90 considered weaknesses, and scores above 109 considered strengths.

8. Determine ipsative strengths and weaknesses, using a criterion of 15 points as indicative of significance and infrequency.

9. Determine the processing deficits and assets. A deficit is both a normative and ipsative weakness, and an asset is both a normative and ipsative strength.

10. Determine whether each factor is unitary. When the range of subtest scores is greater than 22 points, consider the factor to be nonunitary.

11. Conduct pairwise comparisons using a criterion of 20 points as an indication of significance and infrequency.

For example, crystallized intelligence scores should not be included in an analysis of the examinee's processing abilities. In addition to omitting the nonprocessing factors, the full-scale or overall composite score of the battery should not be reported or interpreted as representing overall processing ability whenever it includes any nonprocessing factors or subtests.

3. *Compute clinical factor scores.* This step applies to tests that do not offer factor scores for all of the main processes they assess. The mean of the subtests that measure a specific process can be used as a clinical factor score to represent the functioning level of that process. For example,

the WISC-IV does not produce separate scores for fluid reasoning and visual processing, two processes that it clearly measures. In such instances, the clinician will need to compute *clinical factor* scores before proceeding with the analysis. The subtests that should be used to compute clinical factor scores are identified in the Selective Testing Table for Processes Measured by Cognitive Tests (see Appendix A) and are reported for each test that is reviewed in subsequent chapters. For example, on the WISC-IV, Matrix Reasoning and Picture Concepts should be used to compute a Fluid Reasoning factor score, and Block Design and Picture Completion can be used to compute a Visual Processing score. To calculate clinical factor scores, sum the subtest scores, compute the mean, and round to the nearest whole number. A minimum of two subtests is necessary; a single subtest score should not be used as a clinical factor score. In cases where there are two factor scores for a given process or subtest scores in addition to a separate factor score average all of the subtest scores involved to arrive at a clinical factor score. For any subtest scores that do not have a mean of 100 and a standard deviation of 15, it is necessary to convert them to this common metric before computing the mean (see Appendix D). Because there isn't a normative basis for clinical processing factor scores, practitioners need to interpret clinical processing scores more cautiously than the regular factor scores provided by tests.

4. *Complete columns 1 to 4 of the worksheet.* In the first column, enter the name of the process that was assessed. The names of the processes measured by subtests or factors across several intellectual or cognitive tests can be found in the Selective Testing Table for Processes Measured by Cognitive Tests (Appendix A) and in the information provided for each test in subsequent chapters. In the second column, enter the name of the test or battery that was used. In the third column, enter the names of the processing factors or subtests that were administered. In the fourth column, enter either the processing factor score provided by the test or battery or the clinical processing factor score that was calculated. For factor scores that fall below 40, record a value of 40, and for scores that exceed 160, record a value of 160.

5. *Compute the examinee's processing factor mean.* Sum all of the processing factor scores, calculate the mean, round to the nearest whole number, and enter this number in the fifth column. This value is the individual's processing factor mean. If the examiner completed a comprehensive assessment of processes, this mean can be considered as rep-

resentative of the individual's overall level of processing. However, in most cases the assessment of processing will be less than comprehensive. In these instances, it is best to describe this value as "the average of the processes that were assessed." In cases where only processes suspected of being weak were assessed, it may be better to use a Full Scale IQ or a full composite from a cognitive scale as an indicator of overall processing, especially when the full-scale or composite score is substantially higher than the processing factor mean.

6. *Calculate the difference score for each processing factor.* Subtract the processing factor mean from each processing factor score and enter the difference with a + or – in the sixth column.

7. *Determine normative strengths and weaknesses.* In the seventh column, enter an *S* for processing factor scores that are above 109. Enter a *W* for processing factor scores that are below 90. For scores in the average range (90 to 109), simply put an *A* for average. For the sake of consistency, classify all scores on this basis, even scores from tests that describe the average range as 85 to 115.

8. *Determine ipsative strengths and weaknesses.* When using tests that measure only processing, such as the CAS, the critical values found in the test's manual should be used to determine statistical significance. Whenever clinical factors have been computed or only part of a test has been administered, tables for determining significance and base rates are unavailable. In these instances, a 15 point or greater difference from the individual's processing factor mean may be considered as indicative of a strength or weakness. An arbitrary critical value of 15 points was selected because a difference of 15 points is almost always significant at the .05 level. On most tests, factors with high reliability often require differences of only 8 to 12 points for significance. Thus, a criterion of 15 points should be indicative of significance, even when clinical factors are being compared. In the Ipsative column, enter a *W* for weakness when a processing factor score is 15 or more points lower than the individual's processing mean, and enter an *S* for strength when the factor score is 15 or more points higher than the mean. Before interpreting a significant difference as meaningful, it is standard procedure to evaluate how abnormal, uncommon, rare, or infrequent the difference is among the normal population (see discussion in previous section). The magnitude of the discrepancy exhibited by 15 percent or less of the population varies widely, depending on the test and the factors being compared, but

generally a difference from the mean of about 15 to 20 points will be uncommon. Because base rates are not available for most comparisons made with clinical processing scores, all scores that are 15 points or more different from the individual's mean should be considered relatively uncommon and interpreted as meaningful, especially when the process is determined to be a deficit (see next step) because the occurrence of a deficit is itself rare.

9. *Determine the processing deficits and assets.* As discussed previously, most people have cognitive strengths and weaknesses. Thus, a processing weakness, either normative or ipsative alone, does not necessarily impair learning or other types of functioning. However, it is unusual for a process to be both a normative and ipsative weakness or strength. In instances where a process is a normative and ipsative weakness, it is most likely an impairment and should be classified as a deficit by entering a *D* in the last column. In instances where a process is both a normative and ipsative strength, enter an *A* for asset.

10. *Determine whether each factor is unitary.* After subtest scores have been converted to a metric with a mean of 100 and a standard deviation of 15, compare the lowest and highest subtest scores. When the difference is greater than 22 points (greater than 1.5 standard deviations), consider the factor to be nonunitary. Cautiously interpret nonunitary factors that are normative or ipsative weaknesses alone, but interpret nonunitary factors that are determined to be deficits (see previous discussion). Nonunitary factors should be used to compute the individual's processing mean but should not be included in pairwise comparisons.

11. *Conduct pairwise comparisons.* Compare the scores of pairs of logically related processes, such as short-term memory versus long-term retrieval, visual processing versus auditory processing, and simultaneous processing versus successive processing. Some tests provide statistical tables for pairwise comparisons. When these are not available or when clinical factors have been computed, use a 20-point discrepancy as indicative of significance and infrequency. (With pairs, a higher critical value is necessary than when comparing scores to an overall mean.)

## Analyzing Scores from More Than One Test

As discussed in Chapter 3, a cross-battery approach is often necessary when conducting an assessment of processing, especially when a comprehensive evaluation is desired. A carefully planned and implemented cross-battery assessment increases the efficiency of testing; for example, avoiding redundant testing of factors reduces testing time and keeps analysis of the results manageable. A well-planned cross-battery assessment will also facilitate interpretation of the results and provide an in-depth understanding of the individual. Combining and comparing scores from different tests should not be done haphazardly; practitioners should follow the Selective Testing Table for Processes Measured by Cognitive Tests in Appendix A and advice provided in subsequent chapters. Given the concerns about cross-battery assessment and analysis (Flanagan & Ortiz, 2001), it is best to adhere to a structured approach.

The cross-battery method is well suited for assessment of processing, but a cautious interpretation of cross-battery results is necessary because of the inherent weaknesses of the method. The lack of cross-battery norms is the main concern. There are no norms for any of the numerous cross-battery scales that can be arranged. The factor and subtest scores obtained from different tests are based on standardization samples, distributions, and norms unique to each test. Caution is particularly needed when conducting ipsative analysis based on averaging the factor and subtest scores from different batteries. This cross-battery mean has no standardized distribution as a basis, and there are no statistical tables for determining significant discrepancies between individual factor or subtest scores and the mean. In lieu of this, Flanagan and Ortiz (2001) recommend using a standard normal curve with a mean of 100 and a standard deviation of 15 and using a 1 standard deviation discrepancy as indicative of a significant difference. The potential error introduced by crossing norm groups also can be minimized by using tests that were normed about the same time. For example, with cognitive tests, norms are thought to shift as much as 3 points per decade due to the Flynn Effect (Flynn, 1999). Despite the concerns, a structured, systematic procedure to cross-battery interpretation is preferable to informal methods. For a further discussion of strengths and weaknesses of cross-battery assessment and interpretation, see Flanagan and Ortiz (2001).

The procedures for a cross-battery analysis of processing assessment results are the same as those recommended for analyzing results from a single test or battery; the same worksheet, steps, and criteria apply. The main difference is that practitioners need to be more cautious in interpreting cross-battery results (see Rapid Reference 4.5).

## Illustration of Processing Analysis Steps

Scores from a cross-battery processing assessment case study are used to illustrate the clinical analysis steps. Also, see the completed worksheet (Rapid Refer-

## ≡ Rapid Reference 4.5

### Cross-Battery Assessment Concerns and Suggestions

1. USE as few tests or batteries as possible; the use of only two or three is recommended.

2. USE tests that were normed at about the same time period.

3. REMEMBER that there are no cross-battery norms, and the distribution of the cross-battery mean and distributions of discrepancies between scores are unknown.

4. REPORT that the cross-battery mean does not have any norms, and report how the mean was computed.

5. DO NOT interpret cross-battery factor scores as if they represent actual factor scores from a single norm group.

6. REPORT that the determination of ipsative strengths and weaknesses was arrived at by comparing factor scores to the individual's cross-battery mean.

7. REPORT a confidence interval (68, 90, or 95 percent) for each factor score. When unnormed factor scores have been computed, assign a confidence interval value by using a general standard error of measurement (SEM) of 5. Thus, a 95 percent confidence interval for cross-battery factors would be the score plus and minus 10.

8. INTEGRATE the significant cross-battery results with other assessment findings, drawing conclusions only when other data corroborate test scores.

ence 4.6) at the end of the explanation. A comprehensive written interpretative report that incorporates these test scores can be found in Chapter 9.

1. *Calculate subtest, factor, and composite scores using age norms.* In this case, the WISC-IV and the WJ III COG were administered. The WJ III COG Fluid Reasoning and Processing Speed clusters were not administered.

   WISC-IV Index and Subtest Scores
   Verbal Comprehension—95
   Perceptual Reasoning—77
      Block Design—4 (70)
      Picture Concepts—9 (95)
      Matrix Reasoning—6 (80)
   Working Memory—94
      Digit Span—8 (90)
      Letter-Number Sequencing—10 (100)

Processing Speed—80
   Coding—7 (85)
   Symbol Search—6 (80)
<u>WJ III COG Cluster Scores</u>
Comprehension-Knowledge—92
Long-Term Retrieval—76
   Visual-Auditory Learning—82
   Retrieval Fluency—78
Visual-Spatial Thinking—96
   Spatial Relations—98
   Picture Recognition—96
Auditory Processing—117
   Sound Blending—114
   Auditory Attention—111
Short-Term Memory—101
   Numbers Reversed—103
   Memory for Words—100

2. *Exclude nonprocessing scores from the analysis.* Exclude Verbal Comprehension from the WISC-IV and Comprehension-Knowledge from the WJ III COG. Also, the WISC-IV Perceptual Reasoning score is not used because it consists of two processes—fluid reasoning and visual processing.

3. *Compute clinical factor scores.* First, convert the WISC-IV subtest scores to the common metric by using the table in Appendix D.
   Block Design     $4 = 70$
   Picture Concepts   $9 = 95$
   Matrix Reasoning  $6 = 80$
   Then compute a Fluid Reasoning clinical factor:
   Picture Concepts $95 +$ Matrix Reasoning $80 = 175/2 = 88$
   Then compute a broader Visual Processing clinical factor by incorporating Block Design with the WJ III COG Visual-Spatial subtests:
   Block Design $70 +$ Spatial Relations $98 +$ Picture Recognition $96 = 264/3 = 88$

4. *Complete columns 1 to 4 of the worksheet.* In the third column, the names of factors are entered when the actual factor scores are used. When clinical factors are computed, the names of the subtests used to compute the clinical factor are entered.

5. *Compute the examinee's processing factor mean.* Average the factor scores: $117 + 88 + 76 + 80 + 101 + 88 + 94 = 644/7 = 92$.

6. *For each factor, calculate the difference from the mean.* For example, Auditory Processing 117 – the Processing factor mean 92 = +25.

7. *Determine normative strengths and weaknesses.* Auditory Processing is a strength, Short-Term Memory and Working Memory are in the average range, and the remaining factors are normative weaknesses.

8. *Determine ipsative strengths and weaknesses.* Auditory Processing is an ipsative strength and Long-Term Retrieval is a weakness.

9. *Determine the processing deficits and assets.* Auditory Processing is an asset because it is both a normative and ipsative strength; Long-Term Retrieval is a deficit because it is both a normative and ipsative weakness.

10. *Determine whether each factor is unitary.* Visual Processing is the only nonunitary factor. The range between the Block Design score of 70 and Spatial Relations of 98 is greater than 22 points. Visual Processing should be interpreted cautiously, and it should not be used in pairwise comparisons.

11. *Conduct pairwise comparisons.* A couple of logical comparisons, for example, Visual Processing versus Auditory Processing are eliminated because Visual Processing is nonunitary. Long-Term Retrieval is found to be significantly lower than Short-Term Memory, but the difference between Processing Speed and Working Memory is not significant.

## REPORTING RESULTS ORALLY

Even when the clinician writes thoroughly comprehensive and coherent evaluation reports, it is necessary to provide an understandable face-to-face explanation of the assessment results to the learner, the learner's parents, the learner's teachers, and other members of the multidisciplinary team at a postevaluation conference. Although this is standard practice, an explanation of processing assessment results can be especially challenging to the evaluator, given the uncertainties, complexity, and controversies surrounding processing assessment. As dictated by professional ethics, practitioners should present assessment results in language that the client(s) can understand. Completing the Processing Analysis Worksheet is an ideal manner of structuring the test results in preparation for a postevaluation conference. The remaining columns of the Processing Assessment Organizer that was used in the planning stages of the assessment should now be completed in final preparation for interpreting results.

At the postevaluation conference, the evaluator should structure and sequence

## Processing Analysis Worksheet

### Case Study #1

Examinee's Name: _____    DOB: _____    Age: 11    Grade: 5    Dates of Testing: _____

| Name of Process | Name of Test/ Battery | Name of Factor/ Subtests | Processing Factor Score | Processing Factor Mean | Difference from Mean | Normative S or W | Ipsative S or W | Deficit or Asset |
|---|---|---|---|---|---|---|---|---|
| Auditory Processing | WJ III COG | Auditory Processing | 117 | 92 | +25 | S | S | A |
| Fluid Reasoning | WISC-IV | Picture Concepts; Matrix Reasoning | 88 | 92 | –4 | W | — | — |
| Long-Term Retrieval | WJ III COG | Long-Term Retrieval | 76 | 92 | –16 | W | W | D |
| Processing Speed | WISC-IV | Processing Speed | 80 | 92 | –12 | W | — | — |

| Short-Term Memory | WJ III COG | Short-Term Memory | 101 | 92 | +9 | A | — |
| Visual Processing | WISC-IV & WJ III COG | Block Design; Spatial Relations; Picture Recognition | 88 | 92 | –4 | W | — |
| Working Memory | WISC-IV | Working Memory | 94 | 92 | +2 | A | — |

*Note:* Dashes indicate the absence of an S or W, or an A or D.

Directions: (1) Use factor scores for analysis, not subtest scores. (2) When a factor score is not available from a test, convert subtest scores to a mean of 100 and an SD of 15. (3) For each factor, compute the mean of the subtest scores and round to the nearest whole number. Use the subtest means as clinical factor scores. (4) Compute the mean of all available factor scores (this is the processing mean). (5) Subtract the processing mean from each processing factor score and enter amount in Difference column. (6) Indicate whether the factor score is a normative weakness or strength (90–109 is average). (7) Using a criterion of 15 points, determine ipsative strengths and weaknesses. (8) Determine deficits and assets. A deficit is both a normative and ipsative weakness. (9) Determine which factors are nonunitary. When the range between the highest and lowest subtest scores exceeds 1.5 SDs the factor is nonunitary. Nonunitary factors should be interpreted cautiously and should not be used in pairwise comparisons. (10) Compare related pairs for significant differences, using a 20-point difference as an indication of significance.

| Factor Score | Factor Score | Difference | Significant:Y/N |
|---|---|---|---|
| Long-Term Retrieval—76 | Short-Term Memory—101 | 25 | Y |
| Processing Speed—30 | Working Memory—94 | 14 | N |

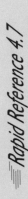

# *Rapid Reference 4.7*

## Processing Assessment Organizer

### Case Study #1

Student: _____ DOB: _____ Age: 11 Grade: 5 Date of Referral: _____ Form Completed By: _____ Date: _____

| Referral Concerns | Processing Hypotheses | Assessment Methods | Assessment Results | Conclusions |
|---|---|---|---|---|
| 1. Struggles in math | 1.A. Has a weakness/ deficit in fluid reasoning | 1.A.1. WISC-IV Fluid Reasoning subtests | Has a normative weakness in fluid reasoning | Normative weakness could make it difficult to keep up with peers in math. |
| | 1.B. Has a weakness/ deficit in visual processing | 1.B.1. WJ III Visual Processing cluster<br>1.B.2 WISC-IV Block Design subtest | Visual processing overall appears average, based on WJ III cluster, but narrow ability measured by Block Design is significantly weaker | Inconclusive |
| 2. Is slow to complete homework | 2.A. Has a weakness/ deficit in planning | 2.A.1. Interview parent<br>2.A.2. Interview student<br>2.A.3. Observe student | Does not appear to have a weakness in planning per se; motivation may be a factor | Hypothesis not supported |
| | 2.B. Has a weakness/ deficit in processing speed | 2.B.1. WISC-IV Processing Speed Index | Has a normative weakness in processing speed | Normative weakness could partially account for slower homework completion time. |

| Behavior | Hypothesis | Test/Method | Finding | Conclusion |
|---|---|---|---|---|
| 3. Does poorly on classroom exams | 3.A. Has a weakness/deficit in long-term retrieval | 3.A.1. WJ III Long-Term Retrieval cluster | Has a deficit in long-term retrieval; Interview data support this finding. | Hypothesis supported |
| 4. Has difficulty learning new concepts | 4.A. Has a weakness/deficit in long-term retrieval | 4.A.1. WJ III Long-Term Retrieval cluster | Has a deficit in long-term retrieval; Interview data support this finding. | Hypothesis supported |
| | 4.B. Has a weakness/deficit in fluid reasoning | 4.B.1. WISC-IV Fluid Reasoning subtests | Has a normative weakness in fluid reasoning | Normative weakness in fluid reasoning may add to the learning difficulty that is primarily due to a deficit in long-term retrieval. |
| 5. Has weak reading comprehension | 5.A. Has a weakness/deficit in working memory | 5.A.1. WISC-IV Working Memory Index | No weakness in working memory | Hypothesis not supported |
| | 5.B. Has a weakness/deficit in executive processing | 5.B.1. Interview parent<br>5.B.2. Interview teacher<br>5.B.3. Observe student | Parent and teacher provided examples of weak executive processing. Difficult to observe | Inconclusive: Possible executive processing weakness could relate to poor use of comprehension strategies. Should be assessed with standardized measure. |

the oral interpretation of assessment results on a domain-by-domain basis instead of a method-by-method basis. With a processing evaluation, the domains would be the different processes or factors that were assessed. For instance, if the learner's working memory was assessed, all available data on working memory should be discussed before moving on to a discussion of the next factor. That is, data from observations, interviews, history, and other informal methods would be integrated with the working memory test scores. This is in contrast to a method-by-method approach, where all of the observation data is reported, then all of the information gathered through interviews is reported, and then all of the test scores are reported. The method-by-method approach can be terribly confusing to the examinee and other conference participants because it requires them to integrate the data that is relevant to each processing factor. The clinician should especially organize test scores by domain or processing factor when more than one test or battery was administered. For example, if both a WJ III COG and a WISC-IV were used to measure processing speed, the processing speed scores from both tests should be discussed at the same time, instead of presenting all of the WJ III COG results and then all of the WISC-IV results. Test results will already be organized process by process if the evaluator follows the analysis steps previously recommended. Other multidisciplinary team members should be encouraged to participate in the domain-by-domain presentation of results. For instance, if long-term retrieval is a concern, invite all participants to present their data on long-term retrieval when the long-term retrieval scores are discussed. Changing the structure of postevaluation conferences may require a special effort on the part of the clinician, as the method-by-method and turn-taking approaches are ingrained, and some multidisciplinary team members may offer resistance to changing the procedure.

The following are step-by-step guidelines for oral interpretation of results. (Also see Rapid Reference 4.8.) Although the sequence may vary somewhat, all of the components are important and should be included even when the client(s) and other participants appear to be well versed in processing and standardized testing. The same steps should also be included when a reevaluation has been conducted. It should not be presumed that those who have already been diagnosed with an LD understand the nature of their disability and their processing strengths and weaknesses.

# DON'T FORGET

It is easier for participants to understand evaluation results when all assessment data related to a processing factor is integrated and presented at one time, as opposed to presenting results method by method.

## Rapid Reference 4.8

### Oral Interpretation Steps

1. Clarify the purpose of the meeting.
2. Provide an overview of what will be discussed.
3. Explain processing and its relationship with learning.
4. Review the referral concerns and the hypotheses that were generated to account for those concerns.
5. Explain why certain tests were selected.
6. Use graphs to present test results.
7. Describe and display the average range and confidence intervals.
8. Display and report only factor scores.
9. Report percentile ranks instead of other scores.
10. Define each factor before reporting its score.
11. Interpret each factor score from a normative and ipsative perspective.
12. Discuss the implications of deficits.
13. Discuss strengths and assets.
14. Integrate other data with the test scores.
15. Relate other team members' results to processing.
16. Confirm or disconfirm hypotheses.
17. Summarize the findings.
18. Explain the diagnosis if applicable.

1. *Clarify the purpose of the meeting.* Stating the purpose of the meeting can prevent misconceptions, put the results in proper perspective, and avoid the discussion of unrelated information. A prevalent purpose is to review the learner's strengths and weaknesses and to incorporate that information into the design of an educational program.
2. *Provide an overview of what will be discussed.* Providing an overview of the meeting accomplishes much the same as stating the purpose. In situations where the learner or learner's parent(s) seem overly anxious, it may be beneficial to reassure them by explaining that everyone is unique and that we all have strengths and weaknesses. If the meeting involves sharing information from several sources or participants, it is very helpful to provide participants with a written agenda or out-

## ≡Rapid Reference 4.9

### Example of a Postevaluation Conference Agenda

1. Introductions
2. Purpose and overview of meeting
3. What processing is and how it relates to learning
4. Referral concerns and hypotheses
5. Background information
6. Assessment results
   a. Auditory processing
   b. Fluid reasoning
   c. Long-term retrieval
   d. Processing speed
   e. Short-term memory
   f. Visual processing
   g. Working memory
7. Review of strengths or weaknesses and deficits or assets
8. Review hypotheses
9. Summary of assessment results
10. Diagnosis
11. Intervention ideas

---

line, with space for taking notes (see Rapid Reference 4.9 for an example of a meeting agenda).

3. *Explain processing and its relationship with learning.* An explanation of processing and its relationship with learning is critical; to proceed without this explanation can derail the entire meeting, as participants will not understand the relevance of the processing results. The explanation of processing should be kept simple, such as describing it as how we take in information, manipulate and transform that information, store that information, and then later retrieve it. The second part of the explanation should describe how learning is dependent on various processes and that learners often have learning problems or disabilities because of processing problems.

4. *Review the referral concerns and the hypotheses that were generated to account for those concerns.* Most participants at the meeting will be aware of the referral concerns although their perspectives of the concerns may vary. A brief review of the concerns helps to put the assessment results in context. The most relevant hypotheses should also be stated because

the hypotheses directly connect the testing to the concerns. For example, you might explain that initial data from the learner's history, interviews, and observations led the team to hypothesize that the learner was having difficulty learning math facts because he or she has a weakness in short-term memory or long-term retrieval, and that is why testing of the learner's short-term memory and long-term retrieval was conducted.

5. *Explain why certain tests were selected.* Those who are unfamiliar with processing assessment may not understand why certain tests were selected. For example, you might need to explain that an IQ test measures more than IQ and that you selected it because it also provides valid information about processing speed and working memory.

6. *Use graphs to present test results.* Even professionals who are familiar with testing and statistics can easily be overwhelmed with the plethora of numbers that result from standardized testing. Simply reporting numbers orally is not an effective method of communicating test results. Even displaying the numbers on a test record, worksheet, or computer generated printout may cause confusion. A visual display of the scores on a graph is almost always appreciated by participants and certainly offers the best chance that they will understand and recall the scores.

7. *Describe and display the average range and confidence intervals.* Most software designed for analyzing test scores will include graphs that display the scores with confidence intervals. If not, such graphing is easily accomplished with standard personal computer software. When using a graph it is important that the average range (90 to 109) be demarcated and used as a reference point for each score. Confidence intervals (90 percent or 95 percent are preferred) can be explained as the range within which the learner's true ability is most likely to lie. When the evaluator has used the Processing Analysis Worksheet (see Appendix C), only those scores should be reported and displayed on a graph, along with their confidence intervals. When clinical factor scores have been computed, the evaluator should estimate the SEM to be 5 points, which means that the 95 percent confidence intervals for clinical factor scores would range from plus and minus 10 points from the obtained score. For example, a clinical factor score of 90 would have a 95 percent confidence interval of 80 to 100.

8. *Display and report only factor scores.* Similar to oral reporting of other types of testing, we should usually not report all available test scores.

The maxim is to keep it simple and focused on the scores most relevant to the hypotheses under investigation. Factor scores that corre-
spond to processes should be the emphasis of the discussion. It may
be necessary to reduce some of the standard graphs generated by test
scoring software to eliminate subtest scores and other less relevant
data.

9. *Report percentile ranks instead of other scores.* Because most individuals can
quickly become overwhelmed by test scores and statistics, it is best to
consistently report just one type of test score. For most people, percentile ranks are more understandable than standard scores and other
types of test scores. Emphasizing percentiles when the learner has
scores well below or well above average can really help to drive home
the point about weaknesses and strengths. When introducing percentiles, be sure to define *percentiles* so that they are not confused with
percentages.

10. *Define each factor before reporting its score.* Even when the name of the factor or process appears self-explanatory, we should not assume that all
participants possess a correct concept of the construct. A straightforward definition should be offered, along with an example that illustrates how the process usually functions. The tasks that were used to
measure the factor might also be described but actual test items
should not be revealed.

11. *Interpret each factor score from a normative and ipsative perspective.* Introduce
each factor score by stating which normative range it falls within, for
example, average, below average, or above average. For those factors
that are ipsative strengths or weaknesses, clarify that these are
strengths or weaknesses within the child, relative to the child's own
average processing level. It might be more understandable for participants if you first complete a normative explanation of all the factor
scores then discuss the results of the ipsative analysis.

12. *Discuss the implications of deficits.* At the conclusion of the normative and
ipsative description, emphasize the factors that are deficits, explaining
that the learner not only has a weakness relative to peers but also a
weakness within him- or herself. Elaborate by clarifying the implications of a processing deficit; for example, you might express how severe the deficit is and the high likelihood that it is having a detrimental impact on learning.

13. *Discuss strengths and assets.* In assessment, we are often so concerned
about analyzing the examinee's problems that we forget to consider

or discuss strengths and assets. Like weaknesses, processing strengths should also be described from both a normative and ipsative perspective. The meaning and significance of assets should be emphasized, especially the importance of incorporating assets into treatment design.

14. *Integrate other data with the test scores.* The convergence of data from a variety of sources enhances the validity of the examinee's test results. In any assessment, test scores should be supported by corroborating data. At a postevaluation conference, it is important to explicitly connect the supporting data with related test scores. Explaining the connections among the data helps participants more fully understand the learner's strengths and weaknesses and the educational implications. The integration of data across evaluation team members is facilitated when assessment information is organized and presented by domains instead of by assessment methods.

15. *Relate other team members' results to processing.* When a multidisciplinary evaluation has been conducted, the clinician can further enhance understanding of the learner's processing, by explicitly pointing out connections between the processing assessment results and functioning in other domains. For example, the word retrieval problems reported by a speech therapist may relate to general long-term retrieval difficulties, or a child's difficulty with phonemic awareness may also be evident during reading achievement testing.

16. *Confirm or disconfirm hypotheses.* Support or lack of support for hypotheses should be directly stated, even when the assessment findings are not clear. This step brings closure to the meeting and to the evaluation itself. Avoidance of this step may leave participants confused about the meaning of the results and the implications for learning. When inconsistent or unclear findings occur, it is best to honestly state that you don't know exactly how the learner is functioning in a particular area of processing.

17. *Summarize the findings.* Summarizing is an effective communication strategy that not only forces the presenter to review and integrate the results and to express the key findings but also allows the client(s) to hear the essence of the interpretation again. One method of summarizing is to list all of the identified processing strengths and weaknesses.

18. *Explain the diagnosis, if applicable.* If the clinician diagnoses the examinee as having an LD, it is crucial that the clinician explain what an LD

is and the basis of the determination. It is especially important to discuss how processing deficits are part of the LD and how they are impacting learning.

Practitioners should be mindful that the client(s) may easily become overwhelmed by the information presented and the implications of the evaluation findings, if not intimidated by the group of professionals facing them. Throughout the process, it is important to keep the clients involved in a dialogue by inviting their participation, asking them to contribute information, and asking them to react to specific findings. It is also crucial to periodically check for understanding by asking them if they can give examples of the finding being discussed; for example, what behaviors indicative of a short-term memory deficit have they observed. In general, individuals who present assessment results should utilize effective communication strategies, such as paraphrasing and summarizing.

## DIAGNOSING LEARNING DISABILITIES (LDs)

With the passage of the federal IDEA act of 2004, the diagnostic criteria, at least the educational criteria, for a specific learning disability (SLD) is in the process of changing. The law eliminates the ability-achievement discrepancy requirement while retaining the identifying characteristic of SLD as a processing disorder. Consequently, there may be a renewed emphasis and interest in assessing processing with norm-referenced instruments when conducting LD evaluations. The traditional ability-achievement discrepancy approach was inconsistent with a processing approach to the identification of LD; thus, its departure will not be missed by those who advocate for cognitive processing assessment.

### Consistency Approach versus Discrepancy Approach

Naglieri (1999) was one of the first to advocate for a new approach to diagnosing LDs. The traditional approach has been to use an ability or achievement discrepancy, based on the assumption that a student with an LD is an individual whose academic skills are significantly lower than his or her intellectual or cognitive ability level. However, an approach that is more consistent with a processing model of LDs is to look for consistency between processing scores and related achievement scores. (See Rapid Reference 4.10.) To apply the consistency method with processing and achievement scores, each processing score should be compared with specific achievement scores. If a processing weakness is accounting for an academic skill deficit, then both scores should be low, instead of related aptitudes

## ≋Rapid Reference 4.10

**Example of Consistency Approach to SLD Identification—
Evidence of a Basic Reading Skills Disability**

| Factor | Score | Achievement Difference |
|---|:---:|:---:|
| | *Processing* | |
| Fluid Reasoning | 105 | Discrepant |
| Simultaneous Processing | 98 | Discrepant |
| Successive Processing | 79 | Consistent |
| Phonemic Awareness | 78 | Consistent |
| Planning | 103 | Discrepant |
| | *Achievement* | |
| Reading Decoding | 75 | — |

or cognitive processing scores being significantly higher than the academic skill score. For example, successive processing is known to be related with reading decoding, or basic reading skills, whereas simultaneous processing has a minimal relationship. Thus, when a Successive Processing score and a Reading Decoding score are both low, there is evidence of an LD in basic reading skills. In contrast, if both Simultaneous Processing and Successive Processing are high (average) scores while the basic reading skills score is low (below average), there is no evidence of an LD from a processing perspective.

In cases of SLDs, there should still be evidence of average functioning in at least some areas of processing. For example, in the case of a reading disability, there might be a discrepancy between a high Simultaneous Processing score and a low Reading Decoding score, because simultaneous processing is less correlated with reading than successive processing. When all processing scores are low and consistent with low achievement scores, it is more likely that the child has generally low cognitive ability or Mental Retardation than an LD. When a processing score is discrepant (higher) instead of being consistent with a related

## DON'T FORGET

The consistency approach to LD identification looks for low processing scores that go with low achievement scores. The approach is based on the premise that processing weaknesses account for SLDs. Thus, there should be consistency between related areas instead of a discrepancy.

achievement area, then other variables, such as environmental variables, that might account for the academic deficit should be investigated, the implication being that a processing deficit is not causing the underachievement. Thus, the most convincing evidence that a processing deficit is accounting for a learning problem is when ipsative processing deficits are all related to the area of academic deficiency and areas of less-related processes are not weaknesses or deficits.

## ⚞ TEST YOURSELF ⚟

1. **Which of the following is a concern about profile analysis?**
   (a) Lack of subtest specificity
   (b) Profiles lack diagnostic validity
   (c) Low subtest reliability
   (d) All of the above

2. **When conducting ipsative analysis, you should focus interpretation on which type of scores?**
   (a) Global
   (b) Factor
   (c) Subtest
   (d) None of the above

3. **A *deficit* is defined as**
   (a) a developmental delay.
   (b) a normative weakness.
   (c) an ipsative weakness.
   (d) both a normative and ipsative weakness.

4. **Statistically significant ipsative weaknesses should be interpreted cautiously when**
   (a) the discrepancy is relatively common in the population.
   (b) the factor score is in the average range.
   (c) the factor is unitary.
   (d) when an a posteriori hypothesis needs to be generated.

5. **Which relies mainly on an analysis of test scores?**
   (a) Clinical analysis
   (b) A diagnosis
   (c) Psychometric analysis
   (d) Hypothesis testing

6. **To determine intra-individual processing strengths and weaknesses, what should each factor score be compared to?**
   - (a) Full Scale IQ
   - (b) The processing mean
   - (c) Achievement test scores
   - (d) The mean of 100

7. **During a postevaluation conference with the examinee, all obtained test scores should be reported.** True or False?

8. **When statistical tables are unavailable for a group of scores being analyzed, what value should be used as indicative of a significant discrepancy?**
   - (a) 10 points
   - (b) 12 points
   - (c) 15 points
   - (d) 22 points

9. **Which factor score should be omitted from a processing analysis?**
   - (a) Fluid Reasoning
   - (b) Phonemic Awareness
   - (c) Verbal Comprehension
   - (d) Visual Processing

10. **When a processing deficit accounts for an SLD you would expect the related processing score and achievement score to be**
    - (a) consistent.
    - (b) discrepant.
    - (c) neither consistent or discrepant.
    - (d) both consistent and discrepant.

*Answers:* 1. d; 2. b; 3. d; 4. a; 5. c; 6. b; 7. False; 8. c; 9. c; 10. a

## Five

## ASSESSING PROCESSING WITH TRADITIONAL INTELLIGENCE SCALES

After more than a century of intellectual assessment, psychologists are still in search of a theory that explains all of intellectual functioning. The construct of intelligence has long been debated (Flanagan & Harrison, 2005; Sternberg & Detterman, 1986), but there is certainly a current consensus that intelligence is not just one thing (a single factor referred to as *g*). Several multiple-factor theories of intelligence have been proposed (see Sattler, 2001, for a review), and some of them form the basis of recently developed intellectual instruments. According to Flanagan et al. (2000), psychometric intelligence theories have recently converged, resulting in a more complete multiple intelligences theory. Currently, the most prominent multiple intelligences theory, CHC theory (discussed in Chapter 2), is the basis of many revised intelligence scales, including the venerable Stanford-Binet. Cattell-Horn-Carroll theory provides a taxonomy for classifying the subtests and factors that make up various scales, and CHC theory also provides a common framework for interpreting results across intelligence scales.

As traditional intelligence scales have evolved over the past century, especially over the past 20 years, they have come to explicitly measure more and more intellectual abilities. In doing so, they have also expanded into more direct measurement of the processes involved in intellectual and cognitive functioning. Given the trend, the next phase of intellectual assessment and interpretation may involve models that describe cognitive performance within a processing framework. Flanagan et al. (2000) refer to this potential next phase as the "fifth wave" of interpretation and cite Woodcock's Cognitive Performance Model as an example. Thus, the time has come to consider intellectual factors from a processing perspective. Viewing performance on intellectual scales from a processing perspective will enlighten and broaden our understanding of the individuals we assess.

This chapter will review the prominent traditional intellectual scales—the three Wechsler scales and the Stanford-Binet—from a processing assessment perspective. While the full composite scores may provide an indication of overall processing, the more direct measures of specific processes are found at the factor and subtest level (see Rapid Reference 5.1). For each scale reviewed, the focus will be on

# ≡ Rapid Reference 5.1

## Processes Measured by Traditional Intellectual Scales

| Process | WPPSI-III | WISC-IV | WAIS-III | SB5 |
|---|---|---|---|---|
| *Fluid Reasoning* | Matrix Reasoning; Picture Concepts; Word Reasoning; Similarities | Matrix Reasoning; Picture Concepts; Word Reasoning; Similarities; Arithmetic | Matrix Reasoning; Similarities | FLUID REASONING |
| *Processing Speed* | PROCESSING SPEED | PROCESSING SPEED | PROCESSING SPEED | |
| *Short-Term Memory* | | Digits Forward | Digits Forward | |
| *Visual Processing* | Block Design; Picture Completion; Object Assembly | Block Design; Picture Completion | Block Design; Object Assembly; Picture Completion; Picture Arrangement | VISUAL-SPATIAL PROCESSING |
| *Working Memory* | | WORKING MEMORY | WORKING MEMORY | WORKING MEMORY |

*Note:* Factors (indexes, quotients, composites) are capitalized; subtests are not.

the processes measured and how to interpret them. Basic information will also be provided on each scale's technical properties, such as reliability and validity, and unique administration features. Readers who desire more details about a test should refer to the test's technical manual or read reviews found in sources such as the *Mental Measurements Yearbook*. Guidelines for selecting factors and subtests to administer in each case are found in Chapter 3, and general interpretive guidelines have been discussed in Chapter 4. The specific interpretive advice given for each scale presumes that the reader will also apply the general interpretation guidelines presented in Chapter 4; for example, factors that are not unitary should be interpreted cautiously.

## WECHSLER ADULT INTELLIGENCE SCALE, THIRD EDITION (WAIS-III)

After the WISC-III (Wechsler, 1991) introduced a Processing Speed Index to the Wechsler scales, the WAIS-III (Wechsler, 1997b) became the first of the Wechsler scales to include a Working Memory Index. The WAIS-III also augmented the measurement of fluid reasoning, by adding a Matrix Reasoning subtest. Subsequent revisions of the WISC and the Wechsler Preschool and Primary Scale of Intelligence (WPPSI) continued the trend of including more subtests that measure processing. Because memory and intellectual ability in adults are often tested concurrently, especially during a neuropsychological assessment, the WAIS-III (see Rapid Reference 5.2) was conormed with the Wechsler Memory Scale, third edition (WMS-III; Wechsler, 1997c), reviewed in Chapter 7.

## Rapid Reference 5.2

### Wechsler Adult Intelligence Scale, Third Edition (WAIS-III)

**Author:** David Wechsler

**Publication date:** 1997

**Theoretical basis:** Traditional Wechsler theory

**Main processes measured:** Visual processing, working memory, fluid reasoning, and processing speed

**Age range:** 16:00–89:11

**Publisher:** The Psychological Corporation

## Processes Measured by the WAIS-III

### Fluid Reasoning

While the WAIS-III enhances the assessment of fluid reasoning with the addition of the Matrix Reasoning subtest, it does not have a fluid reasoning index (see Rapid Reference 5.3). Matrix Reasoning, the primary measure of fluid reasoning on the

## ≡Rapid Reference 5.3

### WAIS-III Structure and Processes Measured

| Index/Subtest | Processes |
|---|---|
| Verbal Comprehension Index (VCI) | — |
|     Similarities* | Fluid reasoning |
|     Vocabulary* | — |
|     Information* | — |
|     Comprehension* | — |
| Perceptual Organization Index (POI) | Visual processing, fluid reasoning |
|     Block Design* | Visual processing |
|     Matrix Reasoning* | Fluid reasoning |
|     Picture Completion* | Visual processing |
|     Picture Arrangement* | Visual processing |
|     Object Assembly | Visual processing |
| Working Memory Index (WMI) | Working memory, short-term memory |
|     Digit Span* | Working memory, short-term memory |
|     Arithmetic* | Working memory |
|     Letter-Number Sequencing | Working memory |
| Processing Speed Index (PSI) | Processing speed |
|     Digit-Symbol Coding* | Processing speed |
|     Symbol Search | Processing speed |

Note: Asterisk (*) indicates core subtest used to calculate Full Scale IQ (FSIQ).

WAIS-III, is part of the Performance Scale and the Perceptual Organization Index. The Similarities subtest, part of the Verbal Scale and Verbal Comprehension Index, also taps fluid reasoning to some extent, especially verbal fluid reasoning. Measures of fluid reasoning are especially relevant for processing assessment in adolescence and throughout adulthood because fluid reasoning comes into its prime in the teens and early twenties and then gradually declines over the remaining life span.

### Visual Processing

The Perceptual Organization Index (POI) is primarily a measure of visual processing, even with the addition of Matrix Reasoning. However, POI is a combination of fluid reasoning and visual processing and thus should not be used to represent either. Consequently, Matrix Reasoning should be removed from the computation of a visual processing factor. That leaves up to four subtests from which a visual processing clinical factor can be derived. The Block Design subtest appears to be the strongest measure of visual processing. Object Assembly, an optional subtest no longer used to compute Performance IQ or the POI, is also a strong measure of visual processing. Thus, the WAIS-III offers an in-depth assessment of visual processing.

### Working Memory and Short-Term Memory

The project directors for the development of the WAIS-III recognized the important role working memory plays in cognitive functioning and in learning. Although the Wechsler Adult Intelligence Scale–Revised (WAIS-R) Digit Span and Arithmetic subtests were already tapping short-term and working memory, it was not a well-known fact because the WAIS-R's third factor was named *Freedom from Distractibility*. Adding Letter-Number Sequencing to the index and changing the name to Working Memory resulted in better sampling of working memory and more recognition of what was actually being measured. Any subtest or index that assesses working memory is, of course, also measuring short-term memory, as the two are interrelated. Straightforward short-term memory, without much working memory involvement, is tapped by Wechsler items that require very little mental manipulation, such as Digits Forward. However, most of the items on the Working Memory Index (WMI) require mental manipulation of the information, and, thus, seem to be tapping working memory more so than short-term memory.

The extent to which the Arithmetic subtest measures working memory is uncertain. According to exploratory and confirmatory factor analytic studies reported in the *WAIS-III WMS-III Technical Manual* (Wechsler, 1997a), Arithmetic has the lowest loading on the Working Memory factor because it also loads somewhat on the Verbal Comprehension factor. Furthermore, the manual also reported a five-factor model in which Arithmetic was associated with a Quantitative ability factor.

### Processing Speed

While the functioning level of most processes begins to decline in the midtwenties, the decline of processing speed seems to be the most precipitous (see Figure 2.3 in Chapter 2). Thus, the assessment of processing speed, like memory and fluid reasoning, is a critical component of any testing designed to assess the functioning and integrity of cognitive processing, especially in later adulthood. Like the other Wechsler scales, the WAIS-III Processing Speed subtests take a rather narrow sample of processing speed; thus, inferences about broader mental processing speed will need to be bolstered by additional data.

## Selected Technical Features

The WAIS-III national standardization sample of 2,450 was selected according to 1995 U.S. census data. Compared to some of the more recently revised and published scales, the WAIS-III norms are several years older. Thus, the Flynn Effect (Flynn, 1999) needs to be taken into account when interpreting WAIS-III results independently or in conjunction with more recently normed tests, such as when conducting a cross battery analysis. Except for the PSI, reliability coefficients for all of the composites are above .90 (see Rapid Reference 5.4). The PSI reliability may be lower because it consists of fewer subtests or items and because it is a speeded test. Subtest split-half reliability coefficients range from a low of .70 for Object Assembly to a high of .93 for Vocabulary.

The WAIS-III technical manual (1997a) reports ample evidence of construct validity and criterion related validity. Regarding processing, the correlations between the WAIS-III and WMS-III provide support for the WAIS-III's WMI. The high correlation (.82) between the WMIs of the two scales demonstrates that they are measuring a similar construct. As expected, the WMS-III Visual Memory scales correlate more highly with the WAIS-III Performance IQ (PIQ) and POI and the WMS-III Auditory Memory scales correlate more highly with the Verbal IQ (VIQ) and VCI.

Clinical studies (Wechsler, 1997b) provide further evidence that the WAIS-III includes a valid measure of working memory and that working memory capacity

## ≡Rapid Reference 5.4

### WAIS-III Average Composite Reliability Coefficients

| Composite | Split-Half | Test-Retest |
|-----------|------------|-------------|
| VCI | .96 | .95 |
| POI | .93 | .88 |
| WMI | .94 | .89 |
| PSI | .88 | .89 |
| VIQ | .97 | .96 |
| PIQ | .94 | .91 |
| FSIQ | .98 | .96 |

Source: Data are from Essentials of WAIS-III Assessment (Kaufman & Lichtenberger, 1999, Rapid Reference 1.4).

is a critical mediator of learning. For both reading and math disabled samples, the WMI mean was the lowest index mean and significantly lower than the Verbal Comprehension and Perceptual Organization means.

## Unique Administration and Scoring Procedures

The examiner will need to administer optional subtests (those not usually included in the calculation of FSIQ) in order to obtain scores for the PSI and WMI. Symbol Search, which can also be used to replace Digit-Symbol Coding when computing the FSIQ, is necessary for the PSI, and Letter-Number Sequencing, which can be used to replace Digit Span when computing the FSIQ, is necessary for the WMI.

In addition to the three new subtests—Matrix Reasoning, Letter-Number Sequencing, and Symbol Search—the WAIS-III also initiated some optional procedures designed to measure incidental learning. Immediately after Digit-Symbol Coding is administered, Pairing and Free Recall may be administered. Both of these tasks involve incidental learning and long-term retrieval, as the examinee is asked to recall symbols from the Digit-Symbol Coding subtest that was just completed. In another optional procedure, Digit-Symbol Copy, the examinee is directed to copy symbols (there is no pairing involved) as quickly as possible. This task is designed to measure the examinee's speed of motor processing, with the effect of memory removed. Because motor skills may impact performance on Digit-Symbol Coding (and thus lower the PSI score), this optional procedure should be administered when motor deficits are suspected or the Digit-Symbol Coding score is a relative weakness.

## Interpretation of the WAIS-III Processing Components

The WAIS-III retains the traditional Verbal-Performance structure while adding four Indexes. The Verbal scale is divided into the VCI and the WMI, while the Performance scale is divided into the POI and the PSI. From a processing perspective, the WAIS-III provides information on four main processes—working memory, processing speed, fluid reasoning, and visual processing.

Begin a processing analysis of WAIS-III results by ignoring the nonprocessing scores—VIQ, PIQ, POI, and VCI. The Processing Analysis Worksheet (Appendix C) should be used to complete the analysis (see Rapid Reference 5.5 for the steps involved and Rapid Reference 5.6 for a completed example). The WMI and PSI scores can be entered directly onto the worksheet. Because the POI taps both fluid reasoning and visual processing, you will need to compute a visual processing clinical factor score and a fluid reasoning clinical factor score from the ap-

≡ *Rapid Reference 5.5*

## WAIS-III Processing Analysis Steps

1. Exclude nonprocessing scores—VIQ, PIQ, VCI, and POI—from the analysis.

2. Calculate a visual processing clinical factor score from at least two of the Perceptual Organization subtests, excluding Matrix Reasoning. First, transform the subtest scores to a metric with a mean of 100 and a standard deviation of 15 using the table in Appendix D. Then compute the mean of the scores and round to the nearest whole number.

3. Calculate a fluid reasoning clinical factor score from the Matrix Reasoning and Similarities subtests, following the same computations as in step 2.

4. Using the WMI and PSI scores obtained from the WAIS-III manual, record the four processing scores on the Processing Analysis Worksheet, and compute the mean of the four processing scores.

5. Compare each processing factor score to the individual's WAIS-III *processing* factor mean, using a 15 point discrepancy as an indication of significance and infrequency. Complete the weakness and deficit columns.

6. Examine subtest scores within each index or factor to determine whether each factor is unitary. When the difference between the highest and lowest subtest scores is 5 points or greater (when using a mean of 10 and standard deviation of 3), consider the factor to be nonunitary. Interpret nonunitary factors cautiously, and do not use them for pairwise comparisons.

7. Compare processing factor pairs, especially working memory versus processing speed and fluid reasoning versus visual processing, using a 20-point discrepancy as the criterion for significance and infrequency.

8. (This step is optional because it does not involve interpretation at the factor level.) Compute the greatest number of digits recalled in both Digits Forward and Digits Backward. Table B.6 in the WAIS-III Administration and Scoring Manual can be used to compare performance to the normative sample. Critical values are not provided, but a significant ipsative difference may be indicated when the spans differ by 3 or more points.

propriate subtests (see the Selective Testing Table for Processes Measured by Cognitive Tests in Appendix A). Only two subtests are required for each factor score, but more can be included in the calculation if they have been administered. For example, it is not necessary to administer the optional Object Assembly subtest in order to obtain a visual processing clinical factor score. The fluid reasoning clinical factor score from the WAIS-III is unusual in that it contains a verbal reasoning subtest (Similarities). After completing the steps on the upper half of the Processing Analysis Worksheet, remember to conduct pairwise comparisons on the lower half. Logical pairs, such as Working Memory versus Processing Speed, should be examined for significant discrepancies. In the case of Working

## Rapid Reference 5.6

### Processing Analysis Worksheet
### WAIS-III Illustration

Examinee's Name: _____    DOB: _____  Age: _____  Grade: _____  Dates of Testing: _____

| Name of Process | Name of Test/ Battery | Name of Factor/ Subtests | Processing Factor Score | Processing Factor Mean | Difference from Mean | Normative S or W | Ipsative S or W | Deficit or Asset |
|---|---|---|---|---|---|---|---|---|
| Working Memory | WAIS-III | WMI | 79 | 93 | –14 | W | — | — |
| Processing Speed | WAIS-III | PSI | 100 | 93 | +7 | — | — | — |
| Visual Processing | WAIS-III | Block Design; Picture Completion; Pic. Arrangement | 98 | 93 | +5 | — | — | — |

| Fluid Reasoning | WAIS-III | Similarities; Matrix Reasoning | 93 | 93 | 0 | — | — | — |
|---|---|---|---|---|---|---|---|---|

*Note:* Dashes indicate the absence of an S or W, or an A or D.

Directions: (1) Use factor scores for analysis, not subtest scores. (2) When a factor score is not available from a test, convert subtest scores to a mean of 100 and an SD of 15. (3) For each factor, compute the mean of the subtest scores and round to the nearest whole number. Use the subtest means as clinical factor scores. (4) Compare the mean of all available factor scores (this is the processing mean). (5) Subtract the processing mean from each processing factor score and enter amount in Difference column. (6) Indicate whether the factor score is a normative weakness or strength (90–109 is average). (7) Using a criterion of 15 points, determine ipsative strengths and weaknesses. (8) Determine deficits and assets. A deficit is both a normative and ipsative weakness. (9) Compare related pairs (below) for significant differences, using a 20-point difference as an indication of significance. (10) Determine which factors are nonunitary. When the range between the highest and lowest subtest scores exceeds 1.5 SDs (22 points), the factor is nonunitary. Nonunitary factors should be interpreted cautiously and should not be used in pairwise comparisons.

| Factor Score | Factor Score | Difference | Significant:Y/N |
|---|---|---|---|
| Working Memory (79) | Processing Speed (100) | 21 | Y |

Memory versus Processing Speed, the WAIS-III has tables for significance and frequency, eliminating the need to use the 20-point guideline. Finally, compare the Digits Forward and Digits Backward spans (there is place for this on the WAIS-III Record Form, or it could be entered on the bottom of the Processing Analysis Worksheet). This step contrasts short-term memory (Digits Forward) with working memory (Digits Backward).

### Illustration of WAIS-III Processing Analysis

Selected scores from a complete WAIS-III administration are used to illustrate the analytical procedures. Use the Supplemental Processing Analysis Worksheet for All Wechsler Scales in Appendix E to complete the computations not shown on the general Processing Analysis Worksheet.

Given the following scores:

Similarities (S) Scaled Score of 6—transformed to a standard score of 80

Matrix Reasoning (MR) Scaled Score of 11—transformed to a standard score of 105

Picture Completion (PC) Scaled Score of 8—transformed to a standard score of 90

Picture Arrangement (PA) Scaled Score of 9—transformed to a standard score of 95

Block Design (BD) Scaled Score of 11—transformed to a standard score of 105

Object Assembly (OA) Scaled Score of 10—transformed to a standard score of 100

Working Memory Index—79
    Arithmetic—6
    Digit Span—7
    Letter-Number Sequencing—7

Processing Speed Index—100
    Digit-Symbol Coding—9
    Symbol Search—11

Longest Digit Span Forward—5

Longest Digit Span Backward—3

1. Compute a visual processing (VP) clinical factor score: (PC) 90 + (PA) 95 + (BD) 105 + (OA) 100 = 390/4 = 97.5 = (rounded) 98.
2. Compute a fluid reasoning (FR) clinical factor score: (S) 80 + (MR) 105 = 185/2 = 92.5 = (rounded) 93.

3. Compute the processing factor mean: (WMI) 79 + (PSI) 100 + (VP) 98 + (FR) 93 = 370/4 = 92.5 = (rounded) 93.

4. Compute the difference from the mean for each factor, for example: (WM) 79 − 93 = −14.

5. Complete the remaining columns. Only Working Memory is a normative weakness. There are no ipsative strengths or weaknesses and, thus, there cannot be any deficits or assets.

6. Check to see if factors are unitary. The subtest scaled scores of S (6) and MR (11) differ by more than 1.5 standard deviations. Thus, the Fluid Reasoning clinical factor is not unitary and should not be used in the pairwise comparisons.

7. Complete pairwise comparisons. PS (100) is significantly higher than WM (79). Base rate for this pair can be found in the WAIS-III manual.

8. Compare forward (5) and backward (3) digit spans. They differ by less than 3 points and thus are not significantly different.

### *Fluid Reasoning Interpretation*

On the WAIS-III, the Matrix Reasoning subtest is the most direct measure of fluid reasoning. The Similarities subtest also measures fluid reasoning to some extent but it is primarily a measure of crystallized intelligence. Thus, calculating a fluid reasoning clinical factor that includes Similarities is the least desirable choice. A preferable alternative is to administer a fluid reasoning subtest or factor from another scale and combine it with the WAIS-III Matrix Reasoning subtest to produce a cross-battery fluid reasoning factor. Clinical interpretation of a fluid reasoning factor needs to take into account the influences on fluid reasoning subtest performance, such as persistence, visual-perceptual problems, cognitive style (field dependence-field independence), flexibility, ability to respond when uncertain, and overly concrete thinking (Kaufman & Lichtenberger, 1999; see Rapid Reference 5.7).

### *Working Memory Interpretation*

When interpreting a working memory factor from any intellectual or cognitive scale, it is important to keep two things in mind: (1) only a narrow and limited sampling of working

*Rapid Reference 5.7*

**Influences Affecting Performance on Fluid Reasoning and Visual Processing Subtests**

Persistence
Visual-perceptual problems
Cognitive style
Flexibility
Ability to respond when uncertain

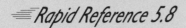

**Rapid Reference 5.8**

**Influences Affecting Performance on Working Memory Subtests**

Short-term memory
Attention
Concentration
Anxiety
Sequential processing
Number ability
Planning ability
Executive processing

memory has been conducted and (2) many abilities, processes, and behaviors can affect performance on working memory subtests. The WMI on the WAIS-III is a narrow measure of working memory because it mainly assesses auditory working memory. It is also difficult to determine the extent to which short-term memory, instead of working memory, is involved (see Chapter 2 for a discussion of the relationship). Furthermore, performance on subtests designed to measure working memory can be influenced by one or more of the following (Kaufman & Lichtenberger, 1999): short-term memory, attention, concentration, anxiety, sequential processing, number ability, planning ability, and executive processing (see Rapid Reference 5.8). Processing speed is also thought to be related to working memory efficiency. However, the WMI and PSI on the WAIS-III may be dissimilar because the Working Memory subtests are auditory and the Processing Speed subtests are mainly visual. Determining the influence these cognitive and behavioral variables have on working memory performance requires clinical interpretation that takes into account testing behaviors, background information, and performance on related scales.

Comparing the length of the span on Digits Forward to the span on Digits Backward may provide some insight into the capacity of the examinee's short-term memory versus working memory. Digits Backward requires mental manipulation of the stimuli; thus, it taps working memory, while rote recall, or basic short-term memory, is the main requirement for adequate performance on Digits Forward. Keep in mind that average examinees produce longer spans (by one to two digits) on Digits Forward than on Digits Backward. Digit Span Backward has been shown to be more affected by aging and impairment than Digit Span Forward (Wechsler, 1997b).

*Processing Speed Interpretation*
It is also necessary to consider the multiple influences on PSI performance, including fine motor ability, motivation, attention, visual memory, planning ability, and working memory (Kaufman & Lichtenberger, 1999; see Rapid Reference

5.9). Coding, one of the PSI subtests, is thought to be especially affected by attention; for example, children with ADHD typically obtain their lowest subtest score on Wechsler Coding subtests (Wechsler, 2003b). Coding is also impacted by fine motor abilities; examinees with fine motor deficits perform poorly on the PSI (Wechsler, 2003b). That's why it is important to administer Coding Copy whenever fine motor deficits are suspected. Finally, all intellectual or cognitive batteries measure processing

### ≡ Rapid Reference 5.9

**Influences Affecting Performance on Processing Speed Subtests**

Fine motor ability

Motivation

Attention

Visual memory

Planning ability

Working memory

speed in the same way—a paper-and-pencil task that requires visual scanning and paired associations. Thus, processing speed should be interpreted narrowly; for example, use the definition provided in the test's manual. Do not interpret the WAIS-III PSI as representative of a broader mental processing speed.

### Visual Processing Interpretation

Isolating visual processing is a challenge because it is extensively involved with the majority of cognitive processes. Performance on a visual processing factor may vary, depending on which of the several subtypes are sampled. Performance may also be affected by several influences, including visual-perceptual problems, cognitive style (field dependence), flexibility, persistence, and ability to respond when uncertain (Kaufman & Lichtenberger, 1999). These are essentially the same influences that affect performance on matrix reasoning tasks (see Rapid Reference 5.7).

### Indications of Learning Disabilities (LDs)

The WAIS-III Technical Manual (Wechsler, 1997a) reports that a sample of learning disabled adults obtained depressed scores on the ACID subtests (Arithmetic, Coding, Information, and Digit Span). Past Wechsler scales research with learning disabled subjects has often found what is referred to as the *ACID profile*. However, Kaufman and Lichtenberger (1999) suggest that the discrepancies among index scores may be a better way to characterize an LD. The WAIS-III standardization study found 30 percent to 40 percent of the LD subjects to exhibit a significantly lower WMI than VCI and a significantly lower PSI than POI. While not diagnostic, such a profile supports an LD diagnosis, especially when the processing deficits correlate highly with the SLD.

## Strengths and Weaknesses as a Measure of Processing

The inclusion of more processing indexes and subtests make the WAIS-III particularly useful in assessing the cognitive processing and neurological functioning of adults. Fluid reasoning, processing speed, and working memory are all critical for routine mental functioning in adulthood. Their inclusion in the WAIS-III allows clinicians to determine when there may be an abnormal decrement in any of these processing abilities. The WAIS-III's linkage with the WMS-III facilitates combining interpretation of results when additional memory assessment is desired. Also, optional Digit-Symbol procedures allow some parsing of abilities or influences that may have impacted performance on Digit-Symbol Coding.

Regarding potential weaknesses, there are no major concerns, as the technical properties of the WAIS-III are sound. However, the dual structure—VIQ and PIQ versus the four Indexes—can make it challenging to interpret results even before attempting interpretation from a processing perspective. There is also the additional challenge of separating and computing estimates of visual processing and fluid reasoning and making clinical judgments when there are no norms for these scores.

## WECHSLER INTELLIGENCE SCALE FOR CHILDREN, FOURTH EDITION (WISC-IV)

The WISC-IV, currently the most widely used measure of children's intelligence (Wechsler, 2003a), originated with David Wechsler's 1949 Wechsler Intelligence Scale for Children. Although the main purpose of the WISC-IV is to measure general intelligence, the WISC-IV measures some prominent cognitive processes. New subtests, the restructuring of the battery, alternative scoring procedures, and the inclusion of more processing subtests in the computation of the Full Scale IQ (FSIQ) make the WISC-IV more of a processing measure than its predecessor, the WISC-III (see Rapid Reference 5.10). Three of the four WISC-IV indexes—the Working Memory Index (WMI), the Processing Speed Index (PSI), and the Perceptual Reasoning Index (PRI)—can be categorized as processing scales. The Verbal Comprehension Index (VCI), generally classified as crystallized intelligence, should not be considered a direct measure of processing, although two of the five Verbal Comprehension subtests (Similarities and Word Reasoning) measure verbal fluid reasoning to some extent. Several additional optional processing subtests are also available in a more comprehensive battery, the WISC-IV Integrated, discussed in Chapter 6.

A factor analytic study by Keith et al. (2004), cited in Flanagan and Kaufman (2004), identified five WISC-IV factors instead of four. With five factors, the Perceptual Reasoning factor is divided into Fluid Reasoning and Visual Processing. Keith and his colleagues also identified several other clinical clusters for interpretative purposes—Verbal Fluid Reasoning, Nonverbal Fluid Reasoning, Lexical Knowledge, General Information, Long-Term Memory, and Short-Term Memory.

> ### ≡ Rapid Reference 5.10
>
> ## Wechsler Intelligence Scale for Children, Fourth Edition (WISC-IV)
>
> **Author:** David Wechsler
> **Publication date:** 2003
> **Main processes measured:** Fluid reasoning, visual processing, working memory, and processing speed
> **Theoretical basis:** Traditional Wechsler theory
> **Age range:** 6:0–16:11
> **Publisher:** PsychCorp

## Processes Measured by the WISC-IV

### Working Memory and Short-Term Memory

The working memory subtests of the WISC-IV require the examinee to actively maintain information in conscious awareness while performing some operation or manipulation with it (Wechsler, 2003b). To some extent, the working memory subtests also involve short-term memory (see Rapid Reference 5.11). For example, the Digit Span subtest can be divided into short-term memory and working memory, with Digit Span Forward involving short-term memory span, while Digit Span Backward, requiring manipulation of the digits, mainly involves working memory. The first several items of Letter-Number Sequencing may also be considered as primarily measuring short-term memory span because examinees are not required to rearrange the stimuli. Arithmetic is classified as a supplemental Working Memory subtest on the WISC-IV. According to the WISC-IV technical and interpretative manual (Wechsler, 2003b) the WISC-IV version of Arithmetic demands more working memory and less math computation than the WISC-III version did. However, Keith et al. (2004) believe that the WISC-IV Arithmetic subtest is primarily a measure of fluid reasoning.

The crucial role of working memory in academic learning and daily functioning is well established. Evidence that the WISC-IV is measuring critical working memory functions is found in a standardization study of children with a Reading Disorder. Compared to a matched normal sample, the children with Reading Disorders obtained significantly lower mean scores for all composites (Wechsler,

## ≡Rapid Reference 5.11

### WISC-IV Structure and Processes Measured

| Index/Subtest | Processes |
| --- | --- |
| Verbal Comprehension | — |
| Similarities* | Fluid reasoning |
| Vocabulary* | — |
| Comprehension* | — |
| Information | — |
| Word Reasoning | Fluid reasoning |
| Perceptual Reasoning | Visual processing, fluid reasoning |
| Block Design* | Visual processing |
| Picture Concepts* | Fluid reasoning |
| Matrix Reasoning* | Fluid reasoning |
| Picture Completion | Visual processing |
| Working Memory | Working memory, short-term memory |
| Digit Span* | Working memory, short-term memory |
| Letter-Number Sequencing* | Working memory, short-term memory |
| Arithmetic | Working memory, short-term memory, fluid reasoning |
| Processing Speed | Processing speed |
| Coding* | Processing speed |
| Symbol Search* | Processing speed |
| Cancellation | Processing speed |

Note: Asterisk (*) indicates core subtest.

2003b), with the largest effect size for the WMI mean of 87.0 (see Rapid Reference 5.12).

### Processing Speed

The core Processing Speed subtests of Coding and Symbol Search were also part of the WISC-III. The updated scale has added Cancellation as a supplemental subtest and now includes Symbol Search in the computation of the FSIQ. Research has documented the dynamic relationship processing speed has with other processes, especially working memory, and mental capacity and neurological development in general, as well as its essential role in academic learning.

## Visual Processing

The WISC-IV does not have a visual processing or a fluid reasoning index but does contain measures of both, as documented by the factor analytic studies of Keith et al. (2004). Visual processing is mainly measured by Block Design and Picture Completion, with Matrix Reasoning partially loading on a visual processing factor as well. Of the three subtests, Block Design is the best measure of visual processing, with a loading of .84; Picture Completion has a loading of .42, and Matrix Reasoning has a loading of .30 (Keith et al., 2004). As indicated in the WISC-IV technical and interpretative manual (Wechsler, 2003b), the Perceptual Reasoning Index should be viewed as a measure of both visual processing and fluid reasoning.

### ≡Rapid Reference 5.12

**WISC-IV Performance of Reading Disorder Group**

| Composite | Mean | SD |
|---|---|---|
| VCI | 91.9 | 9.7 |
| PRI | 94.4 | 11.2 |
| WMI | 87.0 | 12.9 |
| PSI | 92.5 | 11.7 |
| FSIQ | 89.1 | 10.3 |

Source: Data are from WISC-IV technical and interpretative manual (Wechsler, 2003b, p. 83).

## Fluid Reasoning

According to CHC classifications by the WISC-IV project directors (cited in Flanagan & Kaufman, 2004) and factor analysis by Keith et al. (2004), fluid reasoning is measured by more than the Perceptual Reasoning subtests. Keith et al. found Arithmetic to have the highest loading (.79) on fluid reasoning, with Picture Concepts at .59 and Matrix Reasoning at .45. Fluid reasoning measures on the WISC-IV are not limited to the perceptual reasoning or nonverbal domain; fluid reasoning is also required on the Verbal Comprehension subtests of Similarities and Word Reasoning, although these two subtests are intended to primarily assess verbal or crystallized intelligence.

## Selected Technical Features

As with factors on other intellectual scales, processing factor scores tend to be somewhat less reliable than the more g-loaded intellectual factors. For example, both the test-retest (.86) and internal consistency reliability (.88) estimates for PSI are below the desired level of .90 (Wechsler, 2003b). In fact the only Index with a test-retest coefficient above .90 is VCI (see Rapid Reference 5.13). Mean reliability coefficients for the core subtests range from .79 to .89.

≡*Rapid Reference 5.13*

**WISC-IV Composite Average Reliability Coefficients**

| Composite | Internal Consistency | Test-Retest |
| --- | --- | --- |
| VCI | .94 | .93 |
| PRI | .92 | .89 |
| WMI | .92 | .89 |
| PSI | .88 | .86 |
| FSIQ | .97 | .93 |

The full gamut of validity evidence is detailed in the WISC-IV technical and interpretive manual (Wechsler, 2003b). Of the evidence presented, the results of the exploratory factor analysis may be challenged the most, as alternative factor structures have been proffered by Keith et al. (2004) and others. From the national standardization sample of 2,200, 15 validity studies were conducted with clinical groups, such as a group with a Reading Disorder. For each disability, the results of the clinical studies were generally as predicted, supporting the predictive validity and clinical utility of the WISC-IV. Thorough reviews of WISC-IV technical properties can be found in Sattler and Dumont (2004) and Flanagan and Kaufman (2004).

### Unique Administration and Scoring Procedures

The new structure and processing emphasis of the WISC-IV has resulted in some administration and scoring changes from previous WISC versions. There are now five supplemental subtests that can be administered if subtest specific information is desired. The supplemental subtests can also, with limitations, substitute for core subtests when a core subtest is spoiled or there is an a priori justification for making the substitution. When using the supplemental subtests for processing assessment, evaluators should review the Selective Testing Table for Processes Measured by Cognitive Tests (Appendix A) for the processing classifications of the subtests.

Optional alternative scoring procedures for some of the subtests are relevant to processing assessment and interpretation. After the subtests are administered in the usual way, process scores can be obtained for Block Design (with no time bonus) and Digit Span and Cancellation (see the following interpretation section for a fuller discussion). However, these process subtest scores can not be used in the computation of the FSIQ.

Perhaps, the most unique feature of WISC-IV scoring is the option of computing a General Ability Index (GAI) and using this for decision making in lieu of the FSIQ (Raiford, Rolfus, Weiss, & Coalson, 2005). The GAI is based on the WISC-IV norming sample and is derived from the six subtests that comprise the

VCI and PRI. Thus, the GAI represents the more traditional general intellectual ability factor, because the four processing subtests (which tend to load lower on $g$) are removed from the computation. Providing the GAI alternative was, in part, a response to concerns about children with a learning disability not meeting IQ-achievement discrepancy requirements because their low processing scores were pulling down their FSIQ scores. In instances where this phenomenon is expected, it may be beneficial to compute the GAI and contrast it with FSIQ, or use the GAI instead of the FSIQ for diagnosis.

## Interpretation of the WISC-IV from a Processing Perspective

Kaufman (1994) was the first to apply a processing model to interpretation of a Wechsler scale. Kaufman's 1994 book on interpretation of the WISC-III advocated the interpretation of WISC-III results from an information processing perspective. The model divided processing into input, integration, storage, and output. Kaufman also described the extent to which WISC-III subtests measured simultaneous processing, sequential processing, and planning. Kaufman's (Flanagan & Kaufman, 2004) recent advice for interpretation of the WISC-IV does not explicitly address the processing implications of WISC-IV results. Interpretative advice for the WISC-IV can also be found in Prifitera, Saklofske, Weiss, and Rolfhus (2004).

### VCI Interpretation

The VCI should not be interpreted as a direct measure of processing. Although fluid reasoning, long-term retrieval, and other processes are involved in VCI performance, VCI is primarily measuring accumulated verbal knowledge or crystallized intelligence. Processing forms the basis of crystallized or verbal intelligence development, but the WISC-IV VCI subtests are not directly measuring the processes involved. If a cross-battery assessment has been completed, VCI should also be excluded from computation of a cross-battery processing mean. If desired, a clinical verbal fluid reasoning factor may be calculated from the Word Reasoning and Similarities subtests. This clinical factor may then be included in the analysis of processing.

Despite the quandary posed by the VCI, the relationship VCI has with other Indexes should be noted, especially the relationship VCI has with Working Memory, because they are both assessing the auditory/verbal domain. (The WMI subtests are primarily measuring auditory working memory.) Many children with an LD perform poorly on Wechsler verbal/auditory scales, as research on the Bannatyne profile has found. Bannatyne (1974) found that a significant percentage of

# DON'T FORGET

When analyzing WISC-IV results from a processing perspective, VCI should not be interpreted as a processing factor because VCI is primarily a measure of crystallized intelligence. However, the Word Reasoning and Similarities subtests may be interpreted as indicators of verbal fluid reasoning.

children with an LD have a profile where VIQ is between a higher PIQ and lower processing indexes (Processing Speed and Freedom from Distractibility). It is not surprising that many children with an LD would obtain poor Verbal scores, given that many have language delays.

Lower Wechsler Verbal scores may also have been due to the fact that previous Wechsler versions included the Information and Arithmetic subtests in the VIQ and FSIQ. Information and Arithmetic, at least in part, are measures of achievement, and individuals with an LD have deficiencies in achievement. Thus, it could be predicted that examinees with a learning disability will obtain lower Verbal composites when those Verbal composites include measures of achievement. With the introduction of the WISC-IV and the reduction of achievement subtests on the VCI, there is evidence (Dehn, 2004) that many children with a learning disability are obtaining significantly higher scores on VCI than they did in the past.

## PRI Interpretation

To discern the processing implications of the PRI score, it is necessary to separately examine the child's performance on the PRI subtests. PRI is primarily a measure of visual processing and fluid reasoning, and each of the PRI subtests measure both. While the two processes function together, just as other integrated processes do, they are also quite distinct, with fluid reasoning involving more executive processing and verbal components than visual processing involves. Thus, an attempt should be made to examine them separately. Of the three core subtests, Block Design may be the best measure of visual processing, and Matrix Reasoning may be the best measure of fluid reasoning, with Picture Concepts being a moderate measure of both. The Analysis Page in the WISC-IV Record Form may be used for determining subtest strengths and weaknesses within the PRI domain. When doing so be sure to use the Perceptual Reasoning mean and not the mean of all 10 core subtests. An alternative is to align the subtests according to the clinical clusters suggested by Flanagan and Kaufman (2004) and conduct pairwise comparisons. This approach incorporates Word Reasoning and Similarities as measures of verbal fluid reasoning, and has the advantage of discerning whether the differences are common or uncommon, using a statistical table provided by Flanagan and Kaufman.

*Fluid Reasoning and Visual Processing Interpretation*

A more meaningful and cleaner processing interpretation of the WISC-IV is to compute separate clinical factor scores for fluid reasoning and visual processing, as introduced in the previous WAIS-III discussion. The Block Design and Picture Completion subtests can be used to compute a visual processing clinical factor, and the Matrix Reasoning and Picture Concepts subtests can be used to compute a fluid reasoning clinical factor.

*PSI Interpretation*

Although the WISC-IV PSI is intended for direct assessment of processing speed, some interpretive cautions apply. Evaluators should limit their interpretation of the PSI to the WISC-IV definition of processing speed as "the ability to quickly and correctly scan, sequence, or discriminate simple visual information" (Wechsler, 2003b, p. 104). Inferences about a broader mental processing speed should be avoided unless supported by the child's performance on tasks that go beyond the paper-and-pencil tasks found on the Processing Speed subtests of Coding, Symbol Search, and Cancellation. The Processing Speed subtests may be measuring psychomotor speed as much as mental processing speed. Also, performance on processing speed subtests can be influenced by several factors (see Rapid Reference 5.9).

It is especially important to examine how PSI compares with the other three indexes. Just as WMI and VCI often will cluster together because they are both within the verbal/auditory domain, PSI and PRI often will be similar because they are both in the visual/nonverbal domain. The PSI-WMI comparison is also noteworthy because of their interrelated functioning. When PSI and WMI are significantly different, it may be because the PSI tasks are more visual while the WMI tasks are more auditory. In such instances, it is important to examine how VCI aligns with WMI and PRI aligns with PSI. When both alignments exist, the PSI-WMI discrepancy may be part of a broader difference between the visual and auditory domains. See the WISC-IV interpretation book by Prifitera et al. (2004) for additional interpretive insights.

*WMI Interpretation*

Working memory strengths and weaknesses also need to be qualified. The primary distinction that must be

## DON'T FORGET

When the WISC-IV VCI and WMI cluster together, it may be because both are sampling the auditory/verbal domain. In contrast, the PRI and PSI may cluster together because they are both tapping the visual/nonverbal domain. It is important to examine these potential alignments whenever there is a discrepancy between PSI and WMI.

# CAUTION

The WISC-IV WMI is primarily measuring auditory working memory. Interpretive statements about global working memory should be avoided unless there is commensurate performance on subtests of visual working memory.

made is that the WISC-IV standard battery is measuring auditory working memory only. The distinction is especially important for children with learning problems or disabilities because these children often have stronger visual processing abilities and stronger visual working memory. Thus, evaluators should refrain from global statements about working memory; for example, visual working memory may be adequate while auditory working memory is deficient. Quantification of a child's visual working memory can be accomplished by administering the optional visual working memory subtests found in the more comprehensive WISC-IV Integrated battery discussed in Chapter 6.

## Additional Process Analysis

The final type of processing analysis that can be conducted with the WISC-IV standard battery is found on the bottom section of the Analysis Page in the WISC-IV Record Form. Standard scores are provided for Block Design No Time Bonus, Digit Span Forward, Digit Span Backward, Cancellation Random, and Cancellation Structured, as well as the base rates for the longest Digit Span Forward and the longest Digit Span Backward. Isolating the speed factor in Block Design allows one to assess whether slow processing speed or some other limitation, such as fine motor difficulties, may have impacted performance on Block Design. Contrasting the Forward and Backward Digit Spans may illuminate relative differences between short-term (Digits Forward) and working memory (Digits Backward). More in-depth teasing apart of the processes subsumed in each subtest can be accomplished by administering optional subtests in the broader WISC-IV Integrated battery discussed in Chapter 6.

## Analysis of the WISC-IV Processing Components

A processing analysis of the WISC-IV according to the Integrated Processing Model is very similar to the recommended processing interpretation of the WAIS-III, discussed previously in this chapter. Thus, procedural details and the rationale for the steps will not be reiterated here. Readers should refer to Rapid

## ≡Rapid Reference 5.14

### WISC-IV Processing Analysis Steps

1. Exclude VCI and PRI from the analysis.

2. Calculate a visual processing clinical factor score from Block Design and Picture Completion. First, transform the subtest scores to a metric with a mean of 100 and a standard deviation of 15 using the table in Appendix D. Then compute the mean of the scores and round to the nearest whole number.

3. Calculate a fluid reasoning clinical factor score from Matrix Reasoning and Picture Concepts, following the same computations as in step 2. If Arithmetic was administered, it may also be included in the computation of Fluid Reasoning (including Arithmetic is optional and somewhat controversial).

4. Using the WMI and PSI scores obtained from the WISC-IV manual, record the four processing scores on the Processing Analysis Worksheet and compute the mean of the four processing scores.

5. Compare each processing factor score to the individual's WISC-IV *processing* factor mean, using a 15-point discrepancy as an indication of significance and infrequency. Complete the weakness and deficit columns.

6. Examine subtest scores within each index or factor to determine whether each factor is unitary. When the difference between the highest and lowest subtest scores is 5 points or greater (when using a mean of 10 and standard deviation of 3), consider the factor to be nonunitary. Interpret nonunitary factors cautiously, and do not use them for pairwise comparisons.

7. Compare processing factor pairs, especially working memory versus processing speed and fluid reasoning versus visual processing, using a 20-point discrepancy as the criterion for significance and infrequency.

8. Complete the Process Analysis section in the WISC-IV Record Form. (This step is optional because it does not involve interpretation at the factor level.)

Reference 5.14 for a summary of the WISC-IV steps and Rapid Reference 5.15 for a completed Processing Analysis Worksheet, using WISC-IV data.

### Illustration of WISC-IV Processing Analysis

Selected scores from a complete WISC-IV administration are used to illustrate the analytical procedures. Use the Supplemental Processing Analysis Worksheet for All Wechsler Scales in Appendix E to complete the computations not shown on the general Processing Analysis Worksheet. Given the following scores:

═ *Rapid Reference 5.15*

## Processing Analysis Worksheet
### WISC-IV Illustration

Examinee's Name: _____   DOB: _____   Age: _____   Grade: _____   Dates of Testing: _____

| Name of Process | Name of Test/ Battery | Name of Factor/ Subtests | Processing Factor Score | Processing Factor Mean | Difference from Mean | Normative S or W | Ipsative S or W | Deficit or Asset |
|---|---|---|---|---|---|---|---|---|
| Working Memory | WISC-IV | WMI | 74 | 96 | −22 | W | W | D |
| Processing Speed | WISC-IV | PSI | 91 | 96 | −5 | — | — | — |
| Visual Processing | WISC-IV | Block Design; Picture Completion | 113 | 96 | +17 | S | S | A |

| Fluid Reasoning | WISC-IV | Picture Concepts; Matrix Reasoning | 105 | 96 | +9 | — | — | — |

*Note:* Dashes indicate the absence of an S or W, or an A or D.

*Directions:* (1) Use factor scores for analysis, not subtest scores. (2) When a factor score is not available from a test, convert subtest scores to a mean of 100 and an AD of 15. (3) For each factor, compute the mean of the subtest scores and round to the nearest whole number. Use the subtest means as clinical factor scores. (4) Compute the mean of all available factor scores (this is the processing mean). (5) Subtract the processing mean from each processing factor score and enter amount in Difference column. (6) Indicate whether the factor score is a normative weakness or strength (90–109 is average). (7) Using a criterion of 15 points, determine ipsative strengths and weaknesses. (8) Determine deficits and assets. A deficit is both a normative and ipsative weakness. (9) Determine which factors are nonunitary. When the range between the highest and lowest subtest scores exceeds 1.5 SDs, the factor is nonunitary. Nonunitary factors should be interpreted cautiously and should not be used in pairwise comparisons. (10) Compare related pairs (below) for significant differences, using a 20-point difference as an indication of significance.

| Factor Score | Factor Score | Difference | Significant:Y/N |
|---|---|---|---|
| Working Memory (74) | Processing Speed (91) | 17 | Y (based on WISC-IV tables) |
| Visual Processing (113) | Fluid Reasoning (105) | 8 | N |

Picture Concepts (PCn) Scaled Score of 12—transformed to a standard score of 110

Matrix Reasoning (MR) Scaled Score of 10—transformed to a standard score of 100

Arithmetic (A) Scaled Score of 6—transformed to a standard score of 80

Picture Completion (PCm) Scaled Score of 13—transformed to a standard score of 115

Block Design (BD) Scaled Score of 12—transformed to a standard score of 110

Working Memory Index—74
    Digit Span—7
    Letter-Number Sequencing—4

Processing Speed Index—91
    Coding—9
    Symbol Search—8

1. Compute a visual processing (VP) clinical factor score: (PCm) 115 + (BD) 110 = 225/2 = 112.5 = (rounded) 113.
2. Compute a fluid reasoning (FR) clinical factor score. (In this case, it is better to omit Arithmetic because it appears to be measuring something other than what the two primary fluid reasoning subtests are measuring.) (PCn) 110 + (MR) 100 = 210/2 = 105.
3. Compute the processing factor mean: (WMI) 74 + (PSI) 91 + (VP) 113 + (FR) 105 = 383/4 = 95.75 = (rounded) 96.
4. Compute the difference from the mean for each factor, for example: (WM) 74 − 96 = −22.
5. Complete the remaining columns. Working Memory is both a normative and ipsative weakness and, therefore, a deficit, while Visual Processing is both a normative and ipsative strength and, therefore, an asset.
6. Check to see if the factors are unitary. In this case they are all unitary.
7. Complete pairwise comparisons. In this case, there initially do not appear to be any significant discrepancies. But when the WISC-IV manual tables are used, the 17-point WMI/PSI discrepancy is significant at the .05 level for all ages and has a base rate of 16.6 percent, close enough to the 15 percent guideline to interpret. Without further computations, it should be evident that the VP and FR factors must also be significantly higher than WM.

**Strengths and Weaknesses as a Measure of Processing**

The WISC-IV is more of a processing assessment instrument than its predecessor, the WISC-III. While the WISC-IV offers a considerable amount of information on several important processes, interpretation of the processing scores and other embedded processing information can be challenging because the Indexes are not all arranged by processing categories; for example, the Perceptual Reasoning Index includes measures of both visual processing and fluid reasoning. Despite these challenges, the authors of the WISC-IV encourage a process approach to interpretation, as originally advocated by Kaplan, Fein, Morris, and Delis (1991), and, as an alternative, offer an expanded processing assessment instrument in the WISC-IV Integrated.

## WECHSLER PRESCHOOL AND PRIMARY SCALE OF INTELLIGENCE, THIRD EDITION (WPPSI-III)

The origins of the WPPSI-III (Wechsler, 2002a) can be traced back to the publication of the WPPSI in 1967. Whereas the Wechsler Preschool and Primary Scale of Intelligence, Revised (WPPSI-R) maintained the same structure as the WPPSI, the WPPSI-III implemented several structural changes, while maintaining the fundamental Verbal Intelligence Quotient (VIQ) and Performance Intelligence Quotient (PIQ). Similar to the other Wechsler scales, the WPPSI-III incorporates more measures of processing than its predecessors, with the processing speed domain being the main addition (see Rapid Reference 5.16). The WPPSI-III divides the test into two age bands, one for children below the age of 4 and the other for those above the age of 4. For those aged 2:6 to 3:11, there are only four core subtests and only one basic process (visual processing) explicitly measured (see Rapid Reference 5.17). Thus, this discussion of the WPPSI-III will focus on the broader scale, the one for children aged 4 and above.

*≡Rapid Reference 5.16*

**Wechsler Preschool and Primary Scale of Intelligence, Third Edition (WPPSI-III)**

**Author:** David Wechsler

**Publication date:** 2002

**Theoretical basis:** Traditional Wechsler theory

**Main processes measured:** Processing speed, visual processing, and fluid reasoning

**Age range:** 2:6–7:3

**Publisher:** The Psychological Corporation

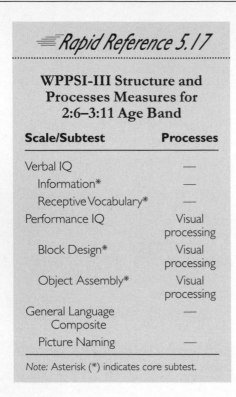

**≋Rapid Reference 5.17**

**WPPSI-III Structure and Processes Measures for 2:6–3:11 Age Band**

| Scale/Subtest | Processes |
|---|---|
| Verbal IQ | — |
| Information* | — |
| Receptive Vocabulary* | — |
| Performance IQ | Visual processing |
| Block Design* | Visual processing |
| Object Assembly* | Visual processing |
| General Language Composite | — |
| Picture Naming | — |

Note: Asterisk (*) indicates core subtest.

**Processes Measured by the Test**

*Processing Speed*

The WPPSI-III measures processing speed with the same two subtests as the WISC-IV—Coding and Symbol Search (adapted for younger children). These two processing speed subtests specifically measure the ability to perform clerical-type tasks quickly and efficiently. Processing speed is especially important to assess in young children, due to its relationship with neurological and cognitive development and learning. The *WPPSI-III Technical and Interpretative Manual* (Wechsler, 2002b) cites studies that have found processing speed in infants to predict future scores on measures of intelligence. However, it is important to keep in mind that at this age level the Processing Speed factor may be as much a measure of fine motor ability or attention and concentration, as of processing speed. It may also be tapping psychomotor speed as much as mental speed.

*Visual Processing*

Similar to the WAIS-III and WISC-IV, the WPPSI-III does not have separate visual processing and fluid reasoning scales; rather, these two processes are embedded in the Performance Scale (see Rapid Reference 5.18). Visual processing is best measured by Block Design, Object Assembly, and Picture Completion. Block Design and Object Assembly both measure spatial relations, a narrow visual processing ability, while Picture Completion quantifies flexibility of visual closure.

*Fluid Reasoning*

On the WPPSI-III, fluid reasoning is assessed mainly by the Performance subtests of Matrix Reasoning and Picture Concepts. On the Verbal scale, Word Reasoning is the best measure of verbal fluid reasoning. The fluid reasoning tasks seem to be age-appropriate, given the profound changes in reasoning that occur in children between the ages of four and seven. Most of the tasks involve the abil-

## ≡Rapid Reference 5.18

### WPPSI-III Structure and Processes Measured for 4:0–7:3 Age Band

| Scale/Subtest | Processes |
|---|---|
| Verbal IQ | — |
| Information* | — |
| Vocabulary* | — |
| Word Reasoning* | Fluid Reasoning |
| Comprehension | — |
| Similarities | Fluid Reasoning |
| Performance IQ | Visual processing, fluid reasoning |
| Block Design* | Visual processing |
| Picture Concepts* | Fluid reasoning[†] |
| Matrix Reasoning* | Fluid reasoning[†] |
| Picture Completion | Visual processing |
| Object Assembly | Visual processing |
| Processing Speed Quotient | Processing speed |
| Coding* | Processing speed |
| Symbol Search | Processing speed |
| General Language Composite | — |
| Receptive Vocabulary | — |
| Picture Naming | — |

Notes: Asterisk (*) indicates core subtest; dagger (†) indicates variation by age.

ity to recognize and form categories. In Matrix Reasoning, the child selects the missing portion from an incomplete matrix. For Picture Concepts, the child chooses pictures that form a group with a common characteristic. The Word Reasoning subtest requires the child to identify the common concept being described.

### Selected Technical Features

The WPPSI-III was standardized on a national sample of 1,700 children, closely matched to demographic variables on the 2000 U.S. census data. Regarding relia-

## *Rapid Reference 5.19*

### WPPSI-III Average Composite Reliability Coefficients

| Composite | Split-Half | Test-Retest |
|---|---|---|
| Verbal IQ | .95 | .91 |
| Performance IQ | .93 | .86 |
| Full Scale IQ | .96 | .92 |
| Processing Speed Quotient | .89 | .90 |
| General Language Composite | .93 | .91 |

*Source:* Data are from *Essentials of WPPSI-III Assessment* (Lichtenberger & Kaufman, 2004, p. 15).

bility, it appears to be adequate for the composite scores. The PIQ, while having adequate internal consistency (.93), is the least stable of the scales, as indicated by its test-retest coefficient of .86 (see Rapid Reference 5.19). Subtest test-retest reliability coefficients range from a low of .74 for Object Assembly to a high of .90 for Similarities.

Factor analytic studies reported in the *WPPSI-III Technical and Interpretative Manual* (Wechsler, 2002b) reveal that the WPPSI-III is a two-factor test (Verbal and Performance) for those under age 4 and a three-factor test (with the addition of Processing Speed) for those above the age of 4. The Picture Concepts subtest (thought to be mostly a measure of fluid reasoning) factor loadings vary by age, indicating that it is measuring different processes at different ages. At ages 6:0 to 7:3, it loads more on the Verbal factor instead of Performance, and at ages 4:0 to 4:11, it loads equally on both the Verbal scale and Processing Speed. Like Picture Concepts, Matrix Reasoning loads on multiple factors—the Performance Scale and Processing Speed at ages 5:0 to 5:11. Given the substantial cognitive changes occurring between the ages of 4 to 7, the shifting loadings are not surprising.

### Unique Administration and Scoring Procedures

When using the WPPSI-III to assess processing, supplemental tests will need to be administered. Symbol Search is not included in the FSIQ computation, but it is necessary for the PS Quotient. In order to estimate visual processing with Matrix Reasoning and Picture Concepts removed, the examiner will need to administer Picture Completion or Object Assembly to pair up with Block Design. Supplemental tests can also be used to substitute for core subtests that have been spoiled or cannot be administered for some reason.

## Interpretation of the WPPSI-III from a Processing Perspective

Because of the age range the WPPSI-III covers and the great developmental variability among children at this age, practitioners who interpret WPPSI-III processing results must be well versed in early childhood development. More than testing conducted at later ages, the results of early childhood and early elementary intellectual testing may be influenced or confounded by unrecognized cognitive processes as well as noncognitive characteristics. Thus, interpretation of WPPSI-III results should include a discussion of developmental expectations and the possible influences of noncognitive characteristics. Qualitative information, especially observations of the child's behavior and processing during testing, is crucial. Hypotheses, predictions, and conclusions about processes should be tenuous, even when there is sufficient corroborating data.

For children at the early childhood, preschool, and early elementary ages, cognitive development is rapidly undergoing substantial changes. The processes a child utilizes to reason and problem solve are changing over time. This developmental phenomenon is demonstrated by shifting subtest factor loadings; as children grow older, the primary processing factor a specific task measures changes. Furthermore, at the early childhood level, it is difficult to separate and identify discreet cognitive factors or processes, especially with an intellectual instrument. For example, factor analytic studies of tests like the WPPSI-III and KABC-II (Kaufman & Kaufman, 2004a) typically are not able to identify more than one or two factors (beyond the global intelligence factor) for children under 4 years of age. Processes are also developing differentially within young children; for example, in early elementary, long-term retrieval and auditory and visual processing are nearing their asymptotes, while processing speed, short-term memory, and fluid reasoning are just beginning to rapidly increase (see Figure 2.3 in Chapter 2).

In fact, development of the higher level processes—fluid reasoning and executive processing—are still in their infancy. Thus, the tasks used to measure these incomplete processes need to be developmentally appropriate. For example, the fluid reasoning tasks on the WPPSI-III involve processing that a preschooler should be capable of, for example, classifying and categorizing. Extreme caution is urged when interpreting a nonverbal fluid reasoning clinical factor derived from WPPSI-III subtests. The shifting factor loadings of Picture Concepts and Matrix Reasoning indicate that these two subtests are measuring other processes as much,

# CAUTION

Because the factor loadings of Picture Concepts and Matrix Reasoning vary by age, computation and interpretation of a nonverbal fluid reasoning clinical factor should be avoided. Instead, compute and interpret a verbal fluid reasoning clinical factor based on Similarities and Word Reasoning.

if not more than, fluid reasoning. Given this uncertainty, it may be more defensible to compute and interpret a verbal fluid reasoning factor based on Word Reasoning and Similarities. If nonverbal fluid reasoning is interpreted, the clinician should explain the usual developmental progression of fluid reasoning and clarify that abstract reasoning, such as inductive and deductive reasoning, will not be fully developed until early adolescence.

One of the main unrecognized cognitive factors is attention. Practitioners know the challenges involved in administering standardized tests to a preschool-aged child and that the child's short attention span is a major concern. The astute examiner needs to be aware of the child's attention to the task at hand and take breaks and employ other tactics to keep the child focused. Because of the major influence of selective and sustained attention, to some extent, the WPPSI-III FSIQ may be viewed as an indicator of broad attention. When lower than normal attentional capacity impacts performance on the scale overall, the clinician must decide whether the test scores should even be reported. The Processing Speed subtests, in particular, are very susceptible to the influence of attention and concentration (see Rapid Reference 5.20). Performance on the Processing Speed subtests may also be influenced by motivation, anxiety, compulsiveness, visual memory, planning ability, and the ability to process abstract symbols (Lichtenberger & Kaufman, 2004).

Another influence, especially on the Performance and Processing Speed subtests, is fine motor development. While the current WPPSI has fewer subtests that are confounded by fine motor development, performance on the paper-and-pencil speeded processing subtests may be severely impacted. Observations and data from other evaluators, such as an occupational therapist, should be weighed before drawing conclusions about results from these subtests.

## ≡ Rapid Reference 5.20

### Influences on WPPSI-III Processing Speed Performance

Attention

Fine-motor ability

Motivation

Anxiety

Compulsiveness

Visual memory

Planning ability

Ability to process abstract symbols

## Analysis of the WPPSI-III Processing Components

A processing analysis and interpretation of WPPSI-III results is very similar to processing interpretation of the other Wechsler intelligence scales, except that there are fewer processes involved. As usual, Verbal IQ and Performance IQ should be omitted from the analysis but the Processing Speed score can be used directly. Verbal IQ is excluded because it is primarily a measure of crystallized intelligence. However, the Word Reasoning and Similarities subtests may be isolated from the other Verbal subtests, and interpreted as verbal fluid reasoning. Of the two main processes measured by the Performance scale, visual processing is more consistent; when fluid reasoning is extracted, it must be interpreted cautiously. See Rapid Reference 5.21 for step-by-step guidelines and Rapid Reference 5.22 for a completed Processing Analysis Worksheet.

*≋Rapid Reference 5.21*

### WPPSI-III Processing Analysis Steps

1. Exclude nonprocessing scores—VIQ and PIQ—from the analysis.

2. Calculate a visual processing clinical factor score from at least two of these three Performance subtests—Block Design, Picture Completion, and Object Assembly. First, transform the subtest scores to a metric with a mean of 100 and a standard deviation of 15 using the table in Appendix D. Then compute the mean of the scores and round to the nearest whole number.

3. Calculate a verbal fluid reasoning clinical factor score from Word Reasoning and Similarities, following the same computations as in step 2. An alternative is to compute a nonverbal fluid reasoning clinical factor based on Picture Concepts and Matrix Reasoning; however, this alternative is not recommended.

4. Compute the mean of the three processing scores—Fluid Reasoning, Visual Processing, and Processing Speed.

5. Compare each processing factor score to the individual's WPPSI-III *processing* factor mean, using a 15-point discrepancy as an indication of significance and infrequency.

6. Examine subtest scores within each index or factor to determine whether each factor is unitary. When the difference between the highest and lowest subtest scores is 5 points or greater (when using a mean of 10 and standard deviation of 3), consider the factor to be nonunitary. Interpret nonunitary factors cautiously, and do not use them for pairwise comparisons.

7. Compare processing factor pairs, especially fluid reasoning versus visual processing, using a 20-point discrepancy as the criterion for significance and infrequency.

# Rapid Reference 5.22

## Processing Analysis Worksheet

### WPPSI-III Illustration

Examinee's Name: _____ DOB: _____ Age: __5__ Grade: __5__ Dates of Testing: _____

| Name of Process | Name of Test/ Battery | Name of Factor/ Subtests | Processing Factor Score | Processing Factor Mean | Difference from Mean | Normative S or W | Ipsative S or W | Deficit or Asset |
|---|---|---|---|---|---|---|---|---|
| Verbal Fluid Reasoning | WPPSI-III | Word Reasoning; Similarities | 110 | 95 | +15 | S | S | A |
| Processing Speed | WPPSI-III | PS | 91 | 95 | −4 | — | — | — |
| Visual Processing | WPPSI-III | Block Design; Object Assembly | 85 | 95 | −10 | W | — | — |

*Note:* Dashes indicate the absence of an S or W, or an A or D.

Directions: (1) Use factor scores for analysis, not subtest scores. (2) When a factor score is not available from a test, convert subtest scores to a mean of 100 and an SD of 15. (3) For each factor, compute the mean of the subtest scores and round to the nearest whole number. Use the subtest means as clinical factor scores. (4) Compute the mean of all available factor scores (this is the processing mean). (5) Subtract the processing mean from each processing factor score and enter amount in Difference column. (6) Indicate whether the factor score is a normative weakness or strength (90–109 is average). (7) Using a criterion of 15 points, determine ipsative strengths and weaknesses. (8) Determine deficits and assets. A deficit is both a normative and ipsative weakness. When the range between the highest and lowest subtest scores exceeds 1.5 SDs, the factor is nonunitary. Nonunitary factors should be interpreted cautiously and should not be used in pairwise comparisons. (10) Compare related pairs (below) for significant differences, using a 20-point difference as an indication of significance.

| Factor Score | Factor Score | Difference | Significant:Y/N |
|---|---|---|---|
| Visual Processing (85) | Verbal Fluid Reasoning (110) | 25 | Y |

## Illustration of WPPSI-III Processing Analysis

Selected scores from a WPPSI-III administration are used to illustrate the analytical procedures. Use the Supplemental Processing Analysis Worksheet for All Wechsler Scales in Appendix E to complete the computations not shown on the general Processing Analysis Worksheet. Given the following scores for a 5-year-old:

Word Reasoning (WR) Scaled Score of 13—transformed to a standard score of 115

Similarities (S) Scaled Score of 11—transformed to a standard score of 105

Block Design (BD) Scaled Score of 6—transformed to a standard score of 80

Object Assembly (OA) Scaled Score of 8—transformed to a standard score of 90

Processing Speed (PS) Quotient—91
    Coding—8
    Symbol Search—9

1. Compute a visual processing (VP) clinical factor score: (BD) 80 + (OA) 90 = 170/2 = 85.
2. Compute a verbal fluid reasoning (FR) clinical factor score: (WR) 115 + (S) 105 = 220/2 = 110.
3. Compute the processing factor mean: (VP) 85 + (PS) 91 + (FR) 110 = 286/3 = 95.3 = (rounded) 95.
4. Compute the difference from the mean for each factor, for example: (VP) 85 – 95 = –10.
5. Complete the remaining columns. Verbal Fluid Reasoning is both a normative and ipsative strength and, therefore, an asset, while Visual Processing is a normative weakness.
6. Check to see if factors are unitary. In this case they are all unitary.
7. Complete pairwise comparisons. In this case, the 25-point difference between Verbal Fluid Reasoning and Visual Processing is clearly significant and infrequent.

### Strengths and Weaknesses as a Measure of Processing

In addition to the concerns, such as the influence of attention span and fine motor skills on subtest performance, discussed in the preceding interpretation section, the main concern about the WPPSI-III is that it explicitly measures only a few processes, even less than the other Wechsler scales. Specifically, there are no direct measures of short-term, working, or long-term memory. This shortfall can be remedied by utilizing the Children's Memory Scale (Cohen, 1997a) or memory subtests from another intellectual or cognitive scale. Memory assessment is especially relevant when a child is referred for a possible LD. Regardless of the referral concerns, at this age level a cross-battery assessment is almost a necessity, especially when the WPPSI-III is used as the primary measure.

As for the processes tapped by the WPPSI-III, they are important to assess at the preschool-age level, and the tasks seem to be developmentally appropriate and appealing to the child. The addition of processing speed and enhancement of fluid reasoning measures makes the test more adaptable for processing assessment that its predecessor, the WPPSI-R. However, the extent to which the WPPSI-III measures fluid reasoning, especially nonverbal fluid reasoning, is questionable. The General Language Composite is mainly intended as a screener for receptive and expressive language development, but it can also be used to evaluate whether language delays may be impacting performance on the scale's other factors. Overall, the WPPSI-III can provide valuable information about some key cognitive processes.

## STANFORD-BINET INTELLIGENCE SCALES, FIFTH EDITION (SB5)

The Stanford-Binet has a long tradition, beginning with Terman's 1916 American version of the Binet-Simon Intelligence Test. Despite four revisions, the test remains true to its origins (see Rapid Reference 5.23). It is still very much a test of $g$ (the proportion of SB5 variance attributed to $g$ ranges from 56 percent to 61 percent). The SB5 (Roid, 2003a) adheres to CHC theory, consisting of five CHC factors, including the CHC Quantitative factor. The SB5 author selected the CHC factors that load highest on $g$, leaving out processing factors with lower $g$, such as processing speed. The result is a test with an emphasis on reasoning. The SB5 is divided evenly into Verbal and Nonverbal Domains, with each of the five fac-

*≡Rapid Reference 5.23*

**Stanford-Binet Intelligence Scales, Fifth Edition (SB5)**

**Author:** Gale Roid

**Publication date:** 2003

**Theoretical basis:** Cattell-Horn-Carroll

**Main processes measured:** Visual processing, working memory, and fluid reasoning

**Age range:** 2:0–85+

**Publisher:** Riverside Publishing

tors consisting of a verbal subtest and a nonverbal subtest. The Nonverbal subtests might better be labeled as *less verbal* as they minimize, but do not eliminate, the need for expressive language. As for assessing processing, the SB5 breaks ranks with other recently revised intellectual scales; it has not become more of a processing measure than previous editions.

## Processes Measured by the Test

The unique structure of the SB5—a verbal and nonverbal subtest for each factor—results in processing factors with different compositions than are usually found on intellectual or cognitive scales (see Rapid Reference 5.24). Consequently, SB5 estimates of processing abilities may vary from estimates derived from other scales that purport to measure the same process. For example, fluid reasoning is often derived form nonverbal tests alone, as is visual processing. Although there are only 10 subtests, there are actually 17 different tasks, as some subtests change tasks with age and difficulty level.

### Fluid Reasoning

The SB5 Fluid Reasoning items were designed to emphasize novel problem solving and be relatively free of dependence on acquired knowledge. The fluid reasoning factor is key to the composition of any *g* measure, such as the SB5, but it is also an important higher level process to assess as it is necessary for successful functioning in the world. A classic Matrices task measures nonverbal fluid reasoning while a sorting task (Early Reasoning), Verbal Absurdities, and Verbal Analogies are used to evaluate verbal fluid reasoning.

*≡Rapid Reference 5.24*

### SB5 Structure and Processes Measured

| Factor | Processes |
|---|---|
| Fluid Reasoning | Fluid Reasoning |
| Knowledge | — |
| Quantitative Reasoning | — |
| Visual-Spatial Processing | Visual Processing |
| Working Memory | Working Memory, Short-Term Memory |

Note: Each factor consists of a Verbal and Nonverbal Subtest with the same name, e.g., Verbal Fluid Reasoning and Nonverbal Fluid Reasoning.

## Visual Processing

The SB5 attempts to measure verbal visual-spatial processing with Position and Direction items in which examinees are told where to position an object or must describe a way to reach a certain location. This SB5 verbal visual-spatial task correlates highly with other spatial tasks (Roid, 2003c). Nonverbal Visual-Spatial Processing items consist of the classic form board at lower levels and the construction of form patterns at higher levels.

## Working Memory and Short-Term Memory

With the recent revision of the Stanford-Binet, there was a shift from short-term memory to working memory, although Memory for Sentences, more of a basic short-term memory task, has been retained. The Last Word task is clearly more challenging and involves working memory as it introduces interference by asking unrelated questions. The Nonverbal Working Memory subtest consists of a Block Span task, a nonverbal analog to the classic digits forward and backward tasks. The SB5 taps both visual and auditory working memory, reducing the need to supplement it with other assessment tools.

The SB5 author recognized the strong relationship that working memory has with academic learning and with reasoning ability. In a standardization study of children with a reading disability, Working Memory and Knowledge were the lowest means (Roid, 2003c) although not by the wide margin found with the WISC-IV. The difference may be that the SB5 Working Memory factor includes both a visual and auditory component.

## Selected Technical Features

The SB5 was normed on a carefully stratified national sample of 4,800 subjects. Students receiving special education comprised 6.8 percent of the normative sample. Regarding reliability, the composites and factors have high internal consistency. However, the test-retest stability of the three processing factors is lower than that of the more intellectual factors (see Rapid Reference 5.25). Average subtest split-half reliabilities are all in the mid-.80s while the test-retest coefficients display more variability, ranging from .76 to .91 at ages 6–20.

Extensive validity evidence is provided in the Technical Manual (Roid, 2003c), including correlations with the Wechsler scales and Woodcock-Johnson III Tests of Achievement and several studies of special populations. The factor profiles for students with specific learning disabilities came out as expected, with Quantitative and Working Memory being the lowest for those with a math disability, Knowledge and Working Memory the lowest for those with a reading disability,

# ≡Rapid Reference 5.25

## SB5 Average Composite Reliability Coefficients

| Composite | Split-Half | Test-Retest* |
|---|---|---|
| Full Scale | .98 | .93 |
| Nonverbal | .95 | .90 |
| Verbal | .96 | .93 |
| Fluid Reasoning | .90 | .85 |
| Knowledge | .92 | .92 |
| Quantitative Reasoning | .92 | .92 |
| Visual-Spatial Processing | .92 | .86 |
| Working Memory | .91 | .88 |

Note: Asterisk (*) indicates ages 6–20.

Source: Data are from Essentials of Stanford-Binet Intelligence Scales (SB5) Assessment (Roid & Barnum, 2004, p. 13).

and Working Memory the lowest for those with a written language disability. Also, factor analytic studies (Roid, 2003c) support the structure of the scale.

## Unique Administration and Scoring Features

The SB5 is unique among intellectual scales in that it uses two routing subtests— Nonverbal Fluid Reasoning and Verbal Knowledge—to determine the levels of item difficulty to administer to the individual on the remaining subtests (there are up to six levels of difficulty). This type of adaptive testing increases the precision of measurement and efficiency of testing. There is routing for both verbal and nonverbal domains; thus, the domains may have different entry levels. This adaptability makes for efficient testing of individuals with verbal-nonverbal discrepancies. Instead of the usual basal and ceiling rules, the SB5 uses performance on item sets, referred to as *testlets,* to determine when to administer a lower or higher testlet or discontinue testing (Roid, 2003b). After the routing subtests are completed, all of the nonverbal subtests are administered; then all of the verbal subtests are administered. The two routing subtests can also be used to compute an Abbreviated Battery IQ for screening purposes.

The SB5 uses subtest scaled scores with a mean of 10 and a standard deviation of 3 and factor standard scores with a mean of 100 and a standard deviation of 15, the same as other intellectual scales. In order to better track cognitive development over time, the SB5 also introduced change-sensitive scores. This metric has a mean of 500 for age 10:0 and ranges from about 430 to 520 on average. While typical stan-

> **DON'T FORGET**
>
> The SB5 change-sensitive scores can be used to track growth or decline of processes over time.

dard scores remain the same over time because they are tied to rank in the distribution, change-sensitive scores will increase as the child performs better upon retesting.

## Interpretation of the Processing Components

When conducting a processing interpretation of the SB5, there is no need to transform subtest scaled scores or compute any clinical factors from subtest scores, even when the SB5 is part of cross-battery assessment. (See Rapid Reference 5.26 for the steps involved and Rapid Reference 5.27 for a completed Processing Analysis Worksheet.) In addition to omitting the SB5 Knowledge factor,

### ≡ Rapid Reference 5.26

#### SB5 Processing Analysis Steps

1. Exclude nonprocessing factor scores—Knowledge and Quantitative Reasoning—from the analysis.

2. Using the standard scores provided by SB5 tables, compute the individual's processing mean from the Fluid Reasoning, Working Memory, and Visual-Spatial Processing scores.

3. Subtract the individual's *processing* mean from each factor, using a 15-point discrepancy as an indication of significance and infrequency. Complete the weakness and deficit columns.

4. Determine whether each of the three factors is unitary. If the difference between the two subtests that comprise each factor is 5 points or greater, then the factor is not unitary. In such instances, interpret the individual subtests instead of the broader factors.

5. For each nonunitary factor, compare the subtests to their respective Verbal and Nonverbal domain scores to determine whether the split within the factor is related to a broader Verbal-Nonverbal discrepancy.

4. Using unitary factors, complete pairwise comparisons. Differences of 20 points or greater can be considered significant and relatively uncommon.

≡ *Rapid Reference 5.27*

## Processing Analysis Worksheet

### SB5 Illustration

Examinee's Name: _____ DOB: _____ Age: _____ Grade: _____ Dates of Testing: _____

| Name of Process | Name of Test/ Battery | Name of Factor/ Subtests | Processing Factor Score | Processing Factor Mean | Difference from Mean | Normative S or W | Ipsative S or W | Deficit or Asset |
|---|---|---|---|---|---|---|---|---|
| Fluid Reasoning | SB5 | Fluid Reasoning | 112 | 94 | +18 | S | S | A |
| Visual Processing | SB5 | Visual-Spatial Processing | 94 | 94 | 0 | — | — | — |
| Working Memory | SB5 | Working Memory | 77 | 94 | −17 | W | W | D |

*Note:* Dashes indicate the absence of an S or W, or an A or D.

Directions: (1) Use factor scores for analysis, not subtest scores. (2) When a factor score is not available from a test, convert subtest scores to a mean of 100 and an SD of 15. (3) For each factor, compute the mean of the subtest scores and round to the nearest whole number. Use the subtest means as clinical factor scores. (4) Compute the mean of all available factor scores (this is the processing mean). (5) Subtract the processing mean from each processing factor score and enter amount in Difference column. (6) Indicate whether the factor score is a normative weakness or strength (90–109 is average). (7) Using a criterion of 15 points, determine ipsative strengths and weaknesses. (8) Determine deficits and assets. A deficit is both a normative and ipsative weakness. (9) Determine which factors are nonunitary. When the range between the highest and lowest subtest scores exceeds 1.5 SDs, the factor is nonunitary. Nonunitary factors should be interpreted cautiously and should not be used in pairwise comparisons. (10) Compare related pairs (below) for significant differences, using a 20-point difference as an indication of significance.

| Factor Score | Factor Score | Difference | Significant: Y/N |
|---|---|---|---|
| Visual Processing (94) | Working Memory (77) | 17 | N |
| Fluid Reasoning (112) | Working Memory (77) | 35 | Y |
| Visual Processing (94) | Fluid Reasoning (112) | 18 | N |

## DON'T FORGET

Significant discrepancies within SB5 factors are unique in that each factor is divided into a verbal and nonverbal subtest. Consequently, subtest interpretation may be appropriate, and the clinician should conduct further assessment of the factor involved.

the Quantitative Reasoning factor should also be excluded from a processing analysis. Although factor analytic studies have demonstrated that quantitative reasoning is a standalone cognitive factor, it is not considered a processing factor because performance partly depends on acquired quantitative concepts and mathematics skills. Subsuming the quantitative subtests under a clinical fluid reasoning factor is unnecessary because the SB5 offers more direct measures of fluid reasoning.

When nonunitary factors arise, the subtests involved should be interpreted separately. Because of the verbal-nonverbal division of subtests within each factor, interpretation of SB5 subtests is informative. The verbal-nonverbal distinction is more meaningful for the Working Memory and Fluid Reasoning factors than it is for the Visual Processing factor. When there are significant verbal-nonverbal differences within a factor, you should evaluate how the split aligns with broader verbal-nonverbal performance on the test. This can be accomplished by first comparing the Verbal and Nonverbal IQs for significance and then determining whether the within factor discrepancy is in the same direction. When nonunitary factors occur, further investigation is called for. For example, when there is a discrepancy within Working Memory, you should administer verbal/auditory and nonverbal/visual subtests from another instrument.

### Illustration of SB5 Processing Analysis

Selected scores from a SB5 administration are used to illustrate the analytical procedures. Given the following scores:

Fluid Reasoning (FR)—112
        Verbal Fluid Reasoning—12
        Nonverbal Fluid Reasoning—12
Visual-Spatial Processing (VP)—94
        Verbal Visual-Spatial Processing—8
        Nonverbal Visual-Spatial Processing—10
Working Memory (WM)—77
        Verbal Working Memory—5
        Nonverbal Working Memory—7

1. Enter the three factor scores in the fourth column of the Worksheet.
2. Compute the processing factor mean: (FR) 112 + (VP) 94 + (WM) 77 = 283/3 = 94.33 = (rounded) 94.
3. Compute the difference from the mean for each factor, for example: (WM) 77 − 94 = −17.
4. Complete the remaining columns. Fluid Reasoning is both a normative and ipsative strength and, therefore, an asset, while Working Memory is both a normative and ipsative weakness and, therefore, a deficit.
5. Check to see if the factors are unitary. In this case they are all unitary.
6. Complete pairwise comparisons. In this case, the 35-point discrepancy between Fluid Reasoning and Working Memory is significant and uncommon. The other two discrepancies are very close to being significant and uncommon. In such instances, the clinician should check the appropriate tables in Appendix B of the SB5 technical manual.

### Strengths and Weaknesses as a Measure of Processing

Even though the SB5 is limited in the number of processing factors it directly assesses, it includes processes that are essential for learning and daily functioning. Furthermore, the structure of the SB5 is theoretically based and is well balanced, with an equal number of subtests in each domain and factor. The result is readily identifiable factors and straightforward, step-by-step interpretation. The structure also allows for a verbal/visual and nonverbal/auditory contrast within each of the factors. In addition to facilitating direct interpretation of the scores, the SB5 has strong technical characteristics, carefully constructed norms, high reliabilities, and ample evidence of validity. Another advantage to the SB5 is that it covers almost the entire life span. The inclusion of change-sensitive scores allows for the tracking of growth and decline in abilities and processes.

## OTHER INTELLECTUAL SCALES

Tests that are based on processing theories or are generally considered to be more cognitive than intellectual are reviewed in the next chapter. Some tests that are primarily designed to measure $g$, such as the Reynolds Intellectual Assessment Scale (Reynolds & Kamphaus, 2003), and tests that are primarily nonverbal measures, such as the Leiter-R (Roid & Miller, 1997) and the Universal Nonverbal Intelligence Test (Bracken & McCallum, 1998), are not reviewed in this book. Only some basic facts about each scale are provided in Rapid Reference 5.28. Readers who wish to utilize these scales for processing assessment are advised to do the

# ≣Rapid Reference 5.28

## Other Intellectual Scales That Assess Processing

**Test:** Differential Ability Scales (DAS)
**Author:** Colin D. Elliott
**Publication date:** 1990
**Age range:** 2:6–17:11
**Publisher:** The Psychological Corporation

**Main processes measured:** Fluid reasoning, long-term retrieval, processing speed, short-term memory, visual processing
**Main processing factor scores (ages 6:0 to 17:11):** Nonverbal Ability, Spatial Ability

---

**Test:** Kaufman Adolescent and Adult Intelligence Test (KAIT)
**Authors:** Alan S. Kaufman and Nadeen L. Kaufman
**Publication date:** 1993
**Age range:** 11–85+
**Publisher:** American Guidance Service

**Main processes measured:** Fluid reasoning, long-term retrieval
**Main processing factor scores:** Fluid, Delayed Recall

---

**Test:** Leiter International Performance Scale-Revised (Leiter-R)
**Authors:** Gale H. Roid and Lucy J. Miller
**Publication date:** 1998
**Age range:** 2:0–20:11
**Publisher:** Stoelting

**Main processes measured:** Attention, fluid reasoning, long-term retrieval, short-term memory, visual processing
**Main processing factor scores:** Fluid Reasoning, Fundamental Visualization, Spatial Visualization, Memory Screen, Associative Memory, Memory Span, Attention, Memory Process, Recognition Memory

---

**Test:** Reynolds Intellectual Assessment Scales (RAIS)
**Authors:** Cecil R. Reynolds and Randy W. Kamphaus
**Publication date:** 2003
**Age range:** 3–94
**Publisher:** Psychological Assessment Resources

**Main processes measured:** Fluid reasoning, short-term memory
**Main processing factor scores:** Nonverbal Intelligence, Composite Memory

---

**Test:** Universal Nonverbal Intelligence Test (UNIT)
**Authors:** Bruce A. Bracken and R. Steve McCallum
**Publication date:** 1998
**Age range:** 5–17
**Publisher:** Riverside Publishing

**Main processes measured:** Fluid reasoning, short-term memory
**Main processing factor scores:** Memory, Reasoning

following: (1) Compare the definitions of the test's factors to the definitions of processes provided in Chapter 2. When there is agreement between the definitions, interpret the selected scale as measuring that process, even when the names may not match. (2) Check the reliability coefficients of the processing factors to be sure they have adequate reliability. (3) Review validity evidence, particularly evidence from studies of students with LDs. (4) When calculating clinical factors by combining subtests not combined by the test, use cross-battery analysis guidelines.

## Differential Ability Scales (DAS)

As this book was going to press, the Differential Ability Scales (Elliott, 1990) was in the process of revision. Given the unknown structure and properties of the revision and the datedness of the current norms, only a brief overview of the DAS is presented here. At the factor level, the structure of the DAS—General Conceptual Ability, Verbal Ability, Nonverbal Reasoning Ability, and Spatial Ability—is very similar to that of the Wechsler scales. However, the DAS structure is unique in that it moves beyond the global scores and adds optional, highly specific diagnostic subtests that tap processes such as short-term memory and processing speed. One of the development goals of the original DAS was diagnostic, aimed at providing reliable ipsative cognitive profiles that could be used to answer questions about learning difficulties. The DAS also is distinct from the Wechsler scales in that it splits the nonverbal domain into Spatial Ability (visual processing) and Nonverbal Reasoning ability (fluid reasoning). If the revision of the DAS retains the current factor structure and diagnostic subtests, it should prove quite useful for assessing processing.

## ⚔ TEST YOURSELF ⚔

1. **Which two processes are measured by Wechsler scales but do not have their own Index scores?**
   (a) Processing speed and working memory
   (b) Short-term memory and verbal comprehension
   (c) Visual processing and fluid reasoning
   (d) Auditory processing and planning

(continued)

2. **The current versions of Wechsler scales directly assess processing more than the earlier versions did.** True or False?

3. **Which test is more of a g measure than a measure of processing?**

    (a) SB5

    (b) WAIS-III

    (c) WISC-IV

    (d) DAS

4. **On the Wechsler scales the most direct measure of auditory short-term memory is _____.**

    (a) Letter-Number Sequencing

    (b) Digits Forward

    (c) Digits Backward

    (d) Arithmetic

5. **Which test does not have a working memory factor?**

    (a) WPPSI-III

    (b) WISC-IV

    (c) WAIS-III

    (d) SB5

6. **When comparing clinical factor scores to a processing mean, a difference of _____ points should be considered significant and uncommon.**

    (a) 3

    (b) 12

    (c) 15

    (d) 22

7. **When conducting a processing interpretation of intellectual scales, which factor should be omitted?**

    (a) Visual processing

    (b) Fluid reasoning

    (c) Short-term memory

    (d) Crystallized intelligence

8. **On any intellectual scale, which factor tends to have the lowest reliability coefficients?**

    (a) Fluid reasoning

    (b) Visual processing

    (c) Processing speed

    (d) Working memory

9. **Developmentally, which processing factor is going through the most change during the school years?**

   (a) Fluid reasoning

   (b) Visual processing

   (c) Long-term retrieval

   (d) Working memory

10. **Performance on processing speed subtests may be influenced by other processes. Which process probably has the most direct impact, especially with younger children?**

    (a) Long-term retrieval

    (b) Executive processes

    (c) Attention

    (d) Phonemic awareness

11. **A Wechsler subtest scaled score of 9 is equal to a standard score (M = 100; SD = 15) of**

    (a) 85.

    (b) 90.

    (c) 95.

    (d) 105.

12. **Which of the following WPPSI-III subtests does not load consistently on any one factor?**

    (a) Block Design

    (b) Picture Concepts

    (c) Matrix Reasoning

    (d) Word Reasoning

*Answers:* 1. c; 2. True; 3. a; 4. b; 5. a; 6. c; 7. d; 8. c; 9. a; 10. c; 11. c; 12. b

## Six

# ASSESSING PROCESSING WITH COGNITIVE SCALES

Beginning in the 1970s, the arrival of theory-based cognitive scales, among them the initial Woodcock-Johnson (Woodcock & Johnson, 1977) and the K-ABC (Kaufman & Kaufman, 1983), began to expand the scope of cognitive assessment. The Woodcock-Johnson was based on Horn-Cattell theory, and the K-ABC was based on Luria's theory. Both of these assessment instruments focused on measuring cognitive processes while de-emphasizing g and crystallized intelligence. These new cognitive scales also revived the debate over the nature of intelligence and the purpose of intellectual or cognitive assessment. To this day, some practitioners do not accept cognitive scales as valid measures of intelligence or as valid predictors of school learning.

In this chapter, there will first be reviews of the KABC-II, the CAS, and the WJ III COG. These instruments, in contrast to the traditional intellectual scales, were designed with cognitive processing assessment in mind. Consequently, they are more suitable for processing assessment, and a processing interpretation of their results is less complicated. Next, there will be a review of the processing component of the WISC-IV Integrated. It is reviewed here instead of with the WISC-IV because cognitive processing assessment is the primary goal of the processing component of the WISC-IV Integrated.

## KAUFMAN ASSESSMENT BATTERY FOR CHILDREN, SECOND EDITION (KABC-II)

The KABC-II (Kaufman & Kaufman, 2004a) is a flexible cognitive assessment instrument that is grounded in two theories—CHC psychometric theory and Luria's neuropsychological theory. While the original K-ABC (Kaufman & Kaufman, 1983) was based on Luria's theory and was composed of two processing factors—simultaneous and successive—the recent revision not only includes more processes but also aligns the processes with CHC factors. The KABC-II operationalizes the Lurian model with measures of planning, learning, and sequential and simultaneous processing. From the CHC perspective, the scales measure visual processing, short-term memory, fluid reasoning, long-term retrieval, and crystallized ability. The main difference between the two models is that the Lurian model excludes crystallized intelligence or acquired knowledge. Examiners should select the model that best applies to each case before administering the battery. With the exception of the Knowledge (Crystallized) subtests, which are omitted when the Lurian model is chosen, the same subtests are administered under both approaches. Thus, model selection affects both interpretation and administration (see Rapid Reference 6.1). The global score for the Lurian model is called the *Mental Processing Index (MPI)*, and the CHC global score is called the *Fluid-Crystallized Index (FCI)*. Regardless of the model selected, the KABC-II provides in-depth evaluation of several important cognitive processes that can be directly interpreted from a processing perspective.

The authors recommend the use of the CHC model in most cases. The Lurian model should be selected whenever the inclusion of crystallized ability would compromise the validity of the global index, such as when the examinee is bilingual. The five-factor KABC-II structure is only applicable for children ages 7 to 18. At age 3, only a general factor emerges. At ages 4 to 6, there is only support for a four-factor model, with Planning / Fluid Reasoning dropping out. The discussion in the remainder of this section will focus on the battery for ages 7 to 18 (see Rapid Reference 6.2).

≡ *Rapid Reference 6.1*

### KABC-II Lurian and CHC Factor Alignment

| Lurian Factor | CHC Factor |
| --- | --- |
| Learning Ability | Long-Term Storage and Retrieval |
| Sequential Processing | Short-Term Memory |
| Simultaneous Processing | Visual Processing |
| Planning Ability | Fluid Reasoning |
| (No Lurian component) | Crystallized Ability |

≡ *Rapid Reference 6.2*

### Kaufman Assessment Battery for Children, Second Edition (KABC-II)

**Authors:** Alan and Nadeen Kaufman

**Publication date:** 2004

**Main processes measured:** Fluid reasoning, visual processing, long-term retrieval, short-term memory, planning, simultaneous, successive

**Theoretical basis:** CHC and Lurian

**Age range:** 3:0–18:11

**Publisher:** AGS Publishing

## Processes Measured by the KABC-II

Of the three main blocks or brain functions proposed by Luria, the KABC-II (Kaufman & Kaufman, 2004b) does not attempt to specifically measure Block 1, which is responsible for arousal and attention. The KABC-II excludes a measure of attention, arousal, and concentration because these processes do not meet the authors' definition of high-level, complex, intelligent behavior. (For a test that purports to measure attention as defined by Luria, see the section on the CAS later in this chapter.) The KABC-II authors also believe that the emphasis should be on the integration of Luria's blocks, rather than on specific measurement of each block or process. This is consistent with Luria's emphasis on the integration of the brain's functional systems; for example, simultaneous and sequential processing interact within the same block (Block 2). The KABC-II authors also state that they did not strive for pure measures of the CHC processes included in the battery.

### *Successive Processing/Short-Term Memory*

These KABC-II subtests involve short-term memory and arranging input in sequential or serial order to solve a problem (see Rapid Reference 6.3). This scale involves the presentation of stimuli in both a visual and auditory format. The Number Recall subtest, which does not include a backward condition, primarily involves auditory short-term memory. Hand Movements primarily involves visual short-term memory. An interference task is included in the higher level items of the Word Order subtest.

### *Planning/Fluid Reasoning*

Because the two subtests that measure planning and fluid reasoning involve high-level decision making and novel problem solving, they both tap executive processing to some extent. The structure of Story Completion, which involves the sequencing of pictures in chronological order, emphasizes planning ability and fluid reasoning rather than visual processing. In Pattern Reasoning, the child completes a logical pattern, a task that clearly requires fluid reasoning.

### *Long-Term Retrieval*

Performance on the Learning scale subtests requires the examinee to learn and retain new information with efficiency. While the KABC-II Learning scale is classified as Long-Term Retrieval, it actually taps several processes, including attention, coding and storing stimuli, executive processing, and visual and auditory processing. The Learning scale does not have a specific Lurian analog although it is included under the KABC-II's Lurian structure. From a processing perspective, the Learning scale is best classified as long-term retrieval, as it is under the CHC

## ≡Rapid Reference 6.3

### KABC-II Structure and Processes Measured at Ages 7–18

| Scale/Subtest | Processes |
| --- | --- |
| Sequential/Short-Term Memory | Successive, short-term memory |
|   Number Recall | Successive, short-term memory |
|   Word Order | Successive, short-term memory |
|   Hand Movements* | Successive, short-term memory |
| Planning/Fluid Reasoning | Planning, fluid reasoning |
|   Story Completion | Planning, fluid reasoning |
|   Pattern Reasoning | Planning, fluid reasoning |
| Learning/Long-Term Storage and Retrieval | Long-term retrieval |
|   Atlantis | Long-term retrieval |
|   Rebus | Long-term retrieval |
| Simultaneous/Visual Processing | Simultaneous, visual processing |
|   Rover | Simultaneous, visual processing |
|   Triangles | Simultaneous, visual processing |
|   Block Counting | Simultaneous, visual processing |
|   Gestalt Closure* | Simultaneous, visual processing |
| Knowledge/Crystallized Ability | — |
|   Verbal Knowledge | — |
|   Riddles | — |
|   Expressive Vocabulary* | — |
| Delayed Recall | Long-term retrieval |
|   Atlantis Delayed* | Long-term retrieval |
|   Rebus Delayed* | Long-term retrieval |

Note: Asterisk (*) indicates supplementary subtests.

model. There are optional delayed recall subtests for both of the Learning scale subtests—Atlantis and Rebus. Atlantis Delayed and Rebus Delayed tap long-term retrieval more specifically than Atlantis and Rebus. A standard score for the supplementary Delayed Recall scale is available.

### Simultaneous Processing / Visual Processing

The KABC-II Simultaneous tasks involve the holistic integration and synthesis of visual-spatial input to produce a solution. The core subtests—Rover, Triangles, and Block Counting—involve perceiving, storing, manipulating, and thinking with visual patterns. Thus, these subtests can also be classified as visual processing.

### Selected Technical Features

The KABC-II norms are based on a stratified national sample of 3,025 subjects between the ages of 3 through 18. The selection of 18-year-olds was determined by the educational placement demographics found in the general population. Overall, approximately 11.1 percent of the standardization sample were in special education or had an ADHD diagnosis, with 5.5 percent of the total sample classified as having an SLD. For a summary of composite score reliability data, see Rapid Reference 6.4.

Confirmatory factor analysis supports the factor structure of the KABC-II (Kaufman & Kaufman, 2004b). As expected, the number of factors increases with age, and the factor loadings of the subtests vary by age. Consistent with cognitive development expectations, Planning Ability/Fluid Reasoning does not emerge as a distinct factor until age 7. The factor analytic results also demonstrate adequate separation between the Planning Ability/Fluid Reasoning factor and the Simultaneous Processing/Visual Processing factor, although these two scales are highly correlated for ages 7 to 18. The consistently high MPI and FCI corre-

---

## ≡ Rapid Reference 6.4

### KABC-II Average Reliability Coefficients for Ages 7–18

| Scale | Internal Consistency | Test-Retest |
|---|---|---|
| Sequential/Short-Term Memory | .89 | .80 |
| Planning/Fluid Reasoning | .88 | .81 |
| Learning/Long-Term Retrieval | .93 | .79 |
| Simultaneous/Visual Processing | .88 | .77 |
| Knowledge/Crystallized Ability | .92 | .92 |
| Nonverbal Index | .92 | .87 |
| MPI | .95 | .90 |
| FCI | .97 | .93 |

Source: Data are from Essentials of KABC-II Assessment (Kaufman, Lichtenberger, Fletcher-Janzen, & Kaufman, 2005, p. 23).

lations with the global scores of other cognitive batteries support the concurrent validity of the KABC-II. The KABC-II's ability to predict achievement is also established because it was conormed with the Kaufman Test of Educational Achievement, Second Edition (Kaufman & Kaufman, 2004c).

Clinical validity studies of students with LDs buttress the KABC-II's claim of being a processing assessment instrument. For example, students with a reading disability obtained a significantly lower mean than the nondisabled group on both the MPI and the FCI, as did those with a mathematics and written expression disability. All three groups also had mean Simultaneous/Visual Processing Indexes that were slightly higher than the other mean indexes. Profiles for specific disabilities were consistent with previous research and profiles from other recently revised intellectual or cognitive scales. For those with a reading disability, Learning and Knowledge were the lowest scores, with Sequential being lower than Simultaneous. Students with a mathematics disability obtained their lowest means on Knowledge and Planning (Kaufman & Kaufman, 2004b).

## Unique Administration and Scoring Procedures

Before testing a child or adolescent, the examiner should select which battery—CHC or Lurian—will best represent the individual's cognitive functioning. According to Kaufman and Kaufman (2004b), CHC is the model of choice unless there is a reason the Crystallized scale would not accurately reflect the individual's cognitive ability level. Cases where the Lurian model should be utilized include a child from a bilingual background, a child with a language disorder, or a child with autism. Although the Kaufmans recommended the CHC model when evaluating children referred for an LD, the Lurian model or a processing interpretation should be applied whenever processing assessment is the goal. However, evaluators can still administer the CHC battery and then interpret the results from a processing perspective.

In addition to the model selected, the set of subtests to administer varies with age. Core subtests should be administered in the order they are presented, but the supplementary tests (except Atlantis Delayed and Rebus Delayed) can be administered in any sequence after the core subtests are completed. In the event a subtest is spoiled, it is permissible to make one substitution of a supplementary subtest for a core

## DON'T FORGET

The KABC-II adheres to both the Lurian and CHC theories. Selection of a model should occur prior to administration. The Lurian model facilitates interpretation from a processing perspective.

subtest. The KABC-II is unique in that it allows further teaching of the task when the child fails teaching items, typically the first and second items of each subtest. On some subtests, it is even permissible to readminister easy items when a child subsequently passes harder items in the same subtest.

There are also other options available that make the KABC-II suitable for students with varying abilities and characteristics. Full-population norms are available for out-of-level testing for children ages 3 through 7 years. For examinees who speak English and Spanish, Spanish directions to all the subtests, sample items, and teaching items are printed in the easels. For bilingual children, a Nonverbal Index comprised of five subtests is another option; however, if processing assessment is desired, the four-factor Luria battery should be administered, unless the examinee has a very limited grasp of English.

## Analysis and Interpretation of the Processing Components

Because the KABC-II is essentially a processing assessment instrument (although it is also a measure of $g$), normative and ipsative interpretation of the results is relatively straightforward, especially when interpreting the results from the Lurian perspective. Guidelines for general interpretation, not just an interpretation focused on processing, are provided in the KABC-II manual (Kaufman & Kaufman, 2004b) and in *Essentials of KABC-II Assessment* (Kaufman et al., 2005). When conducting a processing analysis, the clinician should use the KABC-II record form and the statistical tables provided in the record form and the KABC-II manual. This will allow precise determination of statistical significance, infrequency, and whether a factor is unitary. The general rules found on the Processing Analysis Worksheet (Appendix C) should not be used with KABC-II results. The processing analysis and interpretation steps for ages 7 to 18 are described in the following section (see Rapid Reference 6.5 for a summary of the interpretation steps).

1. *Interpret the MPI as representing the overall level of cognitive processing.* Because the Lurian model is a comprehensive and inclusive model of processing, the MPI can be depicted as representative of the examinee's overall cognitive processing level. If the Knowledge/Crystallized Ability subtests were administered, exclude the Knowledge factor and the FCI from the processing analysis and interpretation.

2. *Determine normative strengths or weaknesses.* Identify the processing scales that have scores outside the average range and describe them as normative strengths or weaknesses. In doing so, consider scores from 90

## ≡ Rapid Reference 6.5

**KABC-II Processing Analysis and Interpretation Steps for Ages 7–18**

1. Interpret the MPI as representing the overall level of cognitive processing.
2. Determine normative strengths or weaknesses, using 90 to 109 as the average range.
3. Compute the mean of the four processing scales, omitting Knowledge if it has been administered.
4. Determine ipsative strengths and weaknesses, using page 3 of the KABC-II record form.
5. Determine deficits and assets.
6. Examine subtest scores within each factor, including Delayed Recall, to determine whether each factor is unitary, using the table provided in the KABC-II record form.
7. Complete pairwise comparisons of the unitary scales, including Delayed Recall, using the tables provided in the KABC-II manual.

to 109 as average instead of using the KABC-II's broader definition of average, which is 85 to 115. The reason for modifying the KABC-II's average range is to keep it consistent with the general processing interpretation model and also to facilitate cross-battery analysis. There is a box on page 3 of the KABC-II record form for indicating strengths and weaknesses, but it is suggested that it be altered to restrict the average range to 90 to 109.

3. *Compute the mean of the four processing scales.* Using the standard scores, calculate the examinee's mean scale index, excluding the Knowledge scale whenever it has been administered. Round the mean to the nearest whole number. The individual's *processing* mean can be used to determine significant and uncommon individual processing strengths and weaknesses.

4. *Determine ipsative strengths and weaknesses.* Subtract the mean from each of the four processing scale indexes, using the Lurian model critical values for significance and infrequency (10 percent base rate) that are provided on page 3 of the KABC-II record form.

5. *Determine deficits and assets.* Apply the rules found on the Processing Analysis Worksheet (Appendix C). A deficit exists when there is both a normative and ipsative weakness; an asset occurs when there is both

a normative and ipsative strength. There isn't a specific column for marking this on the KABC-II record form.

6. *Examine subtest scores within each factor to determine whether each factor is unitary.* Using the appropriate box on page 3 of the KABC-II record form, compute the difference between the highest and lowest subtest scores within each factor and use the 10 percent base rate table (also provided on page 3 of the record form) to make the determination. In the case of Delayed Recall, use the general 5-point rule to decide if the factor is unitary. Interpret nonunitary factors cautiously, and do not use them in pairwise comparisons.

7. *Complete pairwise comparisons of the unitary scales, including Delayed Recall.* Compare logical pairs of processes, such as Sequential versus Simultaneous and Planning versus Learning/Long-Term Retrieval. If the delayed recall subtests were administered, first compute a supplemental Delayed Recall score, using Table D.3 in the KABC-II manual. Next, compare the Delayed Recall score with the Learning scale index, using Table D.9 in the KABC-II manual. Tables for determining whether differences between other factors are statistically significant and infrequent are also available in the KABC-II manual.

When conducting evaluations of children referred for learning problems, administration and interpretation of the supplemental Delayed Recall scale may provide valuable information about the child's ability to retain previously learned material. The Delayed Recall factor may be a more direct measure of long-term retrieval than the Learning/Long-Term Storage and Retrieval scale itself. The Learning scale, which provides corrective feedback during administration, may be primarily measuring initial learning. Thus, the comparison between the Learning and Delayed Recall scales should not be overlooked.

The processing scales may also be interpreted from a CHC perspective, and the same interpretative steps outlined for a Lurian interpretation would apply. From the perspective of the integrated model of processing proposed in this book, the dual-theoretical model proposed by the KABC-II presents an interpretative challenge because the KABC-II equates processing constructs that are herein defined as *distinct processes*. Learning ability has no counterpart in the integrated model, so this scale should always be interpreted as Long-Term Retrieval. However, three of the scales—Sequential/Short-Term Memory, Simultaneous/Visual Processing, and Planning/Fluid Reasoning—require making a choice. The choice of which construct to use really depends on the referral concerns and hypotheses. For example, if a difficulty in successive processing is a concern or hypothesis, then the Sequential/Short-Term Memory scale can provide information regarding the child's successive processing ability. In contrast, if a deficiency in short-term memory is a concern or hypothesis, then the results of the scale can be used to evaluate short-term memory. Although the Luria and CHC definitions of the processes being measured by each scale are quite different, we have to assume for now (pending the publication of further research) that these KABC-II scales are measuring both processes. For an in-depth discussion of how the KABC-II taps multiple processes with each scale see Kaufman et al. (2005).

### Strengths and Weaknesses as a Measure of Processing

Regardless of the theoretical basis one subscribes to, the KABC-II offers an in-depth assessment of processing. The Lurian theory of mental processing, on which the KABC-II is built, is well established; for example, Luria's theory is also the foundation of neuropsychological assessment (Hebben & Milberg, 2002). Linking the Lurian components to CHC psychometric factors actually facilitates interpretation and allows practitioners to understand the relationships among specific processes and theoretical models in general. The option of computing an MPI is valuable because the Index represents general processing ability. A processing interpretation of the KABC-II is direct because it is not necessary to transform scores, compute clinical factors, or apply general guidelines when making psychometric decisions. The KABC-II also facilitates analysis by providing the necessary statistical tables right in the record form. Finally, the KABC-II is excellent for assessing the processing of students from culturally and linguistically diverse backgrounds. The inclusion of Spanish directions, teaching items, and the option of computing a nonverbal composite or a full-scale composite without culturally loaded Knowledge subtests makes it ideal for assessment of individuals from diverse backgrounds. As with other cognitive instruments, there will be instances in which it is necessary to supplement the KABC-II in a cross-battery fashion. For example, clinicians interested in specific data on an examinee's processing speed, working memory, and other processes that play a critical role in learning may administer additional factors from other assessment instruments.

## COGNITIVE ASSESSMENT SYSTEM (CAS)

The CAS (Naglieri & Das, 1997a) is a theory-based test of cognitive abilities and processing that is highly predictive of academic learning and very useful in identifying processing strengths and weaknesses (see Rapid Reference 6.6). With a

≡ *Rapid Reference 6.6*

## Cognitive Assessment System for Children (CAS)

**Authors:** Jack A. Naglieri and J. P. Das
**Publication date:** 1997
**Main processes measured:** Planning, attention, simultaneous, and successive
**Theoretical Basis:** PASS theory of cognitive processing
**Age range:** 5:0–17:11
**Publisher:** Riverside Publishing

## DON'T FORGET

The CAS is theory based and purports to measure the processes that underlie intellectual functioning. It is an excellent predictor of academic learning.

correlation of .73 (Naglieri & Das, 1997b) between the CAS Full Scale and the Woodcock-Johnson Revised Skills cluster (an overall measure of achievement), the CAS seems to be an excellent predictor of academic learning, probably a better predictor than some traditional intellectual measures. The CAS not only has high predictive validity for learning but also is supported by research linking the CAS processes with specific types of learning (Naglieri & Das, 1997b). Thus, it appears that the cognitive processes the CAS claims to measure are highly related to academic learning.

The four processes measured by the CAS are Planning, Attention, and Simultaneous and Successive processing (PASS). PASS theory (Das et al., 1994) is based on Luria's (1970) theory of brain organization and processing. The PASS processes are found in Luria's three functional units, with Attention in the first unit, Simultaneous and Successive processing in the second unit, and Planning in the third (see Chapter 2 for a fuller discussion of Luria's theory). PASS theory proposes that the basic cognitive processes measured by the CAS are the building blocks of intellectual functioning (Naglieri, 1999). Support for this claim is provided by the high correlations the CAS Full Scale has with traditional IQ measures, for example, .69 with the WISC-III FSIQ.

A major advantage of the CAS for assessing processing is that the CAS is intended mainly for just that, although it's Full Scale score is also accepted as an intellectual composite that can be used for diagnostic decisions that require an IQ. The CAS scales comprehensively measure processing, according to the Lurian and PASS theories. The four CAS scales and all 12 subtests can be categorized as measures of processing; for example, the CAS does not contain measures of verbal ability, acquired knowledge, or crystallized intelligence. Thus, all of the CAS scores can be used for analyzing processing, and interpretation of CAS results alone will identify relative strengths and weaknesses in processing without having to compare the four PASS scores with scores from other processing measures or a processing mean arrived at through a cross-battery approach.

## Processes Measured by the CAS

The four scales of the CAS are intended to measure planning, attention, simultaneous processing, and successive processing (see Rapid Reference 6.7). Each of the PASS scales is composed of three subtests whose loadings on the scales they comprise are supported by exploratory and confirmatory factor analytic studies (Naglieri & Das, 1997b).

### Planning
*Planning,* according to Naglieri and Das (1997b), "is a mental process by which the individual determines, selects, applies, and evaluates solutions to problems"

---

## ≡Rapid Reference 6.7

### CAS Structure and Processes Measured

| Scale/Subtest | Processes |
| --- | --- |
| Planning Scale | Planning, executive processing |
|   Matching Numbers* | Planning, executive processing |
|   Planned Codes* | Planning, executive processing |
|   Planned Connections | Planning, executive processing |
| Simultaneous Scale | Simultaneous processing |
|   Nonverbal Matrices* | Simultaneous processing |
|   Verbal-Spatial Relations* | Simultaneous processing |
|   Figure Memory | Simultaneous processing |
| Attention Scale | Attention |
|   Expressive Attention* | Attention |
|   Number Detection* | Attention |
|   Receptive Attention | Attention |
| Successive Scale | Successive processing |
|   Word Series* | Successive processing |
|   Sentence Repetition* | Successive processing |
|   Speech Rate (ages 5–7) or Sentence Questions (ages 8–17) | Successive processing |

*Note:* Asterisk (*) indicates a subtest that is included in the Basic Battery.

(p. 2). The process is integral to problem solving and draws on other processes, as well as knowledge. The CAS Planning subtests require the selection, implementation, and monitoring of strategies in order to successfully solve novel tasks. Planning and its subcomponents are part of metacognition and executive processing. However, because the CAS Planning tasks are specific to planning, caution is urged when interpreting the Planning scores as indicative of broader executive functioning. Planning is required for many scholastic tasks and plays an important role in mathematical reasoning and written language.

### Attention

Attention processes measured by the CAS Attention Scale consist of focused attention, selective attention, and sustained attention (Naglieri, 1997). All of the CAS Attention subtests present examinees with competing demands on their attention and require sustained focus. A measure of attention is important because most types of scholastic learning place strong demands on attention.

### Simultaneous Processing

The essential aspect of the CAS Simultaneous Processing scale is the integration of separate stimuli into a whole or group (Naglieri, 1999). The Simultaneous processing tasks partly depend on visual-spatial processing, memory, and fluid reasoning. The Simultaneous subtests on the CAS include both verbal and nonverbal content. In order to successfully complete the tasks, the examinee must understand the relationships among the stimuli.

### Successive Processing

The Successive Processing scale of the CAS measures the integration of stimuli into a specific serial order that forms a chainlike progression in which each element is only related to those that precede it (Naglieri, 1999). The CAS successive processing tasks involve both the perception of stimuli in sequence and the formation of sounds and movements into a sequence. The CAS Successive processing subtests require the examinee to repeat or comprehend information that is presented in a specific order. Successive processing is required in both spoken and written language, for example, speech sounds are organized into a consecutive series. Successive processing is also heavily involved in reading decoding.

## Selected Technical Features

The CAS was normed on a stratified, random sample of 2,200 subjects that closely matched the demographics of the U.S. population in 1990. Racial and ethnic sample percentages closely matched the U.S. population percentages, for example,

13.5 percent were Black, and 11.4 percent were Hispanic. The sample included children receiving special services in the following proportions: 5.1 percent learning disabled, 1.1 percent speech or language impaired, 0.8 percent seriously emotionally disturbed, 1.3 percent mentally retarded, and 4.4 percent gifted.

A total of 872 children participated in reliability and validity studies. The average internal consistency and test-retest reliability coefficients for the composite scores are reported in Rapid Reference 6.8. Subtest internal consistency reliabilities ranged from .75 to .89, with a median of .82. The median corrected test-retest coefficient for the subtests was .73. The stability of the four scales is adequate for children ages 8 and above, especially when the standard battery is administered.

Both exploratory and confirmatory factor analytic studies found support for the four-factor PASS structure. However, Keith et al. (2001) have questioned the four-factor structure (see discussion in the strengths and weaknesses section). Criterion validity evidence provided in the manual (Naglieri and Das, 1997b) includes relatively high correlations with specific Woodcock-Johnson Revised achievement scores and typical correlations with intellectual scales. Most importantly, the validity studies provide evidence of unique PASS profiles for children with Mental Retardation, LDs, ADHD, reading disabilities, traumatic brain injury, giftedness, and serious emotional disturbance. For example, a standardization study supports the CAS's usefulness in identifying processing weaknesses related to specific LDs. The study of children with reading disabilities and ADHD reported in the CAS interpretative handbook (Naglieri & Das, 1997b) found that the reading disabilities group performed poorest on the Successive Scale (a mean of 87.8), while they

## ≡ Rapid Reference 6.8

### CAS Average Reliability Coefficients*

| Scale | Internal Consistency | Test-Retest |
|---|---|---|
| Planning | .88 | .85 |
| Attention | .88 | .82 |
| Simultaneous | .93 | .81 |
| Successive | .93 | .86 |
| Full Scale | .96 | .91 |

Note: Asterisk (*) indicates Reliability coefficients for Standard (12 subtest) Battery.

Source: Data are from Cognitive Assessment System Interpretative Handbook (Naglieri and Das, 1997c, pp. 43, 47).

≡ *Rapid Reference 6.9*

·······················································

## CAS Mean Scale Scores of Special Populations

| Scale | Reading Disability | ADHD |
|---|---|---|
| Planning | 93.4 | 88.4 |
| Attention | 91.6 | 92.1 |
| Simultaneous | 95.4 | 99.6 |
| Successive | 87.8 | 100.5 |
| Full Scale | 91.1 | 94.1 |

obtained a mean of 95.4 on the Simultaneous Scale, their best performance. Also consistent with predictions, the ADHD group obtained their lowest mean (88.4) on the Planning Scale (see Rapid Reference 6.9).

### Unique Administration and Scoring Features

The CAS has two options—a 12-subtest Standard Battery and an 8-subtest Basic Battery. Both batteries produce a Full Scale score and are composed of all four PASS scales. CAS subtests must be administered in the prescribed order to maximize the validity of the scales. Beginning with Planning (see Rapid Reference 6.7 for administration sequence), all of the subtests that comprise a given scale are administered before administering the next processing scale.

A unique administration feature of the CAS Planning subtests is the observation of the strategies used by the child to complete the items. The intent of strategy assessment is to help the examiner understand the methods the child used during planning. There are two parts to the strategy assessment. First, the examiner records the strategies the child is observed using while completing the task. Following completion of the items of each Planning subtest, the examiner asks the child to tell how he or she did the items. These strategies are recorded as reported strategies.

### Analysis and Interpretation of the Processing Results

Using an ipsative approach, CAS results should mainly be used to examine variability across the four PASS scores to determine the child's cognitive processing strengths and weaknesses (Naglieri, 1999). This method involves comparing each PASS score to the examinee's average level of performance. The average score is not the Full Scale score but rather the mean of the PASS standard scores. Statistical tables are also available for making pairwise comparisons of PASS scales. For example, comparing Simultaneous with Successive and Planning with Attention may yield important information, especially when evaluating students for a possible LD or ADHD. Pairwise comparisons will often reveal discrepancies that do not appear when scales are only compared to a mean. If subtest level analysis is desired, subtest scores can be compared to the mean subtest score for the PASS scale they comprise. However, interpretation at the subtest level is not recommended unless there is a specific reason for doing so, such as when there is significant variation among subtest scores on a particular scale. Overall, interpretation of the PASS processes should be at factor level; that is, the PASS scale scores provide the most important interpretative information about processing strengths and weaknesses.

Readers may find additional CAS analysis procedures and guidelines in the *Cognitive Assessment System Interpretive Handbook* (Naglieri & Das, 1997c) and the *Essentials of CAS Assessment* (Naglieri, 1999). When conducting a processing analysis, the clinician should use the statistical tables provided in the CAS manual. This will allow precise determination of statistical significance and infrequency. The general rules found on the Processing Analysis Worksheet (Appendix C) are unnecessary, except the rule for determining whether a factor is unitary. However, the clinician may wish to record the CAS analysis results on the Processing Analysis Worksheet so that all the results are on one convenient sheet. The processing analysis and interpretation steps are summarized in Rapid Reference 6.10.

---

## ≡Rapid Reference 6.10

### CAS Processing Analysis and Interpretation Steps

1. Interpret the CAS Full Scale as an estimate of the examinee's overall cognitive processing level.

2. Determine whether any of the processing scales are normative strengths or weaknesses, with scores from 90 to 109 considered average.

3. Compute the mean of the four processing scales.

4. Determine ipsative strengths and weaknesses by subtracting the mean from each of the four processing scale scores. Page 2 of the CAS Record Form contains a table for completing an ipsative analysis, or the analysis can be recorded on this text's Processing Analysis Worksheet (Appendix C). Use Tables D.1 and D.2 or D.3 and D.4 in the CAS administration and scoring manual to determine significance and frequency of occurrence.

5. Determine deficits and assets. Apply the rules found on the Processing Analysis Worksheet (Appendix C). A deficit exists when there is both a normative and ipsative weakness; an asset occurs when there is both a normative and ipsative strength.

6. Determine which of the processing factors are unitary by calculating the range between the lowest and highest subtest scaled scores within each scale. When the range is 5 points or greater, consider the factor to be nonunitary. Interpret nonunitary factors cautiously, and do not use them in pairwise comparison.

7. Complete pairwise comparisons of the unitary scales, using Tables D.5 and D.6 in the CAS administration and scoring manual to determine significance and frequency of occurrence.

If processes other than the PASS processes have been assessed with other scales, then a cross-battery method of analysis should be conducted. Given that the CAS is founded on a comprehensive theory of processing, CAS results should still be analyzed separately before incorporating other factor scores and completing a cross-battery analysis. For the cross-battery analysis, use the Processing Analysis Worksheet (Appendix C) guidelines. For example, the four PASS scores should be added in with other processing scores to obtain a processing mean. All of the processing scores should then be compared to that mean to determine significant strengths and weaknesses. The PASS scores may also be compared with other scores in a pairwise manner. See Rapid Reference 4.6 for an example of how to complete a Processing Analysis Worksheet for a cross-battery assessment.

## Strengths and Weaknesses as a Measure of Processing

One of the main strengths of the CAS is that it is a theory-based measure of the essential cognitive processes that are thought to underlie intellectual functioning and academic learning. Not only is the CAS Full Scale score a powerful predictor of achievement, but research has also found different profiles that support the relationships between PASS scores and SLDs. Another strength is that the interpretative handbook (Naglieri & Das, 1997b) and *Essentials of CAS Assessment* (Naglieri, 1999) provide statistical tables that support the interpretation methods recommended previously and the well-organized record form facilitates ease of computation and interpretation.

A potential weakness of the CAS is the claim by some that the CAS Planning and Attention scales are actually measures of processing speed. When Keith et al. (2001) conducted confirmatory factor analytic studies of the CAS, they found the Planning and Attention scales to collapse into a single factor that they believe is measuring processing speed. In contrast, the original confirmatory factor analytic studies of CAS standardization data found strong support for the four-factor PASS configuration of the 12 subtests. Perhaps, Keith et al. results can be explained by the fact that Planning and Attention are interrelated processes and that the tasks that measure them both involve processing speed. As with any attempt to measure cognitive processes and intellectual abilities, it is impossible to isolate a process or ability when presenting an examinee with a task to complete. That is, numerous processes underlie performance on any task, subtest, or scale. Interpreting the Planning and Attention scales separately has clinical utility, especially with children who have LDs and ADHD. Thus, it is recommended that clinicians interpret the CAS Planning and Attention scales separately, despite this controversy.

## WOODCOCK-JOHNSON III TESTS OF COGNITIVE ABILITIES (WJ III COG)

The WJ III COG (Woodcock et al., 2001b) battery is ideal whenever a comprehensive assessment of processing is warranted because the WJ III COG measures most major processes (see Rapid Reference 6.12). WJ III COG factors can also be used selectively to supplement other instruments when conducting a cross-battery assessment. In addition to CHC processes, the WJ III COG measures processes, such as attention, that the WJ III COG labels as Clinical Clusters (see Rapid Reference 6.11). The WJ III COG examiner's manual (Mather & Woodcock, 2001) provides a selective testing table that identifies the subtests (which the WJ III COG refers to as *tests*) that comprise each cluster.

---

### Rapid Reference 6.11

**Woodcock-Johnson III Tests of Cognitive Abilities**

**Authors:** Richard Woodcock, Kevin McGrew, and Nancy Mather

**Publication date:** 2001

**Main processes measured:** Attention, auditory processing, executive processing, fluid reasoning, long-term retrieval, phonemic awareness, planning, processing speed, short-term memory, visual processing, working memory

**Theoretical basis:** Cattell-Horn-Carroll

**Age range:** 2:0–90+

**Publisher:** Riverside Publishing

---

### Processes Measured by the WJ III COG

The WJ III COG measures seven CHC factors and several more clinical factors (see Rapid Reference 6.12). With the exception of Comprehension-Knowledge, all of the clusters or factors of the WJ III COG are direct measures of processes. The names assigned to the WJ III COG clusters are mostly synonymous with names of processes in the integrated model of processing discussed in Chapter 2. The WJ III COG definitions of abilities or processes measured are also consistent with the process descriptions provided in Chapter 2. Thus, a description of the processes measured by the WJ III COG is unnecessary here.

### Selected Technical Features

After standardizing the test on a large norming sample of 8,818 subjects, norms for each age and grade group were established through a linear transformation of scores, instead of fitting the distribution to a standard normal curve. The WJ III COG derived scores are also unique in that the subtest scores that contribute to

≡ *Rapid Reference 6.12*

### WJ III Cognitive Structure and Processes Measured

| Factor/Cluster | Processes |
|---|---|
| Verbal Ability | — |
| Thinking Ability | Visual processing, auditory processing, fluid reasoning, long-term retrieval |
| Cognitive Ability | Processing speed, short-term memory |
| Comprehension-Knowledge* | — |
| Long-Term Retrieval* | Long-term retrieval |
| Visual-Spatial Thinking* | Visual processing |
| Auditory Processing* | Auditory processing |
| Fluid Reasoning* | Fluid reasoning |
| Processing Speed* | Processing speed |
| Short-Term Memory* | Short-term memory |
| Phonemic Awareness | Phonemic awareness |
| Working Memory | Working memory |
| Broad Attention | Attention |
| Cognitive Fluency | Long-term retrieval, processing speed |
| Executive Processes | Executive processing, fluid reasoning, planning |
| Delayed Recall | Long-term retrieval |

Note: See the WJ III COG examiner's manual for tests (subtests) that comprise each cluster. Asterisk (*) indicates CHC factors or clusters.

each composite or cluster score are weighted according to their loading on that factor. This may result in cluster scores that are quite different from the arithmetic mean of the involved subtests. In designing and selecting subtests for each cluster, the WJ III COG authors chose subtests that measured distinct narrow abilities, as identified by Carroll (1993). The purpose of selecting subtests that measure different narrow abilities was to obtain a broader sampling of each factor.

The reliability coefficients for all but the speeded subtests and subtests with multiple points per item were calculated with a split-half procedure. The cluster median reliability coefficients range from .81 to .96, with three of clusters having reliability coefficients below .90 (see Rapid Reference 6.13).

The *Woodcock-Johnson III Technical Manual* (McGrew & Woodcock, 2001) presents adequate validity evidence of the usual types—content, criterion, and con-

## Rapid Reference 6.13

### WJ III COG Median Reliability Coefficients

| Cluster | Reliability Coefficient |
| --- | --- |
| General Intellectual Ability | .98 |
| Verbal Ability | .95 |
| Thinking Ability | .96 |
| Cognitive Efficiency | .93 |
| Comprehension-Knowledge | .95 |
| Long-Term Retrieval | .88 |
| Visual-Spatial Thinking | .81 |
| Auditory Processing | .91 |
| Fluid Reasoning | .95 |
| Processing Speed | .93 |
| Short-Term Memory | .88 |
| Working Memory | .91 |
| Broad Attention | .92 |
| Executive Processes | .93 |
| Cognitive Fluency | .96 |
| Delayed Recall | .94 |
| Phonemic Awareness | .90 |

Source: Data are from *Essentials of WJ III Cognitive Abilities Assessment* (Schrank et al., 2002, p. 13).

struct—but the most pertinent evidence for processing assessment is the developmental evidence for the seven CHC factors. The developmental growth curves illustrate how development varies across processes (see Figure 2.3 in Chapter 2). The developmental curves for visual processing, auditory processing, and long-term retrieval are similar and display the least amount of change over time. In contrast, the processing speed, fluid reasoning, and short-term memory developmental curves rise steeply into the mid-20s and then show a steady, progressive decline for the rest of the life span.

### Unique Administration and Scoring Procedures

The WJ III COG has a few unique administration and scoring procedures that are relevant to assessing processing. A standardized audio recording is used to administer several of the subtests, but, if necessary, these tests can be presented orally. Items on tests that measure memory cannot be repeated. On subtests where the examinees can see the items, the entire page must be completed even when an apparent ceiling has been reached.

The seven CHC factors are the core of the battery. The General Intellectual Ability (GIA) score requires the administration of the seven CHC tests (subtests) in the standard easel. Administration of the second set of CHC tests in the extended easel results in an Extended GIA and a cluster score for each of the CHC factors. When using the WJ III COG to supplement other scales during a cross-battery assessment, the examiner need only administer the subtests of the desired factors. For example, if a practitioner wants to assess the examinee's auditory processing, he or she only needs to give the Sound Blending and Auditory Attention tests. The computer scoring program (tables for hand scoring are not available) will produce individual cluster scores when only portions of the battery are administered. The fact that an examiner may administer the subtests in any order also facilitates cross-battery assessment.

Another unique feature of the WJ III COG that makes it particularly applicable for assessing individuals with an LD is that it includes controlled learning tasks. Four subtests—Visual-Auditory Learning, Visual-Auditory Learning-Delayed, Concept Formation, and Analysis-Synthesis—are controlled learning tasks that give all examinees an identical opportunity to learn by acknowledging correct responses and providing corrective feedback for incorrect responses for all but the final items. The examinees are presented with a novel task, such as learning a rebus reading code. The structure of these four subtests allows the examiner to obtain important information about an examinee's ability to learn a new task, an ability that is especially relevant when a possible LD is being considered. Because Concept-Formation and Analysis-Synthesis comprise the Fluid Reasoning cluster, an examinee's WJ III COG Fluid Reasoning score may differ from Fluid Reasoning scores obtained on other batteries due to the nature of the task and the effects of providing feedback.

### Analysis and Interpretation of WJ III COG Processing Results

#### Intra-Cognitive Discrepancies Analysis
There are several different approaches that can be employed when interpreting the processing scores obtained from the WJ III COG. The first approach utilizes the Intra-Cognitive Discrepancies table that is generated by the WJ III Compuscore or Report Writer for the WJ III. This table displays the results of an ipsative analysis of the seven CHC broad abilities measured by the 14-subtest extended

## ≡Rapid Reference 6.14

### Example of WJ III COG Intra-Cognitive Discrepancies Table

| Cluster | Standard Scores | | | Discrepancy | | Significant at ± 1.00 |
| | Actual | Predicted | Difference | PR | SD | SD (SEE) |
| --- | --- | --- | --- | --- | --- | --- |
| Comp-Knowledge | 77 | 80 | –2 | 45 | –0.12 | No |
| Long-Term Retrieval | 77 | 78 | –1 | 46 | –0.09 | No |
| Vis-Spatial Thinking | 97 | 82 | +15 | 86 | +1.08 | Yes |
| Auditory Processing | 83 | 82 | +1 | 54 | +0.10 | No |
| Fluid Reasoning | 77 | 79 | –2 | 41 | –0.23 | No |
| Processing Speed | 64 | 86 | –22 | 5 | –1.62 | Yes |
| Short-Term Memory | 64 | 83 | –19 | 6 | –1.58 | Yes |
| Phonemic Awareness | 85 | 82 | +3 | 59 | +0.22 | No |
| Working Memory | 60 | 83 | –23 | 3 | –1.92 | Yes |

battery, as well as any clinical clusters that were administered (see Rapid Reference 6.14). When this table is available, evaluators should examine the discrepancy SD column. The values shown in this column reveal how discrepant a particular score is from the predicted score, based on the mean of the other scores. As a guideline, a difference of 1 standard deviation indicates a significant strength or weaknesses. For instance, from the data in Rapid Reference 6.14, it can be determined that the examinee has a significant individual strength in Visual-Spatial Thinking and individual weaknesses in Processing Speed, Short-Term Memory, and Working Memory. The clinician should then complete the processing analysis by (1) determining which factors are unitary, using the criterion of a 22 point or greater discrepancy between the test scores, (2) conducting pairwise comparisons, using 20 points as an indication of significance and infrequency, and (3) identifying which processes are also normative strengths and weaknesses and which are assets and deficits, using the guidelines from this text's Processing Analysis Worksheet (Appendix C).

However, there are some drawbacks to relying on the Intra-Cognitive Discrepancies Table for analyzing processing strengths and weaknesses: (1) The table is only available when all 14 extended-battery CHC tests are administered; (2) the Comprehension-Knowledge cluster, a nonprocessing factor, is included in the analysis; (3) there is no base-rate data for determining how frequently a given discrepancy occurs; (4) additional steps are required in order to complete the analysis. Consequently, another approach to interpreting the WJ III COG processing scores is often necessary, especially when there has been a partial administration or a cross-battery assessment.

### Using the Processing Analysis Worksheet

The second interpretative approach is to complete an analysis following the steps on the Processing Analysis Worksheet (Appendix C). This method is necessary when the Intra-Cognitive Discrepancies Table is unavailable, only some of the WJ-III COG factors have been administered, and when the WJ III COG is part of a broader cross-battery assessment. Rapid Reference 6.15 details the steps involved.

## ≡ Rapid Reference 6.15

### WJ III COG Processing Analysis and Interpretation Steps Using the Processing Analysis Worksheet

1. If available, interpret the GIA score as an estimate of the examinee's overall cognitive processing level.

2. Exclude the following factors from the analysis: Comprehension-Knowledge, Verbal Ability, Thinking Ability, and Cognitive Efficiency. The latter three may be included in an alternative interpretative approach—the Cognitive Performance Model—discussed later.

3. Examine the processing factor scores and determine which are normative strengths or weaknesses, with 90 to 109 considered average.

4. Compute the mean of the processing factors included in the analysis, and round to the nearest whole number.

5. Determine ipsative strengths and weaknesses by subtracting the *processing* mean from each of the processing factor scores. Use a difference of 15 points as an indication of significance and infrequency.

6. Determine deficits and assets. Apply the rules found on the Processing Analysis Worksheet (Appendix C). A deficit exists when there is both a normative and ipsative weakness; an asset occurs when there is both a normative and ipsative strength.

7. Examine test scores within each cluster to determine which factors are unitary. When the difference between the test scores is 22 points or greater, consider the factor to be nonunitary. Interpret nonunitary factors cautiously, and do not use them for pairwise comparisons.

8. Complete pairwise comparisons of logical pairs (see the suggested list in Rapid Reference 6.16), using a difference of 20 points as an indication of significance and infrequency.

## ≡ Rapid Reference 6.16

### Suggested Pairwise Comparisons of WJ III COG Factors

1. Long-Term Retrieval versus Short-Term Memory
2. Long-Term Retrieval versus Working Memory
3. Long-Term Retrieval versus Delayed Recall
4. Long-Term Retrieval versus Phonemic Awareness
5. Long-Term Retrieval versus Processing Speed
6. Short-Term Memory versus Broad Attention
7. Auditory Processing versus Visual-Spatial Thinking
8. Auditory Processing versus Phonemic Awareness
9. Processing Speed versus Broad Attention
10. Processing Speed versus Short-Term Memory
11. Executive Processes versus Fluid Reasoning
12. Executive Processes versus Working Memory
13. Fluid Reasoning versus Visual-Spatial Thinking

### Illustration of WJ III COG Processing Analysis and Interpretation

Scores from a partial WJ III COG administration are used to illustrate the analytical procedures and interpretation. A completed Processing Analysis Worksheet based on this data is in Rapid Reference 6.17. Given the following scores (the tests that comprise each factor are shown indented under the factor score):

Long-Term Retrieval (LTR)—93
    Visual-Auditory Learning—87
    Retrieval Fluency—114
Visual-Spatial Thinking (VP)—115
    Spatial Relations—111
    Picture Recognition—112
Auditory Processing (AP)—107
    Sound Blending—111
    Auditory Attention—98
Fluid Reasoning (FR)—117
    Concept Formation—114
    Analysis Synthesis—117

# Rapid Reference 6.17

## Processing Analysis Worksheet

### WJ III COG Illustration

Examinee's Name: _____ DOB: _____ Age: _____ Grade: _____ Dates of Testing: _____

| Name of Process | Name of Test/ Battery | Name of Factor/ Subtests | Processing Factor Score | Processing Factor Mean | Difference from Mean | Normative S or W | Ipsative S or W | Deficit or Asset |
|---|---|---|---|---|---|---|---|---|
| Long-Term Retrieval | WJ III COG | Long-Term Retrieval | 93 | 104 | –11 | — | — | — |
| Visual Processing | WJ III COG | Visual-Spatial Thinking | 115 | 104 | +11 | S | — | — |
| Auditory Processing | WJ III COG | Auditory Processing | 107 | 104 | +3 | — | — | — |
| Fluid Reasoning | WJ III COG | Fluid Reasoning | 117 | 104 | +12 | S | — | — |
| Short-Term Memory | WJ III COG | Short-Term Memory | 89 | 104 | –15 | W | W | D |

*Note:* Dashes indicate the absence of an S or W, or an A or D.

<u>Directions:</u> (1) Use factor scores for analysis, not subtest scores. (2) When a factor score is not available from a test, convert subtest scores to a mean of 100 and an SD of 15. (3) For each factor, compute the mean of the subtest scores and round to the nearest whole number. Use the subtest means as clinical factor scores. (4) Compute the mean of all available factor scores (this is the processing mean). (5) Subtract the processing mean from each processing factor score and enter amount in Difference column. (6) Indicate whether the factor score is a normative weakness or strength (90–109 is average). (7) Using a criterion of 15 points, determine ipsative strengths and weaknesses. (8) Determine deficits and assets. A deficit is both a normative and ipsative weakness. When the range between the highest and lowest subtest scores exceeds 1.5 SDs, the factor is nonunitary. Nonunitary factors should be interpreted cautiously and should not be used in pairwise comparisons. (10) Compare related pairs (below) for significant differences, using a 20-point difference as an indication of significance.

| Factor Score | Factor Score | Difference | Significant:Y/N |
|---|---|---|---|
| Visual Processing (115) | Auditory Processing (107) | 8 | N |
| Visual Processing (115) | Fluid Reasoning (117) | 2 | N |

Short-Term Memory (STM)—89
   Numbers Reversed—78
   Memory for Words—102

1. After completing columns 1 to 3, enter the processing factor scores in the fourth column.
2. Compute the mean of the five factor scores: (LTR) 93 + (VP) 115 + (AP) 107 + (FR) 117 + (STM) 89 = 521/5 = 104.2 = (rounded) 104.
3. Compute the difference from the processing mean for each factor, for example: (LTR) 93 − 104 = −11.
4. Complete the remaining columns. Visual Processing and Fluid Reasoning are normative strengths. Short-Term Memory is a both a normative weakness and an ipsative weakness and, therefore, a deficit.
5. Check to see if the factors are unitary by comparing the scores of the two tests that comprise each factor. In order to determine the subtests each factor is composed of, check the Selective Testing Table in the *Woodcock-Johnson III Tests of Cognitive Abilities Examiner's Manual* (Mather & Woodcock, 2001). Use the criterion of greater than 22 points to make the determination. In this case, there is a 27-point test difference between the Long-Term Memory tests and a 24-point discrepancy between the Short-Term Memory tests. Thus, the Long-Term Memory and Short-Term Memory factors should be interpreted cautiously and should not be used in pairwise comparisons.
6. Complete pairwise comparisons. Compare Auditory Processing versus Visual Processing and Fluid Reasoning versus Visual-Spatial Thinking. Exclude Long-Term Memory and Short-Term Memory because they are nonunitary. No significant pairwise discrepancies exist in this case.

Because two of these factors are nonunitary, the interpretation of these results involves examining the subtests involved and developing hypotheses to account for the differences. Within Long-Term Retrieval, Retrieval Fluency is significantly higher than Visual-Auditory Learning. Visual-Auditory Learning is a controlled learning task that entails not only long-term retrieval but also short-term memory and encoding of information into long-term storage, whereas Retrieval Fluency is limited to long-term retrieval. A logical hypothesis that should be investigated further would be that this individual has difficulty with learning new material. Within Short-Term Memory, Numbers Reversed is well below average while Memory for Words is average. Because Numbers Reversed requires more manipulation of stimuli that does Memory for Words, an appropriate hypothesis might be that the examinee has a weakness in working memory but not necessarily a weakness in short-term memory overall. This hypothesis is easily investigated by assessing working memory further.

## WJ III COG Performance Model

An alternative interpretative framework for the WJ III COG is the WJ III Cognitive Performance Model or Information Processing Model (Mather & Woodcock, 2001), which integrates cognitive and noncognitive variables into four types of influence on cognitive performance (see Rapid Reference 6.18). Automatic processing, thinking abilities, and stores of acquired knowledge are the main cognitive influences. The fourth component of the model, facilitators-inhibiters, consists of executive processes and noncognitive variables, such as health, temperament, emotional state, and motivation. The influence of these noncognitive variables is derived from clinical judgment. To interpret results using this model, practitioners should enter the appropriate subtest scores on the diagnostic worksheet shown on page 83 of the *Woodcock-Johnson III Tests of Cognitive Abilities Examiner's Manual* or select the diagnostic worksheet report option in the computer-scored Report Writer for the WJ III. A more psychometric application of this model is to simply interpret the Verbal Ability, Thinking Ability, and Cognitive Efficiency cluster scores (see Rapid Reference 6.18) that result whenever the standard (7 subtests) or extended battery (14 subtests) is administered. In doing so, the examiner should make pairwise comparisons, using a 20-point difference as an indicator of significance. For example, an individual may have a Cognitive Efficiency score that is significantly lower than both Thinking Ability and Verbal Ability. Such a pattern would indicate that a weakness in cognitive efficiency, or automatic processing (as measured by short-term memory and processing speed subtests), may be constraining learning and performance in an individual with adequate, and relatively stronger, verbal and thinking abilities.

## Predicted Achievement Discrepancies Analysis

Another discrepancy table supplied by the WJ III Compuscore and the Report Writer for the WJ III that applies to diagnosis of SLDs is the Predicted Achievement/Achievement Discrepancies table. In addition to a discrepancy analysis that uses general intellectual ability, the WJ III computer scoring programs can predict academic achievement scores in reading, mathematics, and written language using the most relevant predictors for each area of achievement. The predictors (the first seven tests in the WJ III COG Standard Battery) are weighted differentially, according to the correlations they have with each academic domain. The WJ III COG tests with the highest correlations are consistent with the pro-

*≡Rapid Reference 6.18*

## Main Components of the WJ III Cognitive Performance Model

Stores of Acquired Knowledge (score derived from Comprehension-Knowledge tests)
   Crystallized Intelligence
   Quantitative Reasoning
   Reading and Writing Ability

Thinking Abilities (score derived from Long-Term Retrieval, Visual-Spatial Thinking, Auditory Processing, and Fluid Reasoning tests)
   Novel Reasoning
   Long-Term Retrieval
   Auditory Thinking
   Visual-Spatial Thinking

Cognitive Efficiency/Automatic Processing (score derived form Short-Term Memory and Processing Speed tests)
   Short-Term Memory/Working Memory
   Automatic Processing Speed

Facilitators-Inhibiters
   Executive Control
   Organic
   Situational/Cultural

*Source:* Adapted from *Woodcock-Johnson III Tests of Cognitive Abilities Examiner's Manual* (Mather & Woodcock, 2001, p. 80).

cesses that research has identified as playing the most important roles for each type of learning (see Chapter 2). Thus, if the learner has an academic skill deficiency that is caused by a related processing deficit, there should be no significant discrepancy between the predicted score and the obtained achievement score; in other words, they should both be low. Examine the discrepancy SD column to make these decisions, with the assumption that nonsignificant discrepancies are indicative of concordance between an achievement domain and related processes. For example, when the SD is higher than +1.00, it means that the achievement level is higher than would be predicted from the related processing scores. When the SD is lower than –1.00, it indicates that the academic skills are lower than would be predicted from the related processing scores. In instances where the processing scores are average and the discrepancy SD is lower than –1.00, it indicates that something other than processing weaknesses are inhibiting development of the academic skill. For more discussion of this phenomenon, review the section on the consistency approach to diagnosing LDs found in Chapter 4.

## Strengths and Weaknesses as a Measure of Processing

The WJ III COG is not only a very comprehensive measure of cognitive processes but is also based on a theory (CHC) that has extensive empirical support. The WJ III COG is also very compatible with the information processing theory and the integrated model of processing advocated in this book. For example, the WJ III COG includes processing factors, such as phonemic awareness, beyond those classified as CHC factors. The WJ III COG not only offers a thorough processing assessment when needed but also easily adapts for selective testing of processes and blends well with other scales when a cross-battery assessment is conducted. The WJ III COG clusters may also provide a broader measure of processes than some other scales, mainly because the WJ III COG measures at least two distinct narrow abilities (Carroll, 1993) within each factor, instead of using two subtests that measure the same narrow ability or process. Finally, the structure of the WJ III COG is supported by extensive factor analytic studies (McGrew & Woodcock, 2001).

The WJ III COG's usefulness as a diagnostic tool has been established by research that has found that students with an LD obtain significantly lower means on most of the processing factors when compared to a nondisabled peer group (McGrew & Woodcock, 2001). Given its extended norms, the WJ III COG is also a valuable diagnostic tool when assessing adults and college students for processing problems and LDs. Furthermore, the WJ III COG and its conormed WJ III Tests of Achievement (Woodcock, McGrew, & Mather, 2001a) facilitate diagnoses by producing extensive data and statistical analyses in their computer-generated reports.

Most of the concerns relate to potential interpretation challenges. For example, interpreting all of the available data can be challenge for those who are not informed about the various available statistics and discrepancies analyses. In-depth understanding of what each WJ III COG test measures is also crucial because many of the tests contribute to more than one cluster score. Processing interpretation, in particular, can be challenging because a thorough analysis of WJ III COG processing results usually requires hand computations and clinical judgment. Finally, practitioners should be cautious when interpreting results from the Cognitive Performance Model framework, as little validation of the model has been published.

## WECHSLER INTELLIGENCE SCALE FOR CHILDREN, FOURTH EDITION-INTEGRATED (WISC-IV INTEGRATED)

The Wechsler Intelligence Scale for Children, fourth edition—Integrated (WISC-IV Integrated; Wechsler et al., 2004a) is the combination of the WISC-IV

## Rapid Reference 6.19

### WISC-IV Integrated

**Authors:** David Wechsler, Edith Kaplan, Deborah Fein, Joel Kramer, Robin Morris, Dean Delis, and Arthur Maerlander

**Publication date:** 2004

**Processes measured:** Executive processing, fluid reasoning, long-term retrieval, planning, short-term memory, visual processing, working memory

**Theoretical basis:** Neuropsychology

**Age range:** 6:0–16:11

**Publisher:** PsychCorp

(Wechsler, 2003a) and the revision of the Wechsler Intelligence Scale for Children, third edition as a Process Instrument (Kaplan et al., 1999; see Rapid Reference 6.19). The WISC-IV Integrated is the addition of 16 optional process subtests to the WISC-IV standard 15-subtest battery. The process subtests consist of additional scoring procedures, alternate presentation formats, and some novel item content. The development and use of the process portion of the WISC-IV Integrated has its roots in neuropsychological assessment and the belief that the WISC-IV is a valuable clinical instrument.

In part, the process subtests are a standardization of informal testing of limits procedures, thereby allowing an actuarial, as well as a clinical, interpretation of WISC-IV performance. The processing portion of the WISC-IV Integrated is not intended to stand alone; it is intended for use after the usual WISC-IV administration. This section will discuss only the 16 optional process subtests of the WISC-IV Integrated and the relationship these process subtests have with the standard WISC-IV subtests (see Chapter 5 for a discussion of the traditional WISC-IV).

The purpose of the WISC-IV Integrated process subtests is to provide additional information about the cognitive processes that underlie performance on the WISC-IV core and supplemental subtests. Each WISC-IV core and supplemental subtest measures more than one ability or process. Following up with process subtests allows the examiner to parse and distinguish among the cognitive processes involved, potentially leading to identification of a process that accounts for an examinee's poor performance on a particular subtest.

## DON'T FORGET

The WISC-IV Integrated includes the traditional WISC-IV battery, and it is designed to be used in conjunction with the WISC-IV.

When poor performance on a standard WISC-IV subtest or index occurs, an examiner may develop hypotheses to account for the poor performance. The hypotheses can be tested by administering standardized process subtests, instead of utilizing the informal testing of the limits approach. For example, an examiner may hypothesize that a child with a relative weakness on the Information subtest performed poorly because of a weakness in long-term retrieval. Readministering the Information subtest with the process version of Information in multiple-choice format may reveal the extent to which a long-term retrieval weakness impacted performance on the standard Information subtest. Administration of WISC-IV Integrated process subtests also allows more in-depth assessment of suspected or identified processing strengths and weaknesses. For example, ipsative analysis of the standard WISC-IV scores and corroborating data from other sources may indicate that a child has a significant weakness in working memory. By administering additional working memory subtests, the examiner may be able to determine the type of working memory deficit; for example, the examiner will be able to assess visual as well as auditory working memory. Other processing hypotheses may originate from observations of the child's testing behaviors. The WISC-IV Integrated affords the opportunity to quantify these observations.

## Processes Measured by the WISC-IV Integrated

The WISC-IV Integrated groups the 16 process subtests under four domains— Verbal, Perceptual, Working Memory, and Processing Speed (see Rapid Reference 6.20). Process subtests within a cognitive domain are not necessarily designed to measure the same construct as the core or supplemental subtest from which they are derived. In fact, some of the process subtests tap additional processes. No domain scores or processing factor scores can be calculated; only subtest scores with the usual mean of 10 and standard deviation of 3 are available. There are more than 16 process scores available because some subtests split into two scores, such as one with bonus points for speed and one without. Also, scaled scores are not available for all of the specific subtest components; some subtest components have only base rates.

### Long Term Retrieval

There is no doubt that performance on the standard WISC-IV verbal subtests requires retrieval of stored information from long-term memory. However, because several abilities and processes are involved, it is difficult to determine the influence of long-term retrieval on the standard WISC-IV Verbal Comprehension subtests. The multiple-choice format of the Verbal processing subtests reduces the demands for verbal expression and long-term memory retrieval (Wechsler et al., 2004c). When a child's performance improves significantly from the

≡ *Rapid Reference 6.20*

### WISC-IV Integrated Structure and Processes Measured

| Domain/Subtest | Processes |
| --- | --- |
| Verbal Domain | |
| Similarities Multiple Choice | — |
| Vocabulary Multiple Choice | — |
| Picture Vocabulary Multiple Choice | — |
| Comprehension Multiple Choice | — |
| Information Multiple Choice | — |
| Perceptual Domain | |
| Block Design Multiple Choice | Visual Processing |
| Block Design Process Approach | Visual Processing |
| Elithorn Mazes | Planning, Executive Processing |
| Working Memory Domain | |
| Visual Digit Span | Short-Term Memory |
| Spatial Span | Short-Term Memory, Working Memory |
| Letter Span | Short-Term Memory |
| Letter-Number Sequencing Process Approach | Working Memory |
| Arithmetic Process Approach | Fluid Reasoning |
| Written Arithmetic | — |
| Processing Speed Domain | |
| Coding Recall | Long-Term Retrieval |
| Coding Copy | — |

standard Verbal subtest to the multiple-choice format, one hypothesis to account for the difference is that a long-term retrieval deficit interfered with performance on the standard subtests. While improved performance on the Verbal process subtests may lend support to a long-term retrieval deficit, the Verbal process subtests are still not direct or specific measures of long-term retrieval. Consequently, a practitioner should still follow up with an instrument that evaluates long-term retrieval in a more direct fashion.

The WISC-IV Integrated lists two process subtests under the Processing Speed domain—Coding Recall and Coding Copy. However, these two subtests are really designed to measure incidental learning and the influence of motor skills on Coding, not processing speed per se. The two process subtests in the Processing Speed domain are both follow-ups to the Coding B subtest. The first subtest, Coding Recall, must be completed immediately following the administration of Coding B. Coding Recall has three items, each of which requires the child to recall members of the paired associates from Coding B. While intended to measure incidental learning (learning that occurs without a directed effort to do so), Coding Recall can be classified as a measure of long-term retrieval. The other subtest, Coding Copy, helps to parse out the influence of motor skills on Coding performance. It is neither a measure of long-term retrieval nor processing speed as it is usually defined.

### Working Memory and Short-Term Memory

The Working Memory process subtests offer more in-depth assessment of working memory than the standard WISC-IV Working Memory subtests, and they provide opportunities to distinguish among different aspects of working memory. The most significant contribution of the Working Memory process subtests is the inclusion of visual working memory; only auditory working memory is required on the regular WISC-IV Working Memory subtests. The distinction is particularly important when evaluating students for a learning disability, as they often have deficient verbal-auditory working memory but adequate visual-spatial working memory.

The WISC-IV Integrated also divides the Working Memory process subtests into Registration and Mental Manipulation tasks, with all of the Span subtests, except the two Span Backward subtests, classified as Registration subtests and the remaining subtests classified as Mental Manipulation subtests. The WISC-IV Integrated technical and interpretative manual (Wechsler et al., 2004c) defines registration as "temporarily retain[ing] information for the purpose of repeating that information without modification" (p. 196) and defines mental manipulation as "performing a transformation of the information" (p. 197), such as reversing the order of digits. The registration definition and tasks are consistent with the construct of short-term memory while the manipulation tasks are clearly working memory.

A couple of the Working Memory process subtests may serve to confound, rather than clarify, the strengths and weaknesses within a child's working memory. That is because these subtests incorporate processes not explicitly included in the standard WISC-IV Working Memory subtests. For example, the Letter Span subtest divides into items that have rhyming letters and items that have non-rhyming letters. Students with phonemic processing difficulties will often find the rhyming items more challenging. The Letter-Number Sequencing Process Approach subtest only scores the items that have embedded words. Although the embedded words may provide memory cues, the child is not alerted to the possibility of embedded words. To determine the impact of such cues on the child's working memory capacity, the examiner would first need to verify whether the child was even aware of the cues and attempted to utilize them.

### Fluid Reasoning

The WISC-IV Integrated does not identify any of the process subtests as specific measures of fluid reasoning. Furthermore, there are no follow-up process versions of the WISC-IV Perceptual Reasoning subtests—Matrix Reasoning and Picture Concepts—that are thought to measure fluid reasoning. However, if the WISC-IV Arithmetic subtest's primary classification is fluid reasoning instead of Working Memory (Keith et al., 2004), then the process versions of Arithmetic are even stronger measures of fluid reasoning because they have been restructured in a manner that reduces the load on working memory.

### Visual Processing

As with the standard WISC-IV Battery, the process versions of Block Design are primarily measures of visual processing. Block Design Multiple Choice measures visual perceptual organization abilities and nonverbal concept formation. The main difference between Block Design and Block Design Multiple Choice is that the latter eliminates a motor response. The Block Design Process Approach subtest also measures visual perceptual organization abilities and nonverbal concept formation. In Part B, the items that were scored 0 in Part A are readministered with a transparent grid overlay placed over the design pictures to assist the child in constructing the design. The grid overlays in part B provide additional information regarding the child's spatial reasoning and ability to analyze and synthesize abstract visual stimuli.

### Planning and Executive Processing

Elithorn Mazes is the only process subtest that is completely unrelated to any of the WISC-IV core and supplemental subtests. For each item, the child must draw a path that passes through a specified number of dots en route to an exit. Elithorn Mazes is designed to measure scanning ability, visual and motor sequential processing, planning, organization, motor execution, and the ability to inhibit impulsive responses. For purposes of processing assessment, it can be more broadly classified as a measure of planning and executive processing.

## Selected Technical Features

The WISC-IV Integrated was normed on a national sample of 730 children, stratified by age, sex, race or ethnicity, parent education level, and geographic region.

About 6 percent of the sample consisted of children in special education. Norms for each of the two youngest age groups (ages 6 and 7) were based on only 50 subjects, while the remaining age groups were composed of 70 participants. The Block Design Process Approach subtest was not standardized with the WISC-IV Integrated. Rather, the procedures and norms for the Block Design Process Approach are from the WISC-III as a Process Instrument (WISC-III PI). Because the norms for the Block Design Process Approach subtest are several years older than the WISC-IV Integrated norms, the results from this subtest should be interpreted cautiously.

Averaged across age groups, the internal consistency reliability coefficients for the subtests range from .67 to .91, generally an improvement from the WISC-III PI. Corrected test-retest reliabilities range from .72 to .84 (see Rapid Reference 6.21 for more reliability coefficients). Because there are no composite scores and all of the interpretation is at the subtest level, clinicians need to be aware of which subtests have less than desirable reliability.

The validity evidence presented in the *Wechsler Intelligence Scale for Children Fourth Edition—Integrated Technical and Interpretative Manual* (Wechsler et al., 2004b) consists mainly of correlational studies providing convergent and discriminant evidence. As predicted, scaled scores within a domain generally have significant and higher correlations with each other than with scores from other domains. Studies conducted with special populations support the validity of the processing subtests and the usefulness of the scale as a measure of processing. In these 13 studies, subjects were matched with normal controls from the WISC-IV standardization data. The special groups generally displayed patterns of processing weaknesses that would be predicted for each disability. For example, a WISC-IV Integrated study conducted with a sample of 45 children with a Reading Disorder is particularly relevant, given the body of research that has found processing deficits to be related to reading disabilities. Compared to a matched control group, the reading-disordered sample had significantly lower scores on many of the Working Memory process subtests. They did not, however, differ on Spatial Span Backward, lending support to the claim that children with a Reading Disorder perform better on working memory tasks that are visual-spatial as opposed to auditory-verbal. In fact, all of the learning-disordered groups demonstrated difficulties with tasks involving short-term and working memory. For a group with ADHD, the largest effect sizes were for the Arithmetic process subtests, Information Multiple Choice, Elithorn Mazes, and Coding Copy. No factor analytic studies of the WISC-IV Integrated are reported in the manual.

### Rapid Reference 6.21

## Average Reliability Coefficients of the WISC-IV Integrated Process Scores

| Subtest | Internal Consistency | Test-Retest |
|---|---|---|
| Similarities Multiple Choice | .77 | .71 |
| Vocabulary Multiple Choice | .85 | .77 |
| Picture Vocabulary Multiple Choice | .85 | .79 |
| Comprehension Multiple Choice | .76 | .69 |
| Information Multiple Choice | .85 | .84 |
| Block Design Multiple Choice (BDMC) | .91 | .77 |
| BDMC No Time Bonus | .91 | .77 |
| Elithorn Mazes (EM) | .75 | .65 |
| EM No Time Bonus | .78 | .59 |
| Visual Digit Span | .83 | .75 |
| Spatial Span Forward | .79 | .65 |
| Spatial Span Backward | .81 | .68 |
| Letter Span Nonrhyming | .75 | .72 |
| Letter Span Rhyming | .67 | .70 |
| Letter-Number Sequencing Process Approach | .84 | .74 |
| Arithmetic With Time Bonus | .86 | — |
| Arithmetic Process Approach-A (ARPA-A) | .89 | .87 |
| ARPA-A With No Time Bonus | .90 | .86 |
| Arithmetic Process Approach-B (ARPA-B) | .90 | .88 |
| Written Arithmetic | .89 | .83 |
| Coding Copy | .84 | — |

Note: This Rapid Reference does not include the seven process scores included in the WISC-IV.

Source: Data are from Wechsler Intelligence Scale for Children Fourth Edition—Integrated Technical and Interpretative Manual (Wechsler et al., 2004c, pp. 132, 139).

## Unique Administration and Scoring Procedures

With the exception of some optional administration procedures for the Coding subtest, administration and scoring of the traditional 10 core and 5 supplemental WISC-IV subtests remains the same in the WISC-IV Integrated. Thus, the WISC-IV Integrated can be used to obtain the customary WISC-IV Full Scale IQ and four Index scores. After administering the usual battery, an examiner may elect to administer one or more process subtests. The process subtests consist of additional scoring procedures, alternate presentation formats, and some novel item content. Except for one completely new subtest (Elithorn Mazes), the process subtests are variations of the standard WISC-IV subtests.

> **DON'T FORGET**
>
> ........................................................
>
> Most of the process subtests are variations of the standard WISC-IV subtests. They typically vary the mode of presentation or the response format.

Some of the process subtests use the same items as the core or supplementary subtests but vary the mode of presentation or response format. For example, all of the Verbal process subtests use identical items but use a multiple-choice response or present the items in picture format. Other process subtests are variations that include new item content and changes to response or presentation format. Although they are organized by domain, the process subtests may be administered in any order. Administration of the subtests need not be immediate (except for Coding Recall); they can be administered up to 95 days after the initial WISC-IV administration. Processing subtest scores may not be used to replace WISC-IV standard subtests or be used to compute the Full Scale IQ or an Index score.

## Analysis and Interpretation of the Processing Results

Interpretation of WISC-IV Integrated results, as suggested in the WISC-IV Integrated Record Form, can be complex, especially if all or most of the process subtests are administered. Because no domain or index scores are available for the processing portion of the test, interpretation is designed to take place at the subtest or intrasubtest level. Core and supplemental subtests, as well as process scores that originate with the standard WISC-IV battery, are included in the process analysis found in the WISC-IV Integrated Record Form. The process analysis in the Record Form consists only of pairwise discrepancy comparisons at the subtest and intrasubtest level. There are 6 scaled score discrepancy comparisons included in the process analysis of the Verbal domain, 7 for the Perceptual domain, 15 for the Working Memory domain, and 2 for the Processing Speed domain. Some of the process level discrepancy comparisons are between the scaled score of a core or supplemental subtest and the scaled score of the corresponding process subtest. Other comparisons are between logical pairings of process subtests, such as Registration tasks versus Mental Manipulation tasks within the Working Memory domain. There are also scaled score discrepancy comparisons

# DON'T FORGET

Some unique characteristics of the WISC-IV Integrated that affect interpretation include the following: There are no general composite or factor scores; only base rates are available for some of the processes; and the suggested process analysis in the Record Form involves only pairwise comparisons between subtests and within subtests.

between two scores from the same subtest, such as Letter Span Rhyming versus Letter Span Nonrhyming. Only base rates are available for most of the intra-subtest processes, such as the longest spans, and there are no critical values for discrepancies between base rates. The lack of scaled scores and critical values for all of the process scores and discrepancies somewhat limits the interpretation. The *Wechsler Intelligence Scale for Children Fourth Edition—Integrated Technical and Interpretative Manual* (Wechsler et al., 2004c) provides hypotheses and implications for both possible outcomes for each of the subtest and intrasubtest discrepancy comparisons.

The subtest interpretation approach utilized by the WISC-IV Integrated is at odds with the interpretative model advocated in this book. Interpretation at the subtest level is difficult to justify, given the lower reliability of subtest scores compared to factor scores. Instead of identifying a common underlying processing factor tapped by two or more subtests, the WISC-IV Integrated focuses on the specific processes measured by each subtest. By altering or limiting the tasks, the WISC-IV Integrated probably increases the specificity of some of the subtests (specificity data is not available). On the other hand, despite the stated goal of parsing out subtest processes, some of the WISC-IV Integrated subtests actually add more confounds by introducing new variables, such as rhyming in the Letter Span subtest.

Consequently, this author recommends that practitioners go beyond the subtest process analysis in the WISC-IV Integrated Record Form. Another level of interpretation would be to compute clinical factors scores and use them in an ipsative analysis. For example, comparing a clinically derived short-term memory (Registration) factor with a clinically derived working memory (Manipulation) factor may have more clinical validity and utility than basing such a comparison only on Digit Span Forward versus Digit Span Backward, as suggested in the WISC-IV Integrated Record Form.

## Analysis of WISC-IV Integrated Clinical Factors

To interpret the WISC-IV Integrated results from the perspective of the Integrated Model of cognitive processing, more of a cross-battery and clinical approach is necessary. This approach avoids reliance on interpretation of subtest and partial subtest scores and emphasizes analysis of clinical factor scores. There are two components to this procedure. The first is an in-depth analysis of short-term memory and working memory processes only. The second part incorporates the new short-term memory and working memory clinical factors with the processes derived from the standard WISC-IV battery—fluid reasoning, processing speed, and visual processing.

### Analysis of Short-Term Memory and Working Memory

Only the Working Memory Domain of the WISC-IV Integrated has enough subtests to calculate clinical processing factor scores. In fact there is enough depth in this domain to combine subtest scores into visual and auditory factors within both short-term memory (Registration) and working memory (Manipulation). The worksheet in Appendix F (see completed example in Rapid Reference 6.22) is designed to facilitate computation of these clinical factors. After completing the computations, use the bottom of the worksheet to conduct pairwise comparisons. Because only two processing domains are being analyzed at this point, do not conduct a profile analysis in which these clinical factor scores are compared to their mean.

The data analyzed in Rapid Reference 6.22 clearly illustrate the benefits of using the WISC-IV Integrated when an in-depth assessment of working memory and short-term memory is desired. The Working Memory Index derived from the standard WISC-IV administration can mask differences between visual and auditory functioning within working memory, as well differences between basic short-term memory and the more complex functioning of working memory. For instance, the analysis in Rapid Reference 6.22 reveals that the visual component of both short-term and working memory is stronger than the auditory component. Within short-term memory, the difference is clearly significant and infrequent, while within working memory the 15-point difference is most likely significant as well. The higher short-term memory over working memory scores in the profile also indicate that working memory is weaker than short-term memory in both visual and auditory functions. This hypothesis, however, cannot be confirmed as the discrepancies are not significant and the Short-Term memory factor is nonunitary.

### Comprehensive WISC-IV Integrated Processing Analysis and Interpretation

In the second phase of the analysis, the short-term memory and working memory clinical factors are included in an analysis (using the Processing Analysis Worksheet in Appendix C) with fluid reasoning, processing speed, and visual processing, which have been derived in the usual fashion from the standard WISC-IV subtests (see Chapter 5). This comprehensive analysis is different from the usual WISC-IV analysis in that a Short-Term Memory factor is added and in that

## ≋Rapid Reference 6.22

### Illustration of Short-Term Memory and Working Memory Analysis Using Appendix F Form

<u>Directions:</u> (1) Clinical factor scores can only be calculated when at least two subtest scores that comprise that factor are available. (2) Begin by transforming all subtest scaled scores to standard scores with a mean of 100 and standard deviation of 15, using the table in Appendix D. (3) For each factor, add up the available subtest transformed scores and compute the mean, rounding to the nearest whole number. (4) Next, determine which clinical factors are unitary. If the difference between the highest and lowest subtest standard scores within a factor exceeds 22 points, consider the clinical cluster nonunitary. Interpret nonunitary factors cautiously, and do not use them in pairwise comparisons. (5) Then conduct pairwise comparisons of the unitary factors, using a 20-point discrepancy as an indication of significance and infrequency. (6) Transfer all clinical factors scores to the Processing Analysis Worksheet (Appendix C) for further analysis.

| Short-Term Memory (STM) | Scaled Score | Standard Score |
|---|---|---|
| Digit Span Forward | 8 | 90 |
| Visual Digit Span | 11 | 105 |
| Spatial Span Forward | 12 | 110 |
| Letter Span Nonrhyming | 8 | 90 |
| Letter Span Rhyming | 6 | 80 |

Standard Score Total __475__ ÷ __5__ (No. of subtests) = __95__ STM Factor Score

| Visual Short-Term Memory (VSTM) | Scaled Score | Standard Score |
|---|---|---|
| Visual Digit Span | 11 | 105 |
| Spatial Span Forward | 12 | 110 |

Standard Score Total __215__ ÷ 2 = __108__ VSTM Factor Score

| Auditory Short-Term Memory (ASTM) | Scaled Score | Standard Score |
|---|---|---|
| Digit Span Forward | 8 | 90 |
| Letter Span Nonrhyming | 8 | 90 |
| Letter Span Rhyming | 6 | 80 |

Standard Score Total __260__ ÷ __3__ (No. of subtests) = __87__ ASTM Factor Score

| Working Memory (WM) | Scaled Score | Standard Score |
|---|---|---|
| Digit Span Backward | 5 | 75 |
| Spatial Span Backward | 7 | 85 |
| Letter Number Sequencing PA | 6 | 80 |

Standard Score Total __240__ ÷ __3__ (No. of subtests) = __80__ WM Factor Score

| Visual Working Memory (VWM) | Scaled Score | Standard Score |
|---|---|---|
| Spatial Span Backward | 7 | 85 |
| Arithmetic PA Part A | 10 | 100 |

Standard Score Total __185__ ÷ __2__ = __93__ VWM Factor Score

| Auditory Working Memory (AWM) | Scaled Score | Standard Score |
|---|---|---|
| Digit Span Backward | 5 | 75 |
| Letter Number Sequencing PA | 6 | 80 |

Standard Score Total __155__ ÷ __2__ = __78__ AWM Factor Score

| Pairwise Clinical Comparisons | Difference | Significant: Y/N |
|---|---|---|
| (Short-Term Memory is nonunitary.) | | |
| _____ Short-Term Memory versus _____ Working Memory | _____ | _____ |
| __108__ Visual Short-Term Memory versus __87__ Auditory Short-Term Memory | __21__ | __Y__ |
| __93__ Visual Working Memory versus __78__ Auditory Working Memory | __15__ | __N__ |
| __108__ Visual Short-Term Memory versus __93__ Visual Working Memory | __15__ | __N__ |
| __87__ Auditory Short-Term Memory versus __78__ Auditory Working Memory | __11__ | __N__ |

the clinical Working Memory factor score replaces the one derived from Digit Span and Letter-Numbering Sequencing. The clinical Working Memory factor is possibly a *purer* measure of Working Memory in that it is based on tasks that require more manipulation of the stimuli; for example, it excludes Digits Forward. The clinical Working Memory factor also represents a broader working memory construct in that it includes both visual and auditory working memory. The clinical Short-Term Memory factor also includes both visual and auditory components. See Rapid Reference 6.23 for the steps involved and Rapid Reference 6.24 for a completed Processing Analysis Worksheet that uses the data from Rapid Reference 6.22.

### Strengths and Weaknesses as a Measure of Processing

From a processing assessment perspective, the WISC-IV Integrated offers an efficient and valuable appraisal of short-term memory and working memory. It not only allows a comparison of these two critical processes based on the same norming sample, but it also allows in-depth assessment of the visual and auditory aspects of each. Thus, the WISC-IV Integrated should be particularly useful when additional information about a child's short-term and working memory functioning is desired.

Regarding children with disabilities, they may or may not perform better on the process subtests, even when the process subtests provide accommodations and reduce the cognitive processing demands necessary for successful performance. For example, children with ADHD may be distracted by the multiple-choice format, and those with phonemic processing problems will be hindered by the rhyming letters in Letter Span.

The fact that the WISC-IV Integrated process component is tethered to the standard WISC-IV battery is both an advantage and disadvantage. It is advantageous because it allows further investigation of processing hypotheses that arise from testing observations and poor performance on some WISC-IV subtests, without switching to another battery. On the other hand, the use of the processing component requires prior administration of the customary WISC-IV battery (because it was normed this way); the processing component cannot be used independently. Also, follow-up testing with other scales may still be necessary, depending on the processes of concern.

### DON'T FORGET

The WISC-IV Integrated provides an in-depth evaluation of working and short-term memory subprocesses, such as visual and auditory.

## *≡Rapid Reference 6.23*

### WISC-IV Integrated Processing Analysis and Interpretation Steps

1. Exclude nonprocessing index scores—VCI and PRI—from the analysis. From the processing portion of the WISC-IV Integrated, use only the Short-Term Memory and Working Memory clinical factor scores that were calculated following the procedures on the Appendix F worksheet. The clinical Working Memory factor score should be used to replace the standard WMI. The PSI is included; it is the only factor score that is derived from the tables in the WISC-IV manual.

2. Calculate a visual processing clinical factor score from Block Design and Picture Completion. First transform the subtest scores to a metric with a mean of 100 and a standard deviation of 15 using the table in Appendix D. Then compute the mean of the scores and round to the nearest whole number.

3. Calculate a Fluid Reasoning clinical factor score from Matrix Reasoning and Picture Concepts, following the same computations as in step 2. If Arithmetic was administered, it may also be included in the computation of Fluid Reasoning (including Arithmetic is optional and somewhat controversial).

4. Record the five processing scores on the Processing Analysis Worksheet, compute the mean of the five processing scores, round the nearest whole number, and use this value as the processing factor mean.

5. Compare each processing factor score to the individual's WISC-IV processing factor mean, using a 15-point discrepancy as an indication of significance and infrequency. Complete the weakness and deficit columns.

6. Examine subtest scores within each factor to determine whether each factor is unitary. When the difference between the highest and lowest subtest scores is 5 points or greater (using scaled scores; M = 10, SD = 3) or greater than 22 points (using scaled scores; M = 100, SD = 15) consider the factor to be nonunitary. Interpret nonunitary factors cautiously, and do not use them for pairwise comparisons.

7. Compare processing factor pairs, especially short-term memory versus working memory and fluid reasoning versus visual processing, using a 20-point discrepancy as the criterion for significance and infrequency.

## Processing Analysis Worksheet

### WISC-IV Integrated Illustration

Examinee's Name: _____ DOB: _____ Age: _____ Grade: _____ Dates of Testing: _____

| Name of Process | Name of Test/ Battery | Name of Factor/ Subtests | Processing Factor Score | Processing Factor Mean | Difference from Mean | Normative S or W | Ipsative S or W | Deficit or Asset |
|---|---|---|---|---|---|---|---|---|
| Working Memory | WISC-IV Integrated | Digit Span Backward; Spatial Span Backward; Letter-Number Sequencing PA | 80 | 97 | –17 | W | W | D |
| Processing Speed | WISC-IV Integrated | PSI | 91 | 97 | –6 | — | — | — |
| Visual Processing | WISC-IV Integrated | Block Design; Picture Completion | 113 | 97 | +16 | S | S | A |

| | | | | | | | |
|---|---|---|---|---|---|---|---|
| Fluid Reasoning | WISC-IV Integrated | Picture Concepts; Matrix Reasoning | 105 | 97 | +8 | — | — | — |
| Short-Term Memory | WISC-IV Integrated | Digit Span Forward; Spatial Span Forward; Visual Digit Span; Letter Span Rhyming; Letter Span Nonrhyming | 95 | 97 | −2 | — | — | — |

*Note:* Dashes indicate the absence of an S or W, or an A or D.

Directions: (1) Use factor scores for analysis, not subtest scores. (2) When a factor score is not available from a test, convert subtest scores to a mean of 100 and an SD of 15. (3) For each factor, compute the mean of the subtest scores and round to the nearest whole number. Use the subtest means as clinical factor scores. (4) Compute the mean of all available factor scores (this is the processing mean). (5) Subtract the processing mean from each processing factor score and enter amount in Difference column. (6) Indicate whether the factor score is a normative weakness or strength (90–109 is average). (7) Using a criterion of 15 points, determine ipsative strengths and weaknesses. (8) Determine deficits and assets. A deficit is both a normative and ipsative weakness. (9) Determine which factors are non-unitary. A deficit is both a normative and ipsative weakness. When the range between the highest and lowest subtest scores exceeds 1.5 SDs, the factor is non-unitary. Non-unitary factors should be interpreted cautiously and should not be used in pairwise comparisons. (10) Compare related pairs (below) for significant differences, using a 20 point difference as an indication of significance.

| Factor Score | Factor Score | Difference | Significant:Y/N |
|---|---|---|---|
| Working Memory (80) | Processing Speed (91) | 11 | Y (based on WISC-IV tables) |
| Visual Processing (113) | Fluid Reasoning (105) | 8 | N |

## 🖋 TEST YOURSELF 🖋

1. **Which test has a bitheoretical basis?**
   (a) KABC-II
   (b) CAS
   (c) WJ III COG
   (d) WISC-IV Integrated

2. **Which test measures the most processing factors?**
   (a) KABC-II
   (b) CAS
   (c) WJ III COG
   (d) WISC-IV Integrated

3. **Which test is not designed to be used independently?**
   (a) KABC-II
   (b) CAS
   (c) WJ III COG
   (d) WISC-IV Integrated

4. **Which test purports to measure attention as defined by Luria?**
   (a) KABC-II
   (b) CAS
   (c) WJ III COG
   (d) WISC-IV Integrated

5. **Which test has fewer factors at the preschool-age level?**
   (a) KABC-II
   (b) CAS
   (c) WJ III COG
   (d) WISC-IV Integrated

6. **The WISC-IV Integrated assesses which process in depth?**
   (a) Visual Processing
   (b) Processing Speed
   (c) Working Memory
   (d) Executive Processing

7. **When using the WJ III Cognitive Intra-Cognitive Discrepancy table, which discrepancy SD value should be used as an indication of significance?**

    (a) .05

    (b) .10

    (c) 1.00

    (d) 1.75

8. **Which test has a battery Composite that can be directly used to represent overall cognitive processing ability?**

    (a) WISC-IV

    (b) CAS

    (c) WJ III COG

    (d) WISC-IV Integrated

9. **A study of reading disabled students' performance on the CAS found their lowest mean factor score to be**

    (a) Planning.

    (b) Attention.

    (c) Successive Processing.

    (d) Simultaneous Processing

10. **The WJ III Cognitive Performance Model of processing includes the influence of _____ on processing and test performance.**

    (a) noncognitive factors

    (b) general intelligence

    (c) development

    (d) learning disabilities

*Answers:* 1. a; 2. c; 3. d; 4. b; 5. a; 6. c; 7. c; 8. b; 9. c; 10. a

## Seven

## ASSESSING MEMORY

The functioning of diverse types of memory is the foundation of all cognitive processing and learning. Daily functioning and learning depend on memory encoding, storage, and retrieval processes. Memory is complex and can be conceptualized in many different ways (Cohen, 1997a). There are many different types of memory processes and storage systems distributed throughout the brain (Berninger & Richards, 2002). Within long-term memory alone there are several different types (see Rapid Reference 7.1). Three main processes integrate the various memory mechanisms: (1) coding and encoding in short-term and working memory convert information for long-term storage; (2) storage in one or more types of long-term memory; and (3) retrieval. Working memory, which is involved in thinking, is unique in that it involves both encoding of new information and processing of already stored information. Of course, successful functioning of memory processes depends on directed and sustained attention, a process that should be assessed whenever memory is evaluated.

A plethora of empirical evidence has established the critical role that various types of memory, especially working memory and long-term retrieval, play in academic learning (Berninger & Richards, 2002; Swanson, 1999). In fact, memory difficulties are one of the major difficulties underlying LDs. Yet surveys have found (Cohen, 1997b) that school psychologists seldom test memory in a direct or comprehensive manner when children are referred for learning difficulties. Despite common practice, a psychological evaluation of a child should not be considered complete without an assessment of memory. Evaluations for learning problems should, at the very least, in-

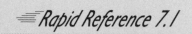

## Rapid Reference 7.1

### Main Categories of Long-Term Memory

Declarative
Semantic
Episodic
Procedural
Associative

clude an assessment of key memory processes (Zurcher, 1995). Assessment of memory is also an essential component of neuropsychological evaluations.

The intellectual and cognitive scales reviewed in Chapters 5 and 6 include a basic sampling of short-term, working, and long-term memory. However, there are times when the referral questions and presenting problems of the examinee necessitate a comprehensive memory evaluation. In these instances, the Wechsler Memory Scale, third edition (WMS-III), the Children's Memory Scale (CMS), or one of the instruments listed in Rapid Reference 7.12 will meet the need. In addition to reviewing the WMS-III and CMS, this chapter provides information on other memory scales, including scales that assess limited aspects of memory.

This chapter focuses on interpretation of memory assessment results, especially the analysis of memory in conjunction with nonmemory processes. Such a cross-battery analysis will identify deficiencies in memory relative to other processes and overall processing. Interpretation of memory results is unique in that a Full Scale or Composite IQ may be used in an ability-memory discrepancy analysis. Of course, examination of the memory scores alone will also provide very meaningful information. Paramount differences to explore are auditory/verbal versus visual/nonverbal memory, immediate (short-term) versus delayed (long-term) memory, and free recall versus recognition. The chapter concludes with a general interpretative model that applies to most memory scales.

> **DON'T FORGET**
>
> An assessment of memory should be part of the psychological evaluation whenever a child is referred for learning problems.

## WECHSLER MEMORY SCALE, THIRD EDITION (WMS-III)

The WMS-III (Wechsler, 1997c) offers a comprehensive, in-depth assessment of memory in adults, aged 16 through 89 (see Rapid Reference 7.2). While designed primarily for neuropsychological assessment, the

> **≣ Rapid Reference 7.2**
>
> **Wechsler Memory Scale for Children, Third Edition (WMS-III)**
>
> **Author:** David Wechsler
>
> **Publication date:** 1997
>
> **Main processes measured:** Long-term retrieval, short-term memory, working memory
>
> **Theoretical basis:** Neuropsychological
>
> **Age range:** 16–89 years
>
> **Publisher:** The Psychological Corporation

WMS-III is the instrument of choice whenever there are serious or multiple concerns about the memory functioning of older students referred for a possible LD. The WMS-III is mainly a measure of declarative episodic memory because it requires the examinee to learn and retrieve information that is novel and contextually bound. *Episodic memory* is defined as personally experienced events or episodes. Tasks that are used to assess episodic memory include text, word lists, geometric designs, and faces.

## Memory Processes Measured by the WMS-III

With the WMS-III, an examiner can assess both the visual and auditory aspects of the three core memory systems—immediate (short-term), working, and long-term. The categorization of the subtests under a visual or auditory index reflects the mode of presentation, not the subtest content. Of the eight available indexes, the most global are Immediate Memory and General Memory. Immediate Memory is composed of the Auditory Immediate and Visual Immediate indexes. General Memory consists of the Auditory Delayed, the Visual Delayed, and the Auditory Recognition Delayed indexes. Thus, the General Memory Index is a global measure of *delayed* memory only; it should not be taken as representing immediate memory or general memory functioning. The Working Memory Index comprises a visually presented subtest and an auditorily presented subtest. There are also four supplemental Auditory Process Composites available (see Rapid Reference 7.3) that are scored only on a percentile metric. Within the Auditory Delayed Index, recognition and recall can be evaluated separately.

### ≡Rapid Reference 7.3

**WMS-III Structure and Types of Memory Measured**

Immediate Memory Index
  Auditory Immediate Index
  Visual Immediate Index
General Memory Index
  Auditory Delayed Index
  Visual Delayed Index
  Auditory Recognition Delayed
    Index
Working Memory Index
Auditory Process Composites*
  Single-Trial Learning*
  Learning Slope*
  Retention*
  Retrieval*

Note: Asterisk (*) indicates supplemental.

### Selected Technical Features

The WMS-III was normed on a nationally stratified sample of 1,250 that was selected according to 1995 U.S. census data. The WMS-III was also conormed with the WAIS-III (Wechsler, 1997b), making it possible to evaluate IQ-memory discrepancies psychometrically with the predicted-difference method or the simple-difference method.

Reliability is a concern with the WMS-III. Not only do some of the index scores have less than desired reliability (see Rapid Reference 7.4), but also five subtests have split-half coefficients of less than .80, and three subtests have test-retest coefficients of less than .70. The low reliability of some of the indexes may be the explanation for an uncommon statistical pattern found with some of the WMS-III discrepancies. For some pairwise comparisons, the discrepancy values needed for a base rate of less than 15 percent are substantially less than the critical values for the .01 level of significance. Given the concerns about subtest profile analysis and the low reliability coefficients of several WMS-III subtests, psychometric interpretation of WMS-III results should be focused on the factor level.

Regarding construct validity, confirmatory factor analytic findings support the underlying immediate and delayed memory dimensions of the WMS-III (Wechsler, 1997d). The findings also support a separate working memory factor, as well as modality-specific (visual and auditory) memory dimensions. Correlations with other memory measures demonstrate convergent validity, further supporting the construct validity of the WMS-III. Studies of the WAIS-III and WMS-III were also conducted with several clinical groups. An LD reading group exhibited average performance on all of the WMS-III memory indexes, obtaining its lowest

## ≡Rapid Reference 7.4

### WMS-III Average Reliability Coefficients

| Index | Internal Consistency | Test-Retest |
|---|---|---|
| Immediate Memory | .91 | .84 |
| Auditory Immediate | .93 | .85 |
| Visual Immediate | .82 | .75 |
| General Memory | .91 | .88 |
| Auditory Delayed | .87 | .84 |
| Visual Delayed | .83 | .76 |
| Auditory Recognition Delayed | .74 | .70 |
| Working Memory | .86 | .80 |

Source: Data are from *Essentials of WMS-III Assessment* (Lichtenberger, Kaufman, & Lai, 2002, Rapid Reference 1.3).

mean on the Working Memory Index. Compared to a normal matched control group, participants with reading disabilities had a significantly higher forgetting rate for auditorily presented material.

## Unique Administration and Scoring Procedures

A partial administration of the WMS-III is allowed, as long as the correct interval between an immediate subtest and the delayed recall version of the subtest is maintained. Memory factors should be selected on the basis of referral concerns and hypotheses (see discussion in Chapter 3). The WMS-III facilitates the testing of specific, directional hypotheses regarding memory; for instance, it is possible to test the hypothesis that the learner's auditory memory is weaker than his or her visual memory. When other scales are administered, duplication of factors should be avoided to maintain efficiency; for example, it is unnecessary to measure working memory twice when both the WAIS-III and WMS-III are administered.

Most of the WMS-III subtests are administered in their entirety, making subtest administration relatively straightforward. Because repeating test items is generally not permissible, it is important that the examinee is paying attention before the item is presented. When administering only portions of the WMS-III, the examiner should avoid administering several auditory memory subtests or several visual memory subtests in a row.

## Interpretation of Results

A complete administration of the WMS-III yields an abundance of data regarding memory processes and potential strengths or assets and weaknesses or deficits within memory systems. Identification of specific memory deficits is extremely important because memory deficits are impediments to learning and potential impairments in daily functioning. The interpretative route to follow mainly depends on whether the WMS-III has been administered in isolation or has been part of a multibattery processing assessment. When the WMS-III is the sole processing assessment instrument, the statistical tables in the WMS-III manual should be used for determining significance and frequency of occurrence. When there has been a multibattery assessment of processing that includes all or some of the WMS-III indexes, the WMS-III scores and other process scores should be analyzed together, using the analysis steps discussed in Chapter 4 and the Processing Analysis Worksheet found in Appendix C. Even when there has been a multibattery processing assessment, it is advisable to also analyze the WMS-III results separately, especially when all of the WMS-III indexes have been administered. The specific steps for interpretation of the WMS-III are detailed below and summarized in Rapid Reference 7.5. For additional interpretative advice and details, see Lichtenberger et al. (2002) or Wechsler (1997d).

Comparing logical or contrasting pairs of WMS-III indexes for significant discrepancies is an essential component of WMS-III interpretation (see Rapid Reference 7.5 for the recommended comparisons). As suggested in Chapter 4, it may also be worthwhile to compare the separate types of memory to the mean of the examinee's WMS-III index scores. When other processes have also been as-

## ≡Rapid Reference 7.5

### Interpretive Steps for the WMS-III

1. If the WAIS-III was administered, compare each WMS-III index with the WAIS-III Full Scale IQ.
2. Using the mean of the WMS-III index scores, conduct a profile analysis of WMS-III memory factors.
3. Conduct a processing analysis that combines WMS-III indexes with other non-memory factors.
4. Examine subtest scores within each index or factor to determine whether each factor is unitary.
5. Conduct pairwise comparisons of WMS-III indexes.

    5a. Compare immediate versus delayed memory indexes.

    Immediate Memory versus General Memory

    Auditory Immediate versus Auditory Delayed

    Visual Immediate versus Visual Delayed

    5b. Compare visual versus auditory memory indexes.

    Visual Immediate versus Auditory Immediate

    Visual Delayed versus Auditory Delayed

    5c. Compare working memory with immediate memory and general (delayed) memory indexes.

    Working Memory versus Auditory Immediate

    Working Memory versus Visual Immediate

    Working Memory versus Immediate Memory

    Working Memory versus General Memory

    5d. Compare the two working memory subtest scores.

    Letter Number Sequencing versus Spatial Span

    5e. Compare auditory delayed recall and auditory delayed recognition indexes.

    Auditory Delayed versus Auditory Recognition Delayed

sessed, comparing the distinct types of memory to an overall processing mean may reveal weaknesses that do not come to light when the WMS-III results are analyzed alone. For instance, an individual may have depressed memory scores in all types of memory. In such a case, the memory deficits may only become evident when the scores are compared to the individual's overall processing mean. In cases where no additional processing analysis is desired, the memory scores may be compared to a Full Scale IQ. A comparison with the WAIS-III Full Scale IQ is particularly informative, as the WAIS-III was conormed with the WMS-III. Of course, if the WAIS-III was administered, then, in fact, other processes have been assessed. Hence, the most unadulterated analysis of processing would be to incorporate the WAIS-III processing factors with the WMS-III indexes, using the Processing Analysis Worksheet found in Appendix C.

### Interpretive Steps for the WMS-III

1.  *If the WAIS-III was administered, compare each WMS-III index with the WAIS-III Full Scale IQ.* Normally, processing scores should not be compared with a Full Scale IQ when conducting an ipsative analysis of processing because IQ scores usually contain nonprocessing factors. An exception is made in this case because these two scales were normed together and because of the high correlations between IQ and memory. As a result, the WAIS-III Full Scale can justifiably be used to predict levels of memory functioning. Resulting discrepancies are strong indicators of memory weaknesses or deficits. However, commensurate scores do not guarantee the absence of a weakness or deficit, as a dysfunction in one or more types of memory may have had a detrimental impact on IQ test performance, especially performance on a verbal scale. Begin by contrasting the WAIS-III Full Scale IQ and the WMS-III General Memory Index, using the predicted-difference tables provided in the WMS-III manual. This should be the initial comparison because the General Memory Index is considered to be the best estimate of an examinee's overall memory functioning. Proceed by comparing each of the remaining WMS-III indexes with Full Scale IQ. The emphasis given to any obtained discrepancies will also depend on the discrepancies found among the pairwise comparisons between different types of memory.
2.  *Using the mean of the WMS-III index scores, conduct a profile analysis of WMS-III memory factors.* Computing a mean and completing a profile analysis of the memory factors should only be conducted when the entire WMS-III has been administered. Using the Processing Analysis

Worksheet from Appendix C and following the procedures outlined in Chapter 4, conduct a clinical analysis of WMS-III index scores. Begin by computing the mean of the specific memory indexes (excluding the Immediate Memory and General Memory composites). This mean represents a global aggregate of memory processes that includes immediate (short-term), working, and long-term memory or retrieval. Comparing the different types of memory to this overall memory mean may expose specific ipsative memory weaknesses. Because the WMS-III does not have statistical tables for this purpose, any 15-point discrepancy should be considered significant and relatively infrequent.

3. *Conduct a processing analysis that combines WMS-III indexes with other non-memory factors.* Whenever the WMS-III is part of a cross-battery processing assessment, the WMS-III scores should be integrated with other processing scores (in addition to step 2), using the Processing Analysis Worksheet in Appendix C and following the procedures outlined in Chapter 4. This type of analysis is especially recommended when only portions of the WMS-III have been administered. With this approach, each WMS-III index score is compared with a processing factor mean that is derived from both memory and nonmemory factors. (Because they are composites, exclude the Immediate Memory and General Memory indexes from this analysis.) The drawback to this approach is that the WMS-III statistical tables will not apply. The advantage is that memory weaknesses or strengths may emerge when they are not found among WMS-III indexes. This step may be conducted even when the only other scale administered is the WAIS-III. In this instance, include only the WAIS-III processing factors in the analysis (see Chapter 5). When the WAIS-III has been administered, the clinician may elect to complete both steps 1 and 3 but, in doing so, should state whether the discrepancies are relative to the general intellectual level or the overall cognitive processing level.

4. *Examine subtest scores within each factor to determine whether each factor is unitary.* When the difference between the highest and lowest subtest scores is 5 scaled score points or greater, consider the factor to be nonunitary. Interpret nonunitary factors cautiously, if at all, and do not use them for pairwise comparisons.

5. *Conduct pairwise comparisons of WMS-III indexes.* For pairs of WMS-III indexes, the statistical tables in the WMS-III manual should be used to determine significance and frequency of occurrence.

5a. *Compare immediate versus delayed memory.* This comparison is perhaps the most common in memory assessment. Begin by checking for significant discrepancies between the most global scores—Immediate Memory versus General Memory (delayed). Then, contrast immediate versus delayed within the auditory and visual modes, by examining Auditory Immediate versus Auditory Delayed and Visual Immediate versus Visual Delayed. Because long-term memory depends on immediate memory, it is often presumed that immediate memory is adequate whenever performance on long-term memory tasks is average. However, initially poor learning followed by strong retention of what was learned may result in a significantly lower immediate memory score. But the more likely discrepancy is long-term memory being significantly lower than immediate memory, indicating difficulties with retention or retrieval of information.

5b. *Compare visual versus auditory memory.* Global visual and auditory scores are not available on the WMS-III. Consequently, the comparisons are between Visual Immediate versus Auditory Immediate and Visual Delayed versus Auditory Delayed. Where significant differences exist within the immediate or delayed domains, the broader memory factor (Immediate or General) should be considered nonunitary and interpreted cautiously, if at all, especially when the differences are 1.5 or greater standard deviations. When memory differences between modalities emerge, they may be associated with relative strengths and weaknesses between broader visual and auditory processes. When a visual-auditory memory discrepancy emerges, visual and auditory processing should be investigated if they were not concurrently assessed.

5c. *Compare working memory with immediate memory and general or delayed memory.* Begin by contrasting the Working Memory Index with all three immediate memory scores, bearing in mind that what the WMS-III labels as immediate memory is equivalent to short-term memory. Also, keep in mind that the Working Memory Index is composed of both visual and auditory tasks. Because working memory serves to encode information into long-term memory, the Working Memory Index should also be contrasted with the General Memory Index.

5d. *Compare the two working memory subtest scores.* Because statistical tables are not available for this comparison, use a scaled score difference of 3 points as an indication that there is a significant difference between visual working memory and auditory working memory. Instead of reporting these individual subtest scores and any discrepancy, the clinician should follow up with a more in-depth assessment of visual and auditory working memory whenever this subtest discrepancy occurs. If the scaled score difference between the two Working Memory Index subtests is 5 or more points, working memory should not be interpreted as a unitary factor.

5e. *Compare auditory delayed recall with auditory delayed recognition.* This step amounts to contrasting the Auditory Delayed Index (recall) with the Auditory Recognition Delayed Index. Because retrieval through recall is more demanding than retrieval through recognition, a significantly lower Auditory Delayed score may indicate some type of long-term retrieval weakness or deficit. That is, the examinee may possess adequate encoding and storage of information but have difficulty spontaneously retrieving that information. When interpreting this discrepancy, the clinician needs to appreciate the fact that this comparison is limited to the auditory mode.

## Strengths and Weaknesses as a Measure of Memory Processes

At the adult level, the WMS-III may be the most comprehensive measure of memory. Its main strength is that is measures both the auditory and visual aspects of short-term, long-term, and working memory. Its main limitation is that it does not formally evaluate procedural memory, which is involved in the learning of academic skills. The structure of the test facilitates analysis of scores and identification of memory difficulties. An ipsative analysis, including pairwise comparisons, is readily accomplished without having to rely on clinical factors. However, additional global scores would have been helpful, for example, a full scale memory score (the General Memory Index includes only delayed measures) and global visual and auditory memory indexes. Finally, the conorming of the WMS-III with the WAIS-III is advantageous because the WAIS-III Full Scale IQ can be used to determine discrepancies.

## CHILDREN'S MEMORY SCALE (CMS)

Until the relatively recent development of the CMS (Cohen, 1997a) and similar scales (Delis, Kramer, Kaplan, & Ober, 1994; Sheslow & Adams, 1990), there were no scales specifically designed for the comprehensive assessment of mem-

≡*Rapid Reference 7.6*

**Children's Memory Scale (CMS)**

**Author:** Morris J. Cohen
**Publication date:** 1997
**Main processes measured:** Attention, long-term retrieval, short-term memory
**Theoretical basis:** Neuropsychological
**Age range:** 5–16 years
**Publisher:** The Psychological Corporation

ory in children. In addition to age-appropriate tasks, the CMS is designed to be sensitive to the developmental changes in memory that take place throughout childhood. The CMS (see Rapid Reference 7.6) bears many similarities to the WMS-III; for example, they both assess the auditory and visual dimensions of memory, and both exclude measures of procedural memory. In contrast to the WMS-III, the CMS taps learning and attention/concentration but does not explicitly measure working memory. Given its structure, the CMS provides valuable information about the memory functioning of children referred for learning difficulties, as well as special populations, such as those with traumatic brain injury.

## Memory Processes Measured by the CMS

The main processes measured by the CMS are attention, short-term memory, and long-term retrieval. Different combinations of subtests yield eight index scores (see Rapid Reference 7.7). The General Memory Index truly represents global memory processing, as it includes immediate and delayed subtests in both the visual and auditory dimensions. Each subtest in the visual/nonverbal domain and the auditory/verbal domain contains an immediate and a delayed version. However, the Delayed Recognition Index includes only auditory/verbal subtests. The names of the indexes generally reflect the tasks involved and the memory components they tap, with the following exceptions: (1) the Attention/Concentration Index also places a heavy demand on

≡*Rapid Reference 7.7*

**CMS Structure and Types of Memory Measured**

General Memory Index
  Verbal Immediate Index
  Visual Immediate Index
  Verbal Delayed Index
  Visual Delayed Index
Attention/Concentration Index
Learning Index
Delayed Recall Index

working memory; (2) the Learning Index is based on the examinee's performance across three learning trials of one visual and one auditory subtest; and (3) the Auditory/Verbal subtests involve semantically related material that is presented in a sequential format.

## Selected Technical Features

The nationally stratified standardization sample consisted of 1,000 in 10 age groups. It appears that the exclusionary criteria eliminated children who were at risk for learning problems and memory impairments. Individuals excluded ranged from those who were reading below grade level or had repeated a grade to those who had suffered a head injury. For linking purposes, a subset of the examinees was also administered the WISC-III or the WPPSI-R.

The reliability of some of the indexes, especially Visual Immediate and Visual Delayed, is less than desirable, for both internal consistency and test-retest reliability (see Rapid Reference 7.8). Due to concerns that the test-retest coefficients gave a misleading impression of stability, the CMS author conducted a consistency of decision classification study in which scores were divided into three groups that coincided with ranges for impaired, borderline to average, and average to above average. The study found that decision consistency was relatively stable over time. Nevertheless, there are concerns about reliability, even at the in-

## ≡ Rapid Reference 7.8

### CMS Reliability Coefficients

| Index | Internal Consistency Average | Test-Retest for Ages 9–12 |
| --- | --- | --- |
| Visual Immediate | .76 | .69 |
| Visual Delayed | .76 | .66 |
| Verbal Immediate | .86 | .82 |
| Verbal Delayed | .84 | .79 |
| General Memory | .91 | .86 |
| Attention/Concentration | .87 | .89 |
| Learning | .85 | .67 |
| Delayed Recognition | .80 | .56 |

Source: Data are from *Children's Memory Scale Manual* (Cohen, 1997b, pp. 98, 99, 101).

dex level. Consequently, diagnostic decisions should not be based on CMS scores alone. Practitioners also need to be aware that there are practice effects of up to one standard deviation when the scale is readministered within 8 weeks.

Regarding validity evidence reported in the manual (Cohen, 1997b), the best fitting confirmatory factor analytic model consists of three factors: attention/concentration, auditory/verbal delayed memory, and visual/nonverbal delayed memory. Although the factor analytic studies do not fully support the structure of the CMS, the pattern of correlations among the indexes supports convergent and divergent validity within the instrument. The pattern of strong correlations between CMS indexes and Wechsler intellectual factors was as predicted, indicating that memory functioning is highly correlated with intellectual functioning. The highest correlations were between the WISC-III Verbal IQ and the CMS auditory/verbal indexes. Perhaps the most pertinent evidence consists of the correlations with academic achievement and grades; except for visual memory, all types of memory have a strong relationship with academic learning (see Rapid Reference 7.9). Correlations with grades, although they are all significant at the .01 level, are, as predicted, lower than correlations with achievement scores. The relationship between executive functioning and aspects of memory was also examined. The results suggested that auditory/verbal memory functions are more related to executive functioning than attention/concentration or visual/nonver-

## ≡Rapid Reference 7.9

### Correlations Between CMS Indexes and Wechsler Individual Achievement Test Scores

| CMS Indexes | Reading | Math | Writing |
|---|---|---|---|
| Visual Immediate | .24* | .29* | .22* |
| Visual Delayed | .08 | .08 | .07 |
| Verbal Immediate | .51* | .55* | .50* |
| Verbal Delayed | .54* | .55* | .52* |
| General Memory | .49* | .51* | .47* |
| Attention/Concentration | .58* | .58* | .57* |
| Learning | .37* | .39 | .38* |
| Delayed Recognition | .38* | .42* | .38* |

*$p < .01$

Source: Data are from *Children's Memory Scale Manual* (Cohen, 1997b, p. 121).

bal memory. A special group study with a learning disabled sample implicates memory dysfunction in children with LDs. Compared to a matched normal sample, the LD sample scored significantly lower on all indexes, except the Visual Immediate, indicating that children with LD have more difficulty with auditory/ verbal than visual/nonverbal memory. Overall, the extensive validity evidence in the CMS manual clearly establishes the critical role that memory processing plays in learning.

## Unique Administration and Scoring Procedures

Testing should be completed in one session, with the appropriate 30-minute delay interval between immediate and delayed recall. Novice administrators should tape record the responses to the Stories subtest until they become familiar with scoring. Correct orientation of the stimulus cards is crucial and should be practiced before actual testing. Because memory is being measured, examiners should pay close attention to which items may be repeated. Examiners may elect to compute supplemental norm-referenced scores that include separate Numbers Forward and Numbers Backward scores and Percent Retention scores that reflect the proportion of items the examinee retains during the interval from the immediate to the delayed recall version of each subtest.

## Interpretation of CMS Results

The traditional top-down model of interpretation applies well to the CMS and most memory scales. The clinician should begin by interpreting the General Memory Index as the best estimate of global memory. Next, the practitioner should conduct a profile analysis of the seven specific CMS memory factors by comparing each index score to the mean of the indexes. The final step is to contrast logical pairs, such as Visual Immediate versus Visual Delayed. When the CMS is the sole processing assessment instrument, the statistical tables in the CMS manual (Cohen, 1997b) should be used for determining significance and frequency of occurrence. Even when there has been a multibattery processing assessment, it is advisable to first analyze the CMS results separately, especially when all of the CMS indexes have been administered. When there has been a cross-battery assessment of processing, then CMS index scores should be analyzed along with the other processes, using the processing analysis steps discussed in Chapter 4 and the Processing Analysis Worksheet found in Appendix C. Whenever discrepancies are discovered, it is crucial that the clinician specifically state what the strength or weaknesses is relative to; for example, a weakness may be relative to (1) a full intellectual or cognitive composite; (2) the mean of the memory factors; (3) an overall processing mean that includes memory and non-memory factors; and (4) another memory or processing factor in a pairwise comparison. The interpretive steps are detailed in the following section and summarized in Rapid Reference 7.10. Additional interpretative guidelines may be found in the CMS manual (Cohen, 1997b).

---

### ⟱Rapid Reference 7.10

#### Interpretive Steps for the CMS

1. Interpret the General Memory Index as an estimate of global memory functioning.
2. (Optional) If an FSIQ or cognitive composite is available, complete an ability-memory discrepancy analysis with the General Memory Index and each of the indexes, using 20 points as an indication of significance and infrequency.
3. Using the mean of the CMS memory indexes, conduct a within memory scale profile analysis.
4. Conduct a processing analysis that combines memory factors with other non-memory factors.
5. Examine subtest scores within each factor to determine whether each factor is unitary.
6. Conduct pairwise comparisons of the memory indexes.
    - 6a. Compare the Attention/Concentration Index with each memory index.
      Attention/Concentration versus General Memory
      Attention/Concentration versus Verbal Immediate
      Attention/Concentration versus Visual Immediate
      Attention/Concentration versus Verbal Delayed
      Attention/Concentration versus Visual Delayed
      Attention/Concentration versus Learning
      Attention/Concentration versus Delayed Recall
    - 6b. Compare short-term memory and long-term retrieval indexes.
      Verbal Immediate versus Verbal Delayed
      Visual Immediate versus Visual Delayed
    - 6c. Compare visual and auditory memory indexes.
      Visual Immediate versus Verbal Immediate
      Visual Delayed versus Verbal Delayed
    - 6d. Compare the Verbal Delayed Index with the Delayed Recognition Index.

## Interpretive Steps for the CMS

1. *Interpret the General Memory Index as an estimate of global memory functioning.* The General Memory Index on the CMS is an adequate representation of overall memory processing because it includes both short-term memory and long-term memory, as well as the visual and auditory dimensions of each. When the range from the lowest to the highest indexes that comprise the General Memory Index exceeds 1.5 standard deviations (22 points), interpret the General Memory Index cautiously, if at all.

2. *(Optional) If a Full Scale IQ or cognitive composite is available, complete an ability-memory discrepancy analysis with the General Memory Index and each of the indexes, using 20 points as an indication of significance and infrequency.* This is an optional step; it is unnecessary when step 4 is followed. Step 2 is allowed because of the strong relationship between memory and general intellectual and cognitive functioning; in other words, an intellectual or cognitive composite adequately predicts general memory and memory components. The 20-point critical value is suggested because CMS discrepancy tables are only available for the outdated WISC-III and WPPSI-R.

3. *Using the mean of the CMS memory indexes, conduct a within-memory scale profile analysis.* Computing a mean and completing a profile analysis with the memory factors should only be conducted when the entire CMS has been administered. Using the Processing Analysis Worksheet from Appendix C and following the procedures outlined in Chapter 4, conduct a clinical analysis of CMS index scores. Begin by computing the mean of the seven specific (excluding General Memory) indexes. Then compare each of the different types of memory to this overall memory mean to determine ipsative memory strengths and weaknesses, using a 15-point difference as an indication of significance and infrequency.

4. *Conduct a processing analysis that combines memory factors with other nonmem-*

> ### DON'T FORGET
>
> When reporting memory strengths and weaknesses, state which of the following the strength or weakness is relative to
>
> 1. a full intellectual or cognitive composite.
> 2. the mean of the memory factors.
> 3. an overall processing mean that includes memory and non-memory factors.
> 4. another memory or processing factor in a pairwise comparison.

*ory factors.* Whenever the CMS is part of a cross-battery processing assessment, the CMS scores should be combined with other processing factor scores (this is in addition to step 3), using the Processing Analysis Worksheet in Appendix C and following the procedures outlined in Chapter 4. This type of analysis is especially recommended when only portions of the CMS have been administered. With this approach, each CMS index score (excluding General Memory) is compared with a processing factor mean that is derived from both memory and nonmemory factors. Again, use a 15-point difference as an indication of significance and infrequency.

5. *Examine subtest scores within each factor to determine whether each factor is unitary.* When the difference between the highest and lowest subtest scores is greater than 1.5 standard deviations, consider the factor to be nonunitary. Interpret nonunitary factors cautiously, and do not use them in pairwise comparisons.

6. *Conduct pairwise comparisons of the memory indexes.* For pairs of CMS indexes, the statistical tables in the CMS manual should be used to determine significance and frequency of occurrence. For any pairings not found in the manual, use a 20-point difference as an indication of significance and infrequency.

6a. *Compare the Attention/Concentration Index with each memory index.* Attention is the foundation of learning and memory. A weakness in attention may influence memory processing.

6b. *Compare short-term memory versus long-term retrieval.* On the CMS, contrast immediate versus delayed within the verbal and visual modes, by examining Verbal Immediate versus Verbal Delayed and Visual Immediate versus Visual Delayed.

6c. *Compare visual versus auditory memory.* Global visual and auditory scores are not available on the CMS. Consequently, the comparisons are between Visual Immediate versus Verbal Immediate and Visual Delayed versus Verbal Delayed.

6d. *Compare the Verbal Delayed Index with the Delayed Recognition Index.* This step amounts to contrasting recall with recognition. (The Verbal Delayed Index is measuring recall.) Because retrieval through recall is more demanding than retrieval through recognition, a significantly lower Verbal Delayed score may indicate a long-term retrieval weakness. That is, the examinee may possess adequate encoding and storage of information but have difficulty spontaneously retrieving the information on demand. When interpreting this discrepancy, be aware that this comparison is limited to the auditory mode.

## Strengths and Weaknesses as a Measure of Memory Processes

Because it is well grounded in theory and research, the CMS provides valuable diagnostic information about an examinee's memory functioning and processing strengths and weaknesses. Although it lacks direct evaluation of working memory and procedural memory, the CMS assesses memory in a comprehensive fashion. The Learning Index also provides standardized data about how a child learns from practice over a number of repeated learning trials, very pertinent information when children are referred for learning difficulties. The main concern is the weak reliability associated with the Visual Memory Indexes. Clinicians should also keep in mind that visual memory has less to do with academic learning than verbal memory.

# OTHER MEMORY SCALES

## Criteria for Selecting Scales

When selecting a psychometric instrument for memory assessment, practitioners need to first examine the reliability and validity evidence. Factor scores with reliability coefficients below .80 are not sufficiently reliable and should not be used to make diagnostic decisions. Even factor scores with reliability coefficients between .80 and .89 require supporting data. Thus, clinicians should only use memory tests that have high reliability coefficients across the majority, if not all, of the memory indexes. (The instruments listed in Rapid Reference 7.12 have adequate evidence of sufficient reliability, at least for the majority of their composite and subtest scores.) Regarding validity, the most pertinent studies are those that document strong relationships between memory factors and specific types of academic learning. Finally, the instrument chosen should measure several dimensions of memory or measure a particular component in depth; for example, a memory scale should always distinguish between visual and auditory memory processes within each broad memory component.

## General Interpretive Guidelines

The interpretive guidelines previously suggested for the WMS-III and the CMS generally apply to the interpretation of any memory scale. Following the inter-

# DON'T FORGET

The following are primary pairwise comparisons when analyzing memory scale results:

1. Auditory/verbal versus visual/nonverbal memory
2. Immediate (short-term) versus delayed (long-term) memory
3. Free recall versus recognition memory
4. Attention versus all types of memory

pretive guidelines in a memory scale's manual should be the first interpretation procedure. However, a thorough interpretation should go beyond within-scale analysis and compare memory factor scores to overall processing. Additional memory strengths and weaknesses are likely to emerge from this additional procedure. At the very least, it will be easier to understand how memory processes relate to the individual's cognitive processing as a whole. The processing analysis and interpretation procedures described on the Processing Analysis Worksheet (Appendix C) apply to the interpretation of memory scales. See Rapid Reference 7.11 for a summary of interpretive steps that can be applied to any memory scale.

## ≡ Rapid Reference 7.11

### General Interpretive Steps for Any Memory Scale

1. Interpret the full scale memory composite (if available) as an estimate of global memory functioning.
2. (Optional) If a Full Scale IQ or cognitive composite is available, complete an ability-memory discrepancy analysis with each of the memory composites and indexes, using 20 points as an indication of significance and infrequency.
3. Using the mean of the memory indexes (excluding composites consisting of indexes), conduct a within memory scale profile analysis, following the steps on the Processing Analysis Worksheet in Appendix C.
4. When there has been a cross-battery assessment, conduct a processing analysis that combines memory factors (excluding composites consisting of factors) with other nonmemory factors, following the steps on the Processing Analysis Worksheet in Appendix C. This may be completed in addition to step 3.
5. Examine subtest scores within each factor to determine whether each factor is unitary. When the difference between the highest and lowest subtest scores is greater than 1.5 standard deviations, consider the factor to be nonunitary. Interpret nonunitary factors cautiously, if at all, and do not use them in pairwise comparisons.
6. Conduct pairwise comparisons of the memory indexes.

The most challenging memory tests to interpret are those that provide only subtest scores and no factor or composite scores. In these situations, aggregating the subtests into clinical factors and computing a mean for each may serve to identify meaningful memory strengths and weaknesses. With memory scales, clinicians also need to pay close attention to the composition of what appear to be global memory scores; for instance, a "General Memory" score may not include all major types of memory. Finally, remember that the chief interpretative step for any memory scale is the comparison of memory process pairs.

## ≡ Rapid Reference 7.12

### Memory Scales

**Test:** California Verbal Learning Test, Children's Version (CVLT-C)
**Authors:** Dean C. Delis, Joel H. Kramer, Edith Kaplan, and Beth A. Ober
**Publication date:** 1994
**Age range:** 5–16
**Publisher:** The Psychological Corporation

**Main processes measured:** Long-term retrieval, short-term memory
**Main processing factor scores:** Only subtest scores available

---

**Test:** California Verbal Learning Test, Second Edition, Adult Version (CVLT-II)
**Authors:** Dean C. Delis, Joel H. Kramer, Edith Kaplan, and Beth A. Ober
**Publication date:** 2000
**Age range:** 16–89
**Publisher:** The Psychological Corporation

**Main processes measured:** Long-term retrieval, short-term memory
**Main processing factor scores:** Only subtest scores available

---

**Test:** Learning and Memory Battery (LAMB)
**Authors:** James P. Schmidt and Tom N. Tombaugh
**Publication date:** 1995
**Age range:** 20–80
**Publisher:** Multi-Health Systems, Inc.

**Main processes measured:** Long-term retrieval, short-term memory
**Main processing factor scores:** Only subtest scores available
**Comment:** Norms based on a Canadian sample, largely from one location

**Test:** Memory Assessment Scales (MAS)
**Author:** J. Michael Williams
**Publication date:** 1991
**Age range:** 18 and over
**Publisher:** Psychological Assessment Resources, Inc.

**Main processes measured:** Long-term retrieval, short-term memory
**Main processing factor scores:** Short-Term Memory Summary, Verbal Memory Summary, Visual Memory Summary, Global Memory

---

**Test:** Swanson-Cognitive Processing Test (S-CPT)
**Author:** H. Lee Swanson
**Publication date:** 1996
**Age range:** 5 to adult
**Publisher:** PRO-ED

**Main processes measured:** Long-term retrieval
**Main processing factor scores:** Semantic, Episodic, Total

---

**Test:** Test of Memory and Learning (TOMAL)
**Authors:** Cecil R. Reynolds and Erin D. Bigler
**Publication date:** 1994
**Age range:** 5–19
**Publisher:** PRO-ED

**Main processes measured:** Long-term retrieval
**Main processing factor scores:** Verbal Memory, Nonverbal Memory, Composite Memory, Delayed Recall

---

**Test:** Wide Range Assessment of Memory and Learning (WRAML)
**Authors:** David Sheslow and Wayne Adams
**Publication date:** 1990
**Age range:** 3–17
**Publisher:** Wide Range, Inc.

**Main processes measured:** Long-term retrieval, short-term memory
**Main processing factor scores:** Verbal Memory, Visual Memory, General Memory

---

**Test:** Working Memory Test Battery for Children (WMTB-C)
**Authors:** Susan Pickering and Sue Gathercole
**Publication date:** 2001
**Age range:** 5–15
**Publisher:** The Psychological Corporation Europe

**Main processes measured:** Working memory
**Main processing factor scores:** Only subtest scores available

---

*Note:* For information on the WMS-III and CMS, see Rapid References 7.2 and 7.6.

##  TEST YOURSELF

1. **Which type of memory is not measured by the CMS and WMS-III?**
   (a) Semantic
   (b) Episodic
   (c) Recognition
   (d) Procedural

2. **Which type of memory has the weakest relationship with academic learning?**
   (a) Visual delayed
   (b) Verbal immediate
   (c) Auditory delayed
   (d) Working memory

3. **When interpreting memory scales, the most emphasis should be placed on**
   (a) interpreting the subtest scores.
   (b) interpreting the global score.
   (c) interpreting pairwise comparisons.
   (d) interpreting the intellectual ability-memory discrepancies.

4. **When you suspect that the examinee's encoding and storage of information is adequate but retrieving that same information is not, you should compare**
   (a) retrieval with intellectual ability.
   (b) recognition with recall.
   (c) immediate memory with long-term retrieval.
   (d) general memory with attention/concentration.

5. **The main concern with the CMS and the WMS-III is**
   (a) the low reliability of some indexes and subtests.
   (b) limited construct validity evidence.
   (c) the high correlations auditory/verbal memory has with IQ.
   (d) individuals with possible memory impairments were excluded from the sample.

6. **The WMS-III was conormed with**
   (a) the WISC-III.
   (b) the CMS.
   (c) the WJ III COG.
   (d) the WAIS-III.

(continued)

**7. In which type of memory do LD samples typically obtain their highest mean?**

(a) auditory memory

(b) working memory

(c) visual memory

(d) delayed memory

**8. Full Scale IQ is a strong predictor of memory.** True or False?

*Answers:* 1. d; 2. a; 3. c; 4. b; 5. a; 6. d; 7. c; 8. True

# Eight

## USING SCALES DESIGNED TO ASSESS PROCESSING

Since 1990, there has been a significant increase in the number of psychological tests designed specifically for the assessment of cognitive processes. These scales range from measuring only one processing domain, such as executive functioning, to comprehensive batteries that can be used to evaluate several processes. After drawing lessons from neuropsychological assessment, this chapter will review a recently developed neuropsychological battery, a recent executive functioning battery, and a teacher rating scale designed to screen for processing problems. The chapter will conclude with basic information on recommended processing tests that were not reviewed in this book (see Rapid Reference 8.11). The reader is also referred to Appendix G for a complete listing of tests that measure each of the 13 processes that have been the focus of this book. The tests selected for inclusion in Rapid Reference 8.11 and Appendix G have been published since 1990 and have evidence of sufficient reliability. To interpret tests that have not been reviewed, follow the manual's guidelines and the procedures recommended in Chapter 4. For tests that do not offer statistical tables for a full ipsative assessment (critical values for pairwise differences and for discrepancies from the individual's mean), apply the procedures found on the Processing Analysis Worksheet (Appendix C).

## NEUROPSYCHOLOGICAL TESTING

Besides neuropsychologists, a variety of professionals use neuropsychological testing in the design of treatment and in the assessment of brain impairment or dysfunction. The list includes clinical psychologists, school psychologists, physical therapists, speech or language therapists, and other related professions. These practitioners often use neuropsychological tests in the evaluation of disorders such as LDs and ADHD. Those who are not trained in neuropsychology can use neuropsychological instruments, such as the NEPSY (Korkman, Kirk, & Kemp, 1998), as long as they interpret such measures at the cognitive processing level

# DON'T FORGET

......................................................

Practitioners who are not trained in neuropsychology may use neuro-psychological tests. However, they should interpret the results only from a cognitive processing perspective and not make inferences about underlying brain pathology.

and do not make inferences about underlying brain pathology.

Traditionally, neuropsychological assessment batteries have been fashioned from numerous brief instruments drawn from different sources and normed on disparate groups of individuals. Neuropsychological batteries have also typically included intellectual scales, such as the WAIS-III. Undoubtedly, neuropsychologists are quite adept at a cross-battery approach to selecting test materials based on referral concerns and hypotheses. The recent norming of comprehensive neuropsychological batteries such as the NEPSY and the Delis-Kaplan Executive Function System (Delis, Kaplan, & Kramer, 2001) reduces the need to assemble different tests as well as expedites the interpretation of results. Neuropsychologists also use brief stand-alone measures, such as the Comprehensive Trail-Making Test (Reynolds, 2002).

Because neuropsychological tests are designed to be sensitive measures of brain functioning, they are ideal measures of processing. While intellectual and most cognitive scales generally focus on abilities, neuropsychological scales attempt to directly assess broad processing domains and the specific processes that comprise those domains. Consequently, clinicians can more confidently interpret neuropsychological test results from a processing perspective. The components of neuropsychological assessment that involve minimal cognitive processing, such as sensory-motor tests are less useful, but most neuropsychological tests tap core cognitive processes such as attention, executive processing, and various dimensions of memory.

Neuropsychology also has much to offer when it comes to interpreting processing assessment results. In fact, interpreting intellectual scales from a processing perspective was pioneered by neuropsychologists (Kaplan et al., 1991). When interpreting test results, neuropsychologists utilize both psychometric and clinical approaches. They appraise functioning in broad domains, such as executive functioning, but also carefully examine numerous specific processes. They utilize subtest, item, and error analysis to identify dysfunctions in specific processes or subprocesses. Neuropsychologists also attempt to detect patterns of deficiencies that assist with diagnosis and intervention planning. However, they recognize that a pattern of scores similar to that typically seen in a disorder does not necessarily mean the examinee has the disorder.

Until now this book has recommended that most test interpretation be at the factor level because a factor is more reliable and provides a broader sampling of a process. Factors are thought to validly represent broad processing domains or systems. However, there are times when interpretation of test results should focus on more specific narrow processes; for instance, there are many types of long-term retrieval. Interpretation at the subtest and item level is especially informative when a factor is nonunitary, indicating that the subprocesses comprising that factor are functioning at different levels. In other words, there are times when we should attempt to isolate the specific dysfunction that is responsible for impairment in the broader process. Given the design of neuropsychological instruments, a more clinical, process-specific approach to interpretation seems justified when using these instruments. This chapter provides only a limited sample of neuropsychological tests. For a more inclusive listing and a more in-depth discussion of neuropsychological assessment, the reader is referred to Hebben and Milberg (2002).

## DON'T FORGET

When interpreting neuropsychological test results, an analysis of subtest performance is usually necessary in order to identify the specific processing dysfunction that may account for impairment in the broader processing domain.

## NEPSY: A Developmental Neuropsychological Assessment

The NEPSY (Korkman et al., 1998) is a neuropsychological instrument designed specifically for children ages 3 to 12 (see Rapid Reference 8.1). It assesses five domains—attention/executive functions, language, sensorimotor, visuospatial, and memory/learning—with 27 subtests (see Rapid Reference 8.2). The subtests are intended to measure the basic subcomponents that contribute to the complex functioning within a domain. When supple-

### Rapid Reference 8.1

### NEPSY: A Developmental Neuropsychological Assessment

**Authors:** Marit Korkman, Ursula Kirk, and Sally L. Kemp

**Publication date:** 1998

**Main processes measured:** Attention, executive processing, long-term retrieval, short-term memory, visual processing

**Theoretical basis:** Lurian; Neuropsychological

**Age range:** 3–12

**Publisher:** The Psychological Corporation

## *Rapid Reference 8.2*

### NEPSY Structure and Processes Measured

| Core Domains and Subtests | Processes Measured |
|---|---|
| Attention/Executive Function | Attention, executive processing, planning |
| Tower | Planning, problem solving |
| Auditory Attention & Response Set | Auditory attention and inhibition |
| Visual Attention | Visual attention |
| Statue | Inhibition of motor response to noise |
| Design Fluency | Planning |
| Language | Long-term retrieval, phonemic awareness |
| Body Part Naming | Retrieval of body part names |
| Phonological Processing | Phonemic awareness |
| Speeded Naming | Retrieval of names |
| Comprehension of Instructions | Receptive language |
| Repetition of Nonsense Words | Phonemic awareness |
| Verbal Fluency | Retrieval of words in categories |
| Sensorimotor | — |
| Fingertip Tapping | Fine motor movements |
| Imitating Hand Positions | Integration of visuospatial with kinesthetic |
| Visuomotor Precision | Graphomotor speed and accuracy |
| Visuospatial | Visual processing |
| Design Copying | Visuomotor integration |
| Arrows | Judgment of orientation of lines and angles |
| Block Construction | Reproduction of three-dimensional constructions |
| Memory and Learning | Long-term retrieval, short-term memory |
| Memory for Faces | Immediate and delayed memory for faces |
| Memory for Names | Name learning and delayed recall |
| Narrative Memory | Story memory |
| Sentence Repetition | Auditory short-term memory |
| List Learning | Supraspan memory; learning over trials |
| Scaled Supplemental Scores | |
| Auditory Attention | Simple, selective auditory attention |
| Auditory Response Set | Complex auditory attention |
| Immediate Memory for Faces | Immediate memory for faces |
| Delayed Memory for Faces | Delayed recall of faces |
| Immediate Memory for Names | Immediate memory for names |
| Delayed Memory for Names | Delayed recall of names |

Note: For the five domains, only processes from the integrated processing model are listed.

mented by an intellectual or cognitive scale, the NEPSY provides a comprehensive assessment of neuropsychological status in children, as well as a comprehensive assessment of processing.

The NEPSY is based on Luria's neuropsychological theory and clinical methods, as well as traditional assessment methods in neuropsychology. Lurian theory proposes that an impairment in one process, even a subprocess, will affect other complex cognitive functions to which that process contributes (Kemp et al., 2001). The Lurian approach emphasizes the identification of the *primary deficit* that underlies impaired performance in one or more functional domains. A deficit in another functional domain that arises from the primary deficit is referred to as a *secondary deficit*. For example, a deficit in mathematics is a secondary deficit that is caused by a primary deficit in visual processing. Lurian theory is very compatible with the processing deficit model on which this book is based.

> # DON'T FORGET
> ............................................
> According to Lurian theory, a *primary deficit* underlies impaired performance (a *secondary deficit*) in one or more functional domains. Clinicians should attempt to distinguish between primary and secondary deficits.

## Selected Technical Features

Unlike many neuropsychological instruments in the past, the NEPSY was normed on a nationally stratified random sample. The standardization sample consisted of 1,000 children, with 100 in each of 10 age groups. Children with potential processing deficiencies, such as those with an LD were excluded. Kemp et al. (2001) consider the exclusion of impaired individuals advantageous, as it allows the NEPSY to detect impairments better than instruments that are normed on impaired individuals.

Reliability varies considerably by domain, subtest, and age level (see Rapid Reference 8.3). Subtest reliabilities range from .50 to .91, and domain reliabilities range from .70 to .91. Some of the lowest reliability coefficients are for attention subtests at the 3 to 4 age level. Given the less than adequate reliability coefficients for most of the domains, diagnostic decisions should not be based on NEPSY scores alone.

## Unique Administration and Scoring Procedures

With its administrative flexibility, the NEPSY was designed with hypothesis-driven, selective testing in mind. It is recommended that a brief core assessment

## ≡Rapid Reference 8.3

### NEPSY Average Reliability Coefficients

| Core Domain | Ages 3–4 | Ages 5–12 |
|---|---|---|
| Attention/Executive Function | .70 | .82 |
| Language | .90 | .87 |
| Sensorimotor | .88 | .79 |
| Visuospatial | .88 | .83 |
| Memory and Learning | .91 | .87 |

Note: The reliability procedure depended on the nature of the subtests involved in each domain.

Source: Essentials of NEPSY Assessment (Kemp et al., 2001, p. 222).

that samples all five domains be administered first. After the core assessment reveals potential deficits, the examiner should select additional subtests in one or more domains in an effort to delineate how pervasive the deficits may be. Additional subtests should also be administered on the basis of referral concerns and related hypotheses. Expanding the assessment allows for an in-depth evaluation of the processing deficits associated with the suspected disorder. The age of the child will also determine the subtests to administer; the available subtests for 3- and 4-year-olds are somewhat different from those for older children. For ages 3 to 4, there are two core subtests for each domain except Language, which has three. For ages 5 to 12, there are three core subtests for each domain except Visuospatial, which has only two. A full NEPSY administration can be lengthy, taking up to 3 hours. Similar to other scales that measure delayed recall, it may be necessary to take a break so that 30 minutes elapses before a delayed memory section is administered.

Observations have always been an essential component of neuropsychological evaluations. Observing how the child accomplishes the task, what strategies were used, and whether the child used verbal mediation are a few examples of behaviors that should be noted (Kemp et al., 2001). The NEPSY encourages close observation of behaviors by allowing the quantification of qualitative observations. For example, clinicians can tally certain behaviors and compare the total to base-rate statistics.

## Interpretation of NEPSY Results

The NEPSY is a unique neuropsychological instrument in that its standardization and structure facilitate a psychometric approach to interpretation. After a normative analysis of the examinee's scores, practitioners should proceed with an ipsative analysis. As discussed previously, neuropsychologists usually scrutinize subtest performance carefully in an effort to identify the specific subprocesses that are contributing to a broader domain deficit. Thus, ipsative analysis of NEPSY results may include subtest analysis, as well as domain or factor analysis. Of course, any conclusions drawn from subtest data need to be supported by assessment data from other sources and methods. Practitioners with expertise in neurocognitive development may proceed with a clinical interpretation that looks for patterns associated with disorders. This amounts to examining the impact of a primary deficit on functions in which it plays a role. Additional advice on interpretation of the NEPSY and neuropsychological instruments may be found in Kemp et al. (2001) and Hebben and Milberg (2002).

Steps for interpreting the NEPSY from a cognitive processing perspective are described in the following section and summarized in Rapid Reference 8.4. Except for the last step, the NEPSY manual provides statistical tables for determining significance and base rate.

1. *Conduct an ipsative analysis of the five domains.* After describing performance on the five domains and conducting a normative analysis of domain scores, proceed with a typical ipsative analysis of the domain scores. Begin by computing the individual's mean of the five domains and comparing each domain score to the mean to determine strengths and weaknesses across domains.

2. *Examine core subtest scores within each domain to determine whether*

---

*≡Rapid Reference 8.4*

### Interpretive Steps for the NEPSY

1. Conduct an ipsative analysis of the five domains.

2. Examine core subtest scores within each domain to determine whether each domain is unitary.

3. Conduct pairwise comparisons of unitary domains.

4. Examine all subtest scores within each domain to determine specific process strengths and weaknesses.

5. Conduct pairwise comparisons of supplemental scores.

6. When other tests or portions of tests have been administered, conduct a broader analysis of processing.

*each domain is unitary.* Whenever the range between the highest and lowest core subtest scores (do not include expanded subtest scores) exceeds 1.5 standard deviations, consider the domain to be nonunitary. Interpret nonunitary domain scores cautiously, if at all, and do not use them in pairwise comparisons. Step 4 is an especially important step for nonunitary domains.

3. *Conduct pairwise comparisons of unitary domains.* Compare all possible pairs of unitary domains. When reporting significant pairwise differences, be sure to state which of the pair has the higher score.

4. *Examine all subtest scores within each domain to determine specific process strengths and weaknesses.* Given the divergent domains measured by the NEPSY, subtest profile analysis should be conducted only within each domain, not across the entire battery. For domains with at least three subtest scores, compute the individual's mean, using both core and expanded subtest scores, and compare each subtest score to the mean for statistical significance and frequency of occurrence. For domains with only two subtests, use the amount of difference between the two to determine significance and frequency. For domains with three or more subtests, compare all pairs for significant differences. For example, a pairwise comparison between Auditory Attention and Visual Attention may provide evidence that an attention problem is more specific to one mode than another.

5. *Conduct pairwise comparisons of supplemental scores.* The NEPSY divides some subtest scores into supplemental scores to distinguish more precisely what contributed to a subtest score. For example, Immediate Memory for Faces should be contrasted with Delayed Memory for Faces.

6. *When other tests or portions of tests have been administered, conduct a broader analysis of processing.* For instance, the WISC-IV might have been administered in conjunction with the NEPSY. In such cases, apply the procedures from the Processing Analysis Worksheet (Appendix C) to a loosely structured cross-battery analysis. The challenge with including the NEPSY in this type of analysis is that its domain scores can not be easily disaggregated to match the processes in the Integrated Model. For example, the Memory and Learning domain includes both short-term memory and long-term retrieval while the Attention/Executive Functioning domain includes both attention and executive processing. Also, language and sensorimotor domains are usually not included in the cognitive processing analysis approach suggested in this book.

Nevertheless, comparing the NEPSY domains with some different domains from the WISC-IV may result in some clinical insights. Therefore, enter the five NEPSY domain scores into a processing analysis along with the processing factor scores derived from other scales, and follow the usual procedures.

## Strengths and Weaknesses as a Measure of Processing

The NEPSY is an ideal processing assessment instrument, especially when it is paired with a broad intellectual or cognitive measure. In addition to its flexible in-depth testing options, it is very comprehensive. The only noteworthy omission is visual memory. Given all of the available subtest scores, supplemental scores, and qualitative observations, it can be somewhat challenging to interpret. To add to the complexity, some subtest and supplemental scores have only cumulative percentages instead of scaled scores. The main interpretative challenge arises from the fact that some of the NEPSY's processing domains are broader than the core processes suggested in the book.

## ASSESSING EXECUTIVE PROCESSING AND PLANNING

Of all the cognitive processes, executive processing may be the most complex and the most difficult to assess. The construct is usually defined rather broadly. One definition of *executive functioning* includes all cognitive abilities that are mediated primarily by the frontal lobe. Undoubtedly, fluid reasoning is intertwined with executive processing; most concepts and measures of fluid reasoning and executive processing do not attempt to separate the two. *Planning,* which this book categorizes as a distinct process for assessment purposes, is also part of executive processing. Among the many identified executive processes are metacognition, problem solving, monitoring, regulating, verbal mediation, and inhibition (see Chapter 2). In general, executive processes manage all other cognitive processes. An individual may possess adequate lower level processes but a dysfunction in some aspect of executive processing, such as poor strategy selection, may result in lower level processes not being fully utilized. Consequently, a weakness or deficit in executive processing can influence cognitive performance and learning.

Given the challenge of assessing these myriad executive processes, assessment of executive functioning has been primarily in the realm of neuropsychology. Neuropsychologists have typically evaluated an individual's executive processing with a variety of separate tasks, each tapping specific aspects of executive functioning. A recent psychometric arrival—the Delis-Kaplan Executive Function System

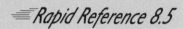

## ≡ Rapid Reference 8.5

### Delis-Kaplan Executive Function System (D-KEFS)

**Authors:** Dean C. Delis, Edith Kaplan, and Joel H. Kramer

**Publication date:** 2001

**Main processes measured:** Executive processing, fluid reasoning, planning

**Theoretical basis:** Neuropsychological

**Age range:** 8–89

**Publisher:** The Psychological Corporation

([D-KEFS] Delis et al., 2001)—purports to comprehensively assess the key components of executive processing (see Rapid References 8.5 and 8.6). The D-KEFS is actually a compendium of nine autonomous tests each measuring a different executive processing domain. The major advantage of the D-KEFS is that these nine tests were all normed together, allowing examiners to evaluate between-test differences with confidence. Nevertheless, it can be difficult to obtain an overall picture from the D-KEFS; there is no global score. To some extent, the examiner must still sift through the results and arrive at interpretations based largely on clinical judgment, similarly to interpreting the traditional pieced-together neuropsychological battery. Another neurocognitive test that has historically been used to assess executive processing (see Rapid Reference 8.7) is the Wisconsin Card Sorting Test, Revised and Expanded (Heaton, Chelune, Talley, Kay, & Curtiss, 1993). Other contemporary scales that tap at least one dimension

## ≡ Rapid Reference 8.6

### Executive Processing Domains Measured by the D-KEFS Tests

| Test | Processes Measured |
| --- | --- |
| Trail Making | Flexibility of thinking on a visual-motor task |
| Verbal Fluency | Fluent productivity in the verbal domain |
| Design Fluency | Fluent productivity in the spatial domain |
| Color-Word Interference | Verbal inhibition |
| Sorting | Problem solving; flexibility of thinking |
| Tower | Planning and reasoning in the spatial modality |
| 20 Questions | Hypothesis testing; abstract reasoning; impulsivity |
| Word Context | Deductive reasoning; verbal abstract thinking |
| Proverb | Metaphorical thinking |

of executive functioning include the NEPSY, the CAS, the KABC-II, the Comprehensive Trail-Making Test, and the WJ-III COG. There is also a behavior rating scale designed to assess executive processing—the Behavior Rating Inventory of Executive Functions (BRIEF; Gioia, Isquith, Guy, & Kenworthy, 2000). The BRIEF is an 86-item parent and teaching rating scale that produces a global executive functioning score as well as two indexes, Behavioral Regulation and Metacognition.

When executive processing assessment is part of a broader evaluation, executive processing test results should be analyzed in conjunction

> ≣ *Rapid Reference 8.7*
> ........................................................
> **Wisconsin Card Sorting Test, Revised and Expanded (WCST)**
>
> **Authors:** Robert K. Heaton, Gordon J. Chelune, Jack L. Talley, Gary G. Kay, and Glenn Curtiss
>
> **Publication date:** 1993
>
> **Main processes measured:** Executive processing, fluid reasoning
>
> **Theoretical basis:** Neuropsychological
>
> **Age range:** 6:5–89
>
> **Publisher:** Psychological Assessment Resources

with scores of other processes, applying the procedures found on the Processing Analysis Worksheet in Appendix C. Because of the influence executive processing has on other processes and on learning, it is especially important to determine whether global executive processing is a strength or weakness relative to overall processing and other processes. When no composite or factor score is available, a clinical estimate of broad executive processing may be arrived at by averaging the subtest scores. Use this clinical factor score in the processing analysis. Clinicians should also conduct an ipsative analysis within the executive processing domain, using whatever test scores are available, including subtest scores. Because of the many distinguishable subprocesses that comprise executive processing, subtest profile analysis is necessary. In the case of the D-KEFS, practitioners should conduct an ipsative analysis of performance across the nine distinct tests.

## SCREENING WITH THE PSYCHOLOGICAL PROCESSING CHECKLIST (PPC)

Recently, a standardized teacher rating scale designed solely for assessing processing became available. The Psychological Processing Checklist (PPC; Swerdlik et al., 2003a) is mainly intended for screening and for developing interventions (see Rapid Reference 8.8). The 35-item PPC seems to be in a class by itself. In contrast, the BRIEF is a rating scale (Gioia et al., 2000), designed to assess exec-

≡ *Rapid Reference 8.8*

## Psychological Processing Checklist (PPC)

**Authors:** Mark E. Swerdlik, Peggy Swerdlik, Jeffrey H. Hahn, and Tim Thomas

**Publication date:** 2003

**Main processes measured:** Attention, auditory processing, visual processing

**Theoretical basis:** Atheoretical

**Age range:** Kindergarten through fifth grade

**Publisher:** Multi-Health Systems, Inc.

utive functioning only, and the Learning Disabilities Diagnostic Inventory ([LDDI] McCarney, 1983), is comprised mainly of items that reflect academic skills.

The PPC produces a Total Score and scores on six scales—Auditory Processing, Visual Processing, Visual-Motor Processing, Social Perception, Organization, and Attention (see Rapid Reference 8.9). It was normed on 944 regular education students and 99 learning disabled students from 10 Illinois school districts. There are grade norms for Kindergarten through eighth grade. The norms are separated by sex because during standardization boys obtained higher ratings on all types of processing problems than girls did.

The PPC has a number of strengths and benefits, especially over the unstandardized checklists and rating scales that are frequently used to assess processing. To begin with, it appears to have excellent internal consistency reliability (see Rapid Reference 8.10). Correlations with factors on direct measures of processing are generally as predicted; for example, there is a strong correlation between the PPC's Attention scale and the Attention factor on the CAS. Confirmatory factor analysis revealed that the items cluster together as hypothesized.

≡ *Rapid Reference 8.9*

### PPC Structure and Processes Measured

| Scale | Processes Measured |
|---|---|
| Auditory Processing | Auditory processing |
| Visual Processing | Visual processing |
| Visual-Motor Processing | Visual-motor processing |
| Social Perception | Perception of body language and other nonverbal cues |
| Organization | Mental manipulation of information, planning |
| Attention | Attention |
| Total Score | — |

## ≋ Rapid Reference 8.10

### PPC Internal Consistency Reliability Coefficients

| Scale | General Education | Special Education |
|---|---|---|
| Auditory Processing | .93 | .82 |
| Visual Processing | .93 | .85 |
| Visual-Motor Processing | .92 | .91 |
| Social Perception | .90 | .85 |
| Organization | .86 | .78 |
| Attention | .90 | .83 |
| Total Score | .98 | .95 |

Source: The Psychological Processing Checklist (Swerdlik et al., 2003, p. 52).

Finally, interpretation of the PPC is straightforward. The authors suggest that a Total Score above a *T*-score of 60 indicates a difficulty in overall processing (Swerdlik, Swerdlik, & Kahn, 2003b). In such instances, clinicians should conduct a follow-up assessment.

Practitioners need to use the PPC judiciously, as it has some limitations. First, making inferences from classroom behaviors to underlying processes is challenging. It is difficult to ascertain which processes the six scales actually measure. For instance, the Organization and Attention scales could not be distinguished during confirmatory factor analysis. Also, the Social Perception and Visual-Motor Processing scales did not correlate with any of the PASS scales on the CAS, a test based on Luria's theory. Although internal consistency reliability coefficients are excellent, no test-retest data is reported in the manual. However, the main concern is that the PPC does not have any memory scales. Memory is not only the most important processing domain, but various aspects of memory are readily observable. The few items that address retrieval are embedded within the Auditory Processing and Visual Processing scales.

Nevertheless, standardized, norm-referenced data have more value than informal data. The PPC could play a role early in an evaluation, whereby it could reveal the extent and severity of potential processing problems. Certainly, a problematic Total Score would indicate the need for a direct measurement of the child's cognitive processes. The PPC can also provide useful guidance when developing classroom interventions. As long as practitioners do not use PPC results as the sole source of data, the PPC could be a welcome addition to a processing assessment toolkit.

## ⚌ Rapid Reference 8.11

### Other Processing Scales

| | |
|---|---|
| **Test:** Comprehensive Test of Phonological Processing (CTOPP)<br>**Authors:** Richard K. Wagner, Joseph K. Torgesen, and Carol A. Rashotte<br>**Publication date:** 1999<br>**Age range:** 5–24<br>**Publisher:** PRO-ED | **Main processes measured:** Long-term retrieval, phonological awareness<br>**Main processing factor scores (ages 7–24):** Phonological Awareness, Phonological Memory, Rapid Naming |
| **Test:** Comprehensive Trail-Making Test<br>**Author:** Cecil R. Reynolds<br>**Publication date:** 2002<br>**Age range:** 11–74<br>**Publisher:** M. D. Angus & Associates | **Main processes measured:** Attention, executive processing<br>**Main processing factor scores:** Composite Index |
| **Test:** Conners Continuous Performance Test-II<br>**Authors:** C. Keith Conners and MHS Staff<br>**Publication date:** 2000<br>**Age range:** 6 and older<br>**Publisher:** Multi-Health Systems, Inc. | **Main processes measured:** Attention<br>**Main processing factor scores:** None<br>**Comment:** Computerized assessment |
| **Test:** The Gordon Diagnostic System<br>**Author:** M. Gordon<br>**Publication date:** 1991<br>**Age range:** 4–16<br>**Publisher:** Clinical Diagnostic Systems | **Main processes measured:** Attention<br>**Main processing factor scores:** None<br>**Comment:** Computerized assessment |
| **Test:** Detroit Tests of Learning Aptitude, Fourth Edition (DTLA-4)<br>**Author:** Donald D. Hammill<br>**Publication date:** 1998<br>**Age range:** 6–0 to 17–11<br>**Publisher:** PRO-ED | **Main processes measured:** Attention, fluid reasoning, simultaneous processing, successive processing<br>**Main processing factor scores:** Attention-Enhanced, Attention-Reduced, Fluid Intelligence, Associative Level, Simultaneous Processing, Successive Processing |

**Test:** Kaplan Baycrest Neurocognitive Assessment (KBNA)
**Authors:** Larry Leach, Edith Kaplan, Dmytro Rewilak, Brian Richards, and Guy-B. Proulx
**Publication date:** 2000
**Age range:** 20–89
**Publisher:** The Psychological Corporation

**Main processes measured:** Attention, fluid reasoning, long-term retrieval, short-term memory, visual processing
**Main processing factor scores:** Attention/Concentration, Immediate Memory Recall, Delayed Memory Recall, Delayed Memory Recognition, Spatial Processing, Reasoning/Conceptual Shifting
**Comment:** 94 component process scores available

---

**Test:** MicroCog: Assessment of Cognitive Functioning
**Authors:** Douglas Powell, Edith Kaplan, Dean Whitla, Sandra Weintraub, Randolph Catlin, and Harris Funkenstein
**Publication date:** 1996
**Age range:** 18–89
**Publisher:** The Psychological Corporation

**Main processes measured:** Attention, fluid reasoning, processing speed, visual processing
**Main processing factor scores:** General Cognitive Functioning, General Cognitive Proficiency, Attention/Mental Control, Memory, Reasoning/Calculation, Spatial Processing, Reaction Time, Information Processing Speed, Information Processing Accuracy
**Comment:** Self-administered computer test

---

**Test:** Phonological Abilities Test (PAT)
**Authors:** Valerie Muter, Charles Hulme, and Margaret Snowling
**Publication date:** 1997
**Age range:** 5–7
**Publisher:** The Psychological Corporation, Europe

**Main processes measured:** Phonemic awareness
**Main processing factor scores:** Subtest scores only
**Comment:** Classified as a screening test; normed on British children

---

**Test:** Process Assessment of the Learner (PAL)
**Author:** Virginia Wise Berninger
**Publication date:** 2001
**Age range:** Grades K–6
**Publisher:** The Psychological Corporation

**Main processes measured:** Long-term retrieval, phonemic awareness
**Main processing factor scores:** General Cognitive Functioning, General Cognitive Proficiency

(continued)

**Test:** Ross Information Processing Assessment—Primary (RIPA)
**Author:** Deborah Ross-Swain
**Publication date:** 1999
**Age range:** 5–0 to 12–11
**Publisher:** PRO-ED

**Main processes measured:** Fluid reasoning, short-term memory, visual processing
**Main processing factor scores:** Memory, Thinking and Reasoning, Information Processing

**Test:** SCAN-A: A Test of Auditory Processing Disorders in Adolescents and Adults
**Author:** Robert W. Keith
**Publication date:** 1994
**Age range:** 12–50
**Publisher:** The Psychological Corporation

**Main processes measured:** Auditory processing
**Main processing factor scores:** Total Test

**Test:** SCAN-C: A Test of Auditory Processing Disorders in Children—Revised
**Author:** Robert W. Keith
**Publication date:** 1999
**Age range:** 5–0 to 11–11
**Publisher:** The Psychological Corporation

**Main processes measured:** Auditory processing
**Main processing factor scores:** Composite

**Test:** Test of Phonological Awareness (TOPA)
**Authors:** Joseph K. Torgesen and Brian R. Bryant
**Publication date:** 1994
**Age range:** 5–8
**Publisher:** PRO-ED

**Main processes measured:** Phonemic awareness
**Main processing factor scores:** Total Score only

**Test:** Woodcock Diagnostic Reading Battery (WDRB)
**Author:** Richard W. Woodcock
**Publication date:** 1997
**Age range:** 4–90+
**Publisher:** Riverside Publishing

**Main processes measured:** Phonemic awareness
**Main processing factor scores:** Phonological Awareness

**TEST YOURSELF**

1. **Measures of executive processing usually do not separate which other process from executive processing?**

   (a) Memory

   (b) Processing speed

   (c) Fluid reasoning

   (d) Auditory processing

2. **When interpreting neuropsychological tests, which level of interpretation is more acceptable than it is for cognitive tests?**

   (a) Global

   (b) Factor

   (c) Subtest

   (d) Item

3. **Which test should be used primarily for screening purposes?**

   (a) PPC

   (b) NEPSY

   (c) D-KEFS

   (d) CTOPP

4. **The NEPSY is unique in that it provides base rates for**

   (a) learning disabilities.

   (b) qualitative observations.

   (c) domain discrepancies.

   (d) subtest discrepancies.

5. **In the Lurian neuropsychological approach, what underlies an impairment in one or more functional domains?**

   (a) Brain pathology

   (b) A processing weakness

   (c) An executive deficit

   (d) A primary deficit

6. **Which test is actually a compendium of nine autonomous tests?**

   (a) NEPSY

   (b) PPC

   (c) D-KEFS

   (d) Wisconsin Card Sorting Test

7. **The domains measured by the NEPSY and D-KEFS are a close match with the processes in this book's Integrated Processing Model.** True or False?

*Answers:* 1. c; 2. c; 3. a; 4. b; 5. d; 6. c; 7. False

# Nine

## ILLUSTRATIVE CASE REPORTS

The purpose of this chapter is to illustrate the applications of this book's concepts and practices, in particular the interpretation of assessment results. The written interpretations will demonstrate how to describe the purpose of a processing assessment, explain the processing analysis procedure, integrate data from more than one test, integrate test data with other sources of data, connect the processes with specific learning concerns, discuss the extent of support for processing hypotheses, and make appropriate recommendations.

The two psychological reports in this chapter are based on actual data from the psychoeducational evaluations of two children. The first, Hannah, does not have an LD but does display a unique profile of processing strengths and weaknesses, as well as a clear deficit that accounts for most of the learning problems she experiences. The second, Gabriel, has average verbal abilities but suffers from Asperger's. His processing profile adds valuable information to understanding his strengths and weaknesses in learning and daily functioning.

### GUIDELINES FOR WRITING A PROCESSING REPORT

To effectively communicate processing assessment results in writing, it is necessary to expand the interpretation (discussion) section of the traditional psychological report. In general, more explanation is needed to help the reader, professional or otherwise, fully understand what was assessed, how it was assessed, how the results were analyzed, and the implications of the results. The additional components and altered structure are similar to the oral interpretation steps discussed in Chapter 4. Illustrations of comprehensive and detailed written reports can be found later in this chapter. For an in-depth discussion of psychological report writing, the reader is referred to Lichtenberger et al. (2004). The suggested modifications and areas of emphasis for a report on a processing assessment are described in the following section and summarized in Rapid Reference 9.1.

## ≡Rapid Reference 9.1

### Guidelines for Writing a Processing Report

1. If IQ testing or cognitive abilities testing was conducted, interpret the global score first.
2. Identify the tests and factors that were used to assess processing.
3. Explain how the processing results were analyzed.
4. Organize the remainder of the interpretation section by processing factors.
5. Distinguish between normative and ipsative.
6. Define terms and use them consistently.
7. Integrate data from other sources or methods.
8. At the end of the processing section, summarize and draw conclusions.

1. *If IQ testing or cognitive abilities testing was conducted, interpret the global score first.* If intellectual or cognitive abilities testing was conducted, begin the interpretation section by reporting information about the global score. Proceed with a discussion of factors only if the instrument contains nonprocessing factors, such as crystallized intelligence; otherwise, discuss the factors under the cognitive processing section that follows. Traditionally, IQ testing has provided an estimate of general intellectual ability that is used to predict academic learning. Because the ability-achievement discrepancy approach is no longer required, the clinician should clarify the purpose of the IQ testing and the use of the full-scale or composite score. When assessing processing, obtaining an IQ score is unnecessary. However, composite scores based only on processing factors, such as the CAS Full Scale or the KABC-II MPI, may be interpreted as representing the examinee's overall level of processing. Also interpret the global score first if an IQ or full composite was obtained during a cross-battery processing assessment.
2. *Identify the tests and factors that were used to assess processing.* The essence of this paragraph is an explanation of what the processing assessment entailed. The purpose of processing assessment, in general, should be stated, followed by a list of the processes selected for assessment. The clinician should then identify the tests and specific factors that were administered, especially when a cross-battery evaluation was completed.

3. *Explain how the processing results were analyzed.* Because of the unique approach to analyzing processing assessment results, it is important that the report writer describes the steps involved, incorporating the guidelines from the Processing Analysis Worksheet (Appendix C). For example, explain that only processing factors were included in the analysis and how clinical factor scores were computed from subtest scores. Most importantly, explain the basis of the processing mean and how it was used in the ipsative analysis.

4. *Organize the remainder of the interpretation section by processing factors.* Traditionally, interpretation of assessment results is organized by method or test. The reader will have a difficult time making sense of the results if this approach is used in a processing assessment. Rather, the interpretation should be organized by the processes assessed; for example, subheadings might be Visual Processing, Working Memory, and so on. Begin each subsection by defining the process involved and identifying the test factor(s) used to measure it. After reporting the traditional data, for example, standard scores and confidence intervals, indicate the extent of support or nonsupport for the hypothesis related to that process and state the implications for learning. An alternative that essentially follows the same organizational structure is to use the actual processing hypotheses as subheadings. For example, the subheading might be Hypothesis 1: The learner has a deficit in phonemic awareness.

5. *Distinguish between normative and ipsative.* As strengths and weaknesses are identified, it is essential that the writer clearly distinguish between normative findings and ipsative findings. For each factor analyzed, the clinician should report both normative and ipsative results.

6. *Define terms and use them consistently.* In particular, differentiate between *weakness* and *deficit* in terms of the degree of severity and the normative or ipsative involvement. The writer should also use frequent terms, such as *process, factor,* and *significant* in a consistent fashion.

7. *Integrate data from other sources or methods.* This step can be challenging for the writer, but it is crucial for the reader's comprehension of the findings. Within the subsections on each process, the writer should incorporate all relevant data, even data that are incompatible with the test scores. For example, after the child's phonemic awareness test scores are interpreted, the writer might report observations of the child reading and information about phonemic awareness obtained from inter-

views and a records review. The writer should then explicitly state the extent to which related data corroborate the tests results and then weigh the evidence for and against the processing hypothesis involved.

8. *At the end of the processing section, summarize and draw conclusions.* A summary at the end of the processing interpretation section provides an opportunity to pull the results together and reiterate the strengths or weaknesses and deficits or assets, as well as the extent of support for a priori hypotheses and any a posteriori hypotheses that may have emerged from the findings. Keep in mind that conclusions drawn about processing should be stated tentatively.

## PSYCHOLOGICAL REPORT FOR HANNAH

*Name:* Hannah
*Grade:* 5
*Age:* 11

### Reason for Referral

The purpose of this evaluation was to determine Hannah's learning aptitudes, her cognitive processing strengths and weaknesses, and her academic skills in order to design and implement an individualized intervention that would be most effective for her. The evaluation was initiated when Hannah's parents enrolled her at a private tutoring center. Hannah was struggling academically, especially in mathematics, science, and social studies. Hannah's mother reported that Hannah was an excellent reader, but her reading comprehension, especially inferential comprehension, was low. Additional concerns reported by Hannah's mother were (1) difficulty retaining new information, for example, not remembering information unless it is frequently reviewed; (2) doing poorly on classroom examinations; (3) difficulty learning new concepts; and (4) difficulty completing homework independently. Hannah's two teachers (for academic subjects) concurred with these concerns. Given these referral concerns, the evaluation team believed that some cognitive processing weaknesses or deficits might be impairing Hannah's learning (see Hannah's completed Processing Assessment Organizer in Rapid Reference 4.10). Thus, the evaluation team hypothesized that Hannah might have a weakness or deficit in one or more of the following cognitive processes: fluid reasoning, long-term retrieval, planning, processing speed, visual processing, short-term memory, and working memory.

**Background Information**

Because Hannah's parents adopted her when she was three months old, prenatal, perinatal, and postnatal information about Hannah is limited. It is known that Hannah's birth mother consumed alcohol and cocaine during her pregnancy. However, it was a full-term pregnancy, and Hannah appeared healthy at birth, with Apgar scores of 9 and 10. The doctors tested the 6 pound, 2 ounce infant for traces of alcohol and cocaine but found none. Hannah's adoptive mother reported that Hannah was an easygoing baby, with no health problems during infancy.

During early childhood Hannah's developmental progression was normal, with the exception of early speech and language development. Hannah toilet trained early and easily and her sensory-motor development seemed fine. She walked at 15 to 17 months of age. Hannah did not babble much as a baby and did not produce her first words until 16 months of age. Her parents became concerned and enrolled her in speech therapy, but by 2 years of age it was determined that her speech and language development was normal, and speech therapy was discontinued. Hannah's parents also observed long-term memory storage and retrieval problems during early childhood; for example, Hannah had difficulty learning colors and couldn't recite common childhood stories despite repeated readings. There were no other concerns during early childhood; for example, Hannah did not have any health problems.

Concerns about Hannah's learning emerged during kindergarten. Due to these concerns and Hannah's summer birthday, Hannah's mother decided to retain Hannah in kindergarten. Despite the additional year in kindergarten, Hannah still struggled with learning in first grade, although her basic reading skills developed normally. General academic learning concerns have persisted throughout Hannah's schooling. She has always attended a Catholic school and has been receiving tutoring since second grade. This is the first time she has received a formal psychoeducational evaluation.

Hannah lives in a two-parent home with a stay-at-home mother. Two older male siblings no longer reside at home. Hannah's mother has been very involved in Hannah's education; it is evident that she wants the best for Hannah. At home, Hannah's mother reads with Hannah and applies effective instructional techniques, such as helping Hannah review basic math facts and recently learned concepts. To enhance Hannah's reading comprehension, she elaborates on the reading material so that Hannah can understand the main ideas and connections between related concepts.

In terms of strengths, Hannah has good social skills, she has a good attitude toward school, and she enjoys athletics, such as basketball. She enjoys video games and playing with dolls. She also enjoys music and seems to learn well from listening. At home, she is very cooperative and responds well to structure and routine.

## Behavioral Observations

There was no opportunity to observe Hannah in her school environment, but anecdotal information from Hannah's teachers indicates that Hannah is well behaved at school and that she makes an effort to learn. For example, she follows directions, is cooperative, attends to instruction, and works on assignments independently.

During several individual testing situations Hannah engaged in appropriate test-taking behaviors and strategies. She followed directions, was cooperative, was persistent, and attended to the task hand. Her verbal expression was adequate, and she elaborated when requested to do so. Hannah seemed to have a realistic self-appraisal of her abilities and skills; for example, recognizing items as easy or difficult. Although she did not display much confidence in her performance, she was not afraid to guess when the items were difficult for her and she did self-correct when she detected errors. She also seemed to work well under time constraints. Throughout testing, Hannah seemed to be making an effort to do her best. Thus, her current test results are considered to be reliable and valid.

## Evaluation Procedures

Parent Interview
Teacher Interview
Woodcock-Johnson III Tests of Cognitive Abilities (WJ III COG)
Woodcock-Johnson III Tests of Achievement (WJ III Achievement)
Wechsler Intelligence Scale for Children-Fourth Edition Integrated
   (WISC-IV Integrated)

## Tests Results and Interpretation

### *Intellectual Functioning*
Because of the possibility that a learning disability is impairing Hannah's acquisition of academic skills, it was necessary to obtain an estimate of her general intellectual ability level. Her intellectual ability score (IQ) could then be used to determine whether her specific academic skills are at the level predicted by her IQ. From her WISC-IV Integrated results, Hannah's general intellectual ability level

**Table 9.1  WISC-IV Integrated Results**

| Index | Standard Score | Percentile | 95% Confidence Interval | Descriptive Category |
|---|---|---|---|---|
| Verbal Comprehension | 95 | 37 | 89–102 | Average |
| Perceptual Reasoning | 77 | 6 | 71–86 | Low Average |
| Working Memory | 94 | 34 | 87–102 | Average |
| Processing Speed | 80 | 9 | 73–91 | Low Average |
| Full Scale | 83 | 13 | 79–88 | Low Average |

appears to be in the low average range. She obtained a WISC-IV Full Scale IQ of 83, which is at the 13th percentile rank. The 95 percent confidence interval for a score of 83 is 79 to 88, meaning that there is a 95 percent chance that Hannah's true IQ is somewhere within the range of 79 to 88. If this intellectual ability estimate is accurate, it indicates that, in general, academic learning is going to be difficult for Hannah.

In addition to measuring general intellectual ability and various cognitive processes, the WISC-IV Integrated groups an individual's abilities into four areas: the Verbal Comprehension Index (VCI), which measures verbal ability and crystallized intelligence; the Perceptual Reasoning Index (PRI), which measures fluid reasoning and visual processing; the Working Memory Index (WMI), which measures manipulation of information in short-term memory; and the Processing Speed Index (PSI), which measures the ability to process visually perceived nonverbal information quickly. Hannah displays considerable variability across these four indexes (see Table 9.1); for example, Hannah's VCI score of 95 is significantly higher than her PRI score of 77. Because of this variability, Hannah's Full Scale IQ may not accurately summarize or represent her overall intellectual or cognitive potential. In fact, Hannah's four index scores cluster into two pairs—the VCI (95) and WMI (94) pair represents a verbal/auditory domain, and the PRI (77) and PSI (80) pair represents a nonverbal/visual domain. This pattern indicates that Hannah's general verbal/auditory functioning is in the average range and significantly higher than her nonverbal/visual functioning, which is in the low average range.

### Cognitive Processing Assessment
An assessment of Hannah's cognitive processing capabilities was conducted in an effort to better understand Hannah's learning strengths and weaknesses. While

the WISC-IV Integrated measures some core processes, a more comprehensive processing assessment was necessary in order to test the processing hypotheses. Consequently, the processing assessment involved the administration of the WISC-IV Integrated and a partial administration of the WJ III COG (see Table 9.2). In addition to the standard WISC-IV battery, some additional working memory and short-term memory processing subtests from the WISC-IV Integrated were also administered to Hannah. The processing factors from these two batteries, including some *clinical* factors, were then combined in a processing analysis. The mean of Hannah's processing factor scores was computed, and then each of her processing scores was compared to that mean. Using a criterion of 15 points, processing scores that were significantly lower than her processing mean were classified as individual weaknesses, and scores that were significantly higher were considered individual strengths (see Table 9.3). Processes that were both normative and individual weaknesses were considered deficits; processes that were both normative and individual strengths were considered assets.

### Table 9.2  WJ III COG Results

| Cluster | Standard Score | Percentile | 95% Confidence Interval | Descriptive Category |
|---|---|---|---|---|
| Long-Term Retrieval | 76 | 5 | 67–85 | Low |
| Visual-Spatial Thinking | 96 | 41 | 88–105 | Average |
| Auditory Processing | 117 | 87 | 106–128 | High Average |
| Short-Term Memory | 101 | 54 | 91–112 | Average |

### Table 9.3  Processing Analysis Results

| Name of Process | Processing Factor Score | Processing Factor Mean | Difference from Mean | Normative S or W | Ipsative S or W | Deficit or Asset |
|---|---|---|---|---|---|---|
| Auditory Processing | 117 | 92 | +25 | S | S | A |
| Fluid Reasoning | 88 | 92 | −4 | W | — | — |
| Long-Term Retrieval | 76 | 92 | −16 | W | W | D |
| Processing Speed | 80 | 92 | −12 | W | — | — |
| Short-Term Memory | 101 | 92 | +9 | A | — | — |
| Visual Processing | 88 | 92 | −4 | W | — | — |
| Working Memory | 94 | 92 | +2 | A | — | — |

Seven key processes were formally assessed: Auditory Processing, Fluid Reasoning, Long-Term Retrieval, Processing Speed, Short-Term Memory, Visual Processing, and Working Memory. For some of these processes, WJ III COG cluster scores or WISC-IV Integrated index scores were used. For other processes, clinical scores were derived by averaging subtest scores (see the interpretation for each process). The mean of Hannah's processing factor scores is 92. Because of the wide range among Hannah's processing scores (76–117), this processing mean may not represent her overall cognitive processing level any better than her Full Scale IQ. Nevertheless, her processing factor mean of 92 is in the average range while her Full Scale IQ is in the low average range.

*Auditory Processing.*   Auditory processing is the ability to perceive, analyze, synthesize, and discriminate auditory stimuli, including the ability to process and discriminate speech sounds. For example, auditory processing includes phonemic awareness and processing. From the score Hannah obtained on the WJ III COG Auditory Processing factor, it appears that Hannah's auditory processing is in the high average range; her Auditory Processing standard score is 117, which is at the 87th percentile. Based on the 95 percent confidence interval, there is a 95 percent chance that Hannah's true Auditory Processing score is within the range of 106 to 128. Relative to her personal mean of 92, her Auditory Processing score is 25 points higher. Thus, Auditory Processing is an individual strength for Hannah. Because it is both an individual strength and a strength compared to her peers, Auditory Processing is also an asset for Hannah.

Other test scores and assessment data are consistent with this finding, beginning with the verbal/auditory strength exhibited in her WISC-IV Index profile. Hannah's mother reported that Hannah seems to learn best by listening, another general indication of a strength in auditory processing. Also, Hannah's enjoyment of music would be consistent with an auditory processing strength. Auditory processing is related to spelling and reading decoding. Thus, it is not surprising that Hannah obtained a WJ III Achievement Spelling score of 116 and a Word Attack (a measure of phonetic decoding) score of 101.

*Fluid Reasoning.*   Fluid reasoning is the ability to reason, form concepts, and solve problems, particularly when confronted with a novel task or unfamiliar situation. For example, fluid reasoning would be required when solving a math story problem. An estimate of Hannah's fluid reasoning was obtained by averaging her scores from the WISC-IV Integrated subtests of Picture Concepts (scaled score = 9) and Matrix Reasoning (scaled score = 6). Transformed to standard scores with a mean of 100 and standard deviation of 15, her rounded clinical fluid reasoning score is 88, a score that is in the low average range. Thus, Hannah has a normative (relative to peers) weakness in fluid reasoning but not an individual weakness.

Hannah's weakness in fluid reasoning has been observed in both the home and school environments. She has difficulty understanding relationships between new concepts and making connections between new material and acquired knowledge. Hannah's teachers, parents, and tutor often explain relationships and connections for her. Hannah's mother has also stated that Hannah's does not cope well, or problem solve, when there are novel situations in everyday life. Fluid reasoning is a process that is related to math reasoning and is also important for inferential reading comprehension. Hannah's Math Reasoning score of 88 and her Reading Comprehension score of 92 are consistent with her Fluid Reasoning score. In conclusion, there is support for the hypothesis that Hannah has a normative processing weakness in fluid reasoning.

*Long-Term Retrieval.*   Long-term storage and retrieval is the ability to store information in long-term memory and fluently retrieve it later. From a processing perspective, storage and retrieval is not the acquired knowledge that is stored in long-term memory but, rather, the *process* of storing or encoding and retrieving information. An example of long-term retrieval is being able to retrieve basic facts when requested. Hannah's WJ III COG Long-Term Retrieval score of 76, which is at the 5th percentile, is in the low range, clearly a normative weakness. There is a 95 percent chance that Hannah's true Long-Term Retrieval score is within the range of 67 to 85. Relative to her personal mean of 92, her Long-Term retrieval score is 16 points lower, a significant individual weakness. Because it is both an individual weakness and normative weakness, long-term retrieval is a deficit for Hannah.

A deficit in long-term retrieval may impair most areas of academic learning, as well as some aspects of daily functioning. The best evidence of Hannah's long-term retrieval deficit is the difficulty she has retaining and retrieving information over time. For example, she does not perform well on classroom examinations despite preparation, and she will forget basic math facts if they are not reviewed on a regular basis. It is quite apparent that Hannah has a deficit in long-term retrieval. Extensive tutoring over several years, as well as parent-guided study at home, may have helped Hannah compensate somewhat for her deficit in long-term retrieval.

*Short-Term Memory.*   Short-term memory is the ability to apprehend and hold information in immediate awareness and then use it within a few seconds, for ex-

**Table 9.4  WISC-IV Integrated Clinical Factors**

| Clinical Factor | Mean Standard Score | Descriptive Category |
|---|---|---|
| Short-Term Memory | 89 | Low Average |
| Visual Short-Term Memory | 85 | Low Average |
| Auditory Short-Term Memory | 90 | Average |
| Working Memory | 100 | Average |
| Visual Working Memory | 93 | Average |
| Auditory Working Memory | 98 | Average |

ample, immediately repeating a list of spoken words. Hannah's short-term memory was assessed with both the WJ III COG and the WISC-IV Integrated. Her WJ III COG cluster score of 101 is at the 54th percentile rank and in the mid-average range. (This score was used in the processing analysis.) There is 95 percent chance that Hannah's true Short-Term Memory score is within the range of 91 to 112. Because the WJ III COG's Short-Term Memory subtest tasks are both auditory, additional short-term memory assessment was conducted with the processing component of the WISC-IV Integrated. From the Integrated, separate visual and auditory short-term memory clinical scores were computed (see Appendix F for the subtests and procedures involved and a completed example in Chapter 7). The estimates of Hannah's visual short-term memory (a score of 85) and her auditory short-term memory (a score of 90) do not reveal any significant differences (see Table 9.4). However, it is noteworthy that the clinically derived overall estimate of short-term memory (a score of 89) from the WISC-IV Integrated is noticeably lower than the norm-referenced score of 101 from the WJ III COG.

Whenever there is a deficit in long-term retrieval, short-term memory and working memory must also be examined because these processes encode information into long-term memory. Given Hannah's average performance in short-term memory and working memory, her memory problem seems to lie not with encoding but rather with retrieval. For example, when her Short-Term Memory score (101) is compared to her Long-Term Retrieval score (76), the 25 point difference is very significant and rarely occurs. Those who teach Hannah must be aware of this discrepancy. Otherwise, Hannah's adequate immediate recall may give the impression that she has no memory or learning problems.

*Working Memory.*    Working memory and short-term memory are interrelated. The main distinction between the two is that working memory is conscious processing and involves manipulation of information, whereas short-term memory is more static in nature. For example, working memory is involved when an individual is organizing information. Hannah's WISC-IV Working Memory Index of 94 was used in the processing analysis. A standard score of 94 is at the 34th percentile rank and in the average range. There is 95 percent chance that Hannah's true Working Memory Index score is within the range of 87 to 102. Because the WISC-IV Integrated's Working Memory subtest tasks are both auditory, additional working memory assessment was conducted with the processing component of the Integrated. From the Integrated, separate visual and auditory working memory clinical scores were computed (see Appendix F for the subtests and procedures involved and a completed example in Chapter 7). The estimates of Hannah's visual working memory (a score of 93) and her auditory working memory (a score of 98) do not reveal any differences (see Table 9.4). However, her visual working memory clinical factor is not unitary because there is more than a 1.5 standard deviation between the Spatial Span Backward scaled score of 11 and the Arithmetic Process Approach Part A scaled score of 6. The difference is most likely due to Arithmetic subtests primarily measuring fluid reasoning instead of working memory. The clinically derived overall estimate of working memory (a score of 100) is consistent with the norm-referenced score of 94.

It was initially hypothesized that working memory would be a weakness or deficit for Hannah. However, it is neither a normative or individual weakness. Similar to short-term memory, there is no anecdotal data that points toward a potential weakness in this area of processing. For example, during testing Hannah did not request any repetition of directions or items, and she seemed comfortable manipulating information in her head, such as mental arithmetic.

*Processing Speed.* Processing speed is the ability to perform simple cognitive tasks quickly. As measured by the WISC-IV Integrated, processing speed is the ability to process visually perceived nonverbal information quickly. Hannah's WISC-IV Processing Speed standard score is 80, which corresponds to a percentile rank of 9 and a 95 percent confidence interval of 73 to 91. Her low average range score denotes a normative weakness and is nearly an individual weakness as well, being 12 points lower than her processing mean.

Thus, there appears to be some support for the hypothesis that Hannah has a deficit in processing speed. Informal data support the test results in that Hannah is often slow to complete tasks, such as tests and homework. It is possible that slow processing speed could be impairing Hannah's learning and academic performance to some extent, as it plays a role in all types of learning and performance. However, there is one indication that Hannah's processing speed is not impacting her acquisition of basic skills. Namely, her academic fluency scores in reading, math, and writing (on the WJ III Achievement) are all in the average or high average range. If Hannah's general processing speed is deficient, it may also exacerbate her long-term retrieval deficit and her fluid reasoning weakness. As mentioned earlier, her low Processing Speed score is consistent with her low Perceptual Reasoning score, both indexes being part of a broader visual/nonverbal domain.

*Visual Processing.* Visual processing is the ability to perceive, analyze, synthesize, and think with visual patterns, including the ability to store and recall visual representations. Mental manipulation and transformation of visual patterns and stimuli are usually involved, for example, constructing a design from a picture of the design. Hannah's visual processing was assessed with both the WJ III COG and the WISC-IV Integrated. When Hannah obtained a Block Design scaled score of 4 on the Integrated, it was decided to investigate further by administering the Visual-Spatial Thinking cluster form the WJ III COG. In contrast, her two visual processing subtest scores on the WJ III COG were substantially higher, producing a cluster score of 96. (Block Design utilizes manipulatives and has time constraints, whereas the WJ III COG tests do not.) The lack of unitary scores indicates that different processes within visual processing were measured and that Hannah has some processing differences within visual processing. It was decided that combining the subtest scores from the two batteries would best represent her overall visual processing level. The resulting cross-battery score is 88, indicating that Hannah has a normative weakness in at least some aspects of visual processing.

It was initially hypothesized that Hannah would have a weakness or deficit in visual processing. There is no anecdotal data to support or disconfirm this hypothesis, other than a parent report that Hannah seems to be more of an auditory than a visual learner. The processing assessment scores are inconsistent but favor a rejection of a weakness hypothesis. Furthermore, Hannah's Math Calculation Skills score is a strong average score at 109. (Math skills are known to be correlated with visual processing.)

*Planning.* It was also hypothesized that planning would be a weaknesses or deficit for Hannah. The evaluation team decided that extensive formal testing of planning was unnecessary. Hannah's mother, teachers, and tutor all reported that Hannah has demonstrated that she has adequate planning, especially when she is motivated. A subtest score from the WISC-IV Integrated is consistent with these reports. Hannah obtained an average scaled score of 9 on Elithorn Mazes, a subtest that is primarily a measure of planning.

## Summary of Processing

Table 9.3 provides a summary of Hannah's processing strengths and weaknesses. Hannah displays an asset in auditory processing. Her short-term memory and working memory appear normal, in both visual and auditory aspects; thus, weakness or deficit hypotheses for these two processes are rejected. She has normative weaknesses in fluid reasoning, long-term retrieval, processing speed, and possibly visual processing. The only clear deficit and the main cause for concern is Hannah's long-term retrieval deficit. Even more unique is Hannah's low long-term retrieval level compared to her average short-term and working memory.

## Summary of Achievement Assessment

Hannah was administered the WJ III Achievement in order to evaluate her academic skills acquisition. With the exception of math reasoning, which is in the low average range, her broad skills in reading, math, and written language are in the average range (see Table 9.5). None of Hannah's academic skills, even the more specific skills, are significantly lower than her Full Scale IQ or her processing factor mean. In fact, her scores in some areas are actually higher than would be predicted, from either her IQ score or from her processing levels. Her only cluster scores in the low average range, and, thus, normative weaknesses, are Math Reasoning and Academic Applications. These two weaknesses would be consistent with her normative processing weakness in fluid reasoning. Teacher and parent

## Table 9.5  WJ III Achievement Results

| Skill | Standard Score | Percentile | 95% Confidence Interval | Category |
|---|---|---|---|---|
| Basic Reading Skills | 100 | 51 | 95–106 | Average |
| Reading Comprehension | 92 | 20 | 87–98 | Average |
| Math Calculation Skills | 109 | 73 | 101–117 | Average |
| Math Reasoning | 88 | 22 | 82–94 | Low Average |
| Written Expression | 108 | 70 | 98–119 | Average |
| Academic Skills | 109 | 72 | 102–116 | Average |
| Academic Fluency | 111 | 76 | 107–115 | High Average |
| Academic Applications | 89 | 23 | 83–94 | Low Average |

reports of Hannah's academic strengths and weaknesses are concordant with the WJ III Achievement scores that she obtained.

## Diagnostic Impressions

Hannah's achievement test scores in reading, mathematics, and written language are all commensurate, if not higher, than her IQ. Thus, the ability-achievement discrepancy diagnostic approach reveals that she does not have a learning disability. Hannah's relatively strong achievement scores also indicate that she is responsive to the interventions that she has received. In conclusion, whereas Hannah does not appear to have a specific learning disability, she does have a processing deficit in long-term retrieval and normative weaknesses in related processes. Her deficit and weaknesses can impair her academic learning if appropriate strategies and accommodations are not utilized.

## Recommendations

1. Given her deficit in long-term retrieval, those who study with Hannah should provide cues that facilitate retrieval. For example, reminding Hannah of the category of the item in question may be helpful. Because Hannah's recall is likely to be stronger than her retrieval, multiple-choice tests may be an appropriate accommodation for her.

2. Given her deficit in long-term retrieval, helping Hannah encode new information in an organized fashion is likely to make retrieval easier later on. For example, making explicit connections, or associations, between new information and related acquired knowledge enhances organization in semantic memory and thereby increases the probability of retrieval on demand. Hannah's adequate working memory should allow her to independently elaborate on and link new information with existing information. Teaching her strategies for doing this independently is important.

3. Given her deficit in long-term retrieval, Hannah will require repeated opportunities to learn and practice new information and procedures. In addition to repetition, she will need frequent reviews, on a daily, weekly, and monthly basis, even reviews of information or skills that she appears to have mastered.

4. Given her normative weakness in fluid reasoning, those who teach Hannah should model and practice problem-solving strategies so that Hannah can automatize commonly used procedures, such as those

used to solve math story problems. Modeling the skills will also enhance Hannah's retention of the steps in the procedures.

5. Given her normative weakness in processing speed, Hannah may need additional testing time in order to fully demonstrate the knowledge and skills she possesses.

## PSYCHOLOGICAL REPORT FOR GABRIEL

*Name:* Gabriel
*Grade:* 5
*Age:* 11

### Reason for Referral

The purpose of this reevaluation was to assess Gabriel's learning aptitudes, his cognitive processing strengths and weaknesses, his academic skills, his adaptive behaviors, and his behavioral and emotional status. The evaluation results will be used to design individualized instruction and behavioral interventions that will address Gabriel's needs. Gabriel, who has autism, remains fully integrated in a regular education classroom at a Catholic elementary school. As Gabriel approaches entry to middle school, his parents, teachers, and tutors are trying to teach Gabriel the skills he will need in order to remain fully integrated. The primary referral concerns relate to characteristics usually associated with autism — communication, social skills, attention, and independent functioning. The evaluation team hypothesized that Gabriel has weaknesses or deficits in all of these areas. Behavioral concerns that interfere with Gabriel's learning include difficulties with staying on task, following directions, organization, distractibility, and completing homework. These behavioral concerns led the evaluation team to hypothesize that Gabriel has processing weaknesses or deficits in attention, auditory processing, short-term memory, long-term retrieval, planning, and successive processing. Current academic concerns center on difficulties in math, reading comprehension, science, and social studies. In mathematics, Gabriel displays no interest, quickly and carelessly completing the assigned work. Tutors also report that he knows the basic math facts but often applies incorrect math calculation procedures. In reading, Gabriel has good decoding skills but lacks comprehension, especially inferential comprehension. In regard to the math and reading problems, the evaluation team hypothesized that Gabriel has a weakness or deficit in fluid reasoning, planning, processing speed, and simultaneous processing. Given a parental report that Gabriel was primarily a visual learner, it was also hypothesized that Gabriel has a strength in visual processing. The focus of the current evaluation was to gain a better understanding of Gabriel's processing strengths and weaknesses so that individualized and effective interventions could be designed for him.

## Background Information

After he was diagnosed with autism at the age of 3, Gabriel received an intensive in-home autism treatment program until the age of 5. During early childhood, he also received speech and language therapy and occupational therapy. At the age of 6, Gabriel obtained a Full Scale IQ in the mid-70s. The psychologist who completed the intellectual evaluation predicted that Gabriel would not be able to succeed in school. However, since entering school Gabriel has been maintained in regular education classrooms, received mostly passing grades, and has acquired average academic skills in many areas. He has never been enrolled in special education and has not been formally reevaluated until now.

All of Gabriel's family members, including grandparents, are involved in his education and care. Gabriel is a member of a two-parent family. He has two female siblings, one older and one younger. Although Gabriel is fairly independent and has well-developed self-care skills, such as dressing and eating, he does require constant supervision. At home, he enjoys drawing, watching TV (especially cartoons), riding his scooter, swimming, and playing computer games. Although Gabriel seldom initiates communication outside of the home, he is quite talkative in the home environment. Other than dealing with some phobias, his behavior in the home environment is not a concern; he is generally cooperative and obedient.

At school, Gabriel's behavior is usually appropriate, and he is generally engaged in learning. He is cooperative and verbally responds during routine communication or when asked a question in class. He is also influenced by reinforcement and tries to please his teachers and peers. Gabriel's peers are accepting of him and assist him during classroom activities and independent study time. Although Gabriel communicates with peers and reports that he has friends, on the playground he withdraws into his own world. Gabriel's classroom teachers also provide him with individual assistance, such as helping him with organization. Each day after school Gabriel receives assistance with his homework from tutors or family members. Gabriel does not have any health concerns. However, he is currently taking Zoloft and Concerta because of attentional concerns in the school environment.

## Behavioral Observations

Gabriel was observed during several after-school tutoring sessions. In general, he was cooperative and followed directions but seldom initiated any conversation or worked independently. At times Gabriel struggled to remain focused; he would be distracted by something in the environment or would talk to himself. Even when he appeared to be paying attention, he frequently asked the tutor to repeat what was just said. At other times, he would become involved in an activity and attend well to the task at hand, even expressing satisfaction when he successfully completed a problem or answered a question. When working on mathematics, he had difficulty keeping the columns lined up, and this often caused a computation error. From these observations, there were signs that Gabriel has processing problems with attention, short-term memory, working memory, and visual processing.

Although Gabriel seemed mostly indifferent to the testing activities, he was compliant throughout several individual testing situations. He followed directions and responded to all of the items presented to him. His verbal responses were adequate and he elaborated when requested to do so. Gabriel's persistence was also adequate; for example, he worked for up to an hour at a time before requesting a termination of testing. However, his attention span was variable; it seemed to be related to how engaging he found the task. Except for the influence of attention span on some tasks, Gabriel's test results should provide reliable and valid estimates of his current cognitive processing levels, as well as his functioning in academics and adaptive behavior.

## Evaluation Procedures

Parent Interviews
Teacher Interviews
Behavior Assessment System for Children (BASC-2)
Woodcock-Johnson III Tests of Cognitive Abilities (WJ III COG)
Woodcock-Johnson III Tests of Achievement (WJ III Achievement)
Kaufman Assessment Battery for Children, second edition (KABC-II)

## Test Results and Interpretation

### Intellectual Functioning

Because of concerns about Gabriel's intellectual potential, two estimates of his current intellectual functioning were gathered, one with the WJ III COG and the other with the KABC-II. With a WJ III COG GIA of 87 and a KABC-II FCI of

93, it can be confidently stated that Gabriel's level of general intelligence is some-where in the low average to average range (see Tables 9.6 and 9.7). The difference between the two scores is most likely due to measurement error and the different composition of cognitive processes the two scales measure. The current estimates are significantly higher than the mid-70's Full Scale IQ he obtained five years ago, indicating that he does have the general intellectual potential to succeed in school.

**Table 9.6  KABC-II Results**

| Index | Standard Score | Percentile | 95% Confidence Interval | Descriptive Category |
|---|---|---|---|---|
| Sequential | 83 | 13 | 74–94 | Low Average |
| Simultaneous | 88 | 21 | 79–99 | Average |
| Learning | 103 | 58 | 95–111 | Average |
| Planning | 102 | 55 | 91–113 | Average |
| Knowledge | 100 | 50 | 92–108 | Average |
| Fluid Crystallized Index (FCI) | 93 | 32 | 87–99 | Average |
| Mental Processing Index (MPI) | 91 | 27 | 85–97 | Average |

**Table 9.7  WJ III COG Results**

| Cluster | Standard Score | Percentile | 95% Confidence Interval | Descriptive Category |
|---|---|---|---|---|
| General Intellectual Ability (GIA) | 87 | 19 | 83–91 | Low Average |
| Verbal Ability | 108 | 69 | 99–117 | Average |
| Thinking Ability | 85 | 16 | 80–90 | Low Average |
| Cognitive Efficiency | 77 | 6 | 71–84 | Low |
| Comp.-Knowledge | 108 | 69 | 99–117 | Average |
| Long-Term Retrieval | 66 | 1 | 58–75 | Very Low |
| Visual-Spatial Thinking | 89 | 24 | 81–97 | Low Average |
| Auditory Processing | 97 | 42 | 86–108 | Average |
| Fluid Reasoning | 88 | 22 | 82–94 | Low Average |
| Processing Speed | 80 | 9 | 74–86 | Low Average |
| Short-Term Memory | 81 | 11 | 72–90 | Low Average |

*Cognitive Processing Assessment*

A comprehensive assessment of Gabriel's cognitive processes was conducted in order to better understand Gabriel's processing strengths and weaknesses and to address the hypotheses regarding the learning challenges that he is experiencing. The cognitive processing assessment involved the administration of the WJ III COG (see Table 9.7) and the KABC-II (see Table 9.6). The processing factors from these two batteries, six from the WJ III COG and three from the KABC-II, were then combined in a processing analysis (see Table 9.8) in which the mean of Gabriel's nine processing factor scores was computed and then each of his processing scores was compared to that mean. Using a criterion of 15 points, processing scores that were significantly lower than his processing mean were classified as individual weaknesses and scores that were significantly higher were considered individual strengths (see Table 9.8). Processes that were both normative and individual weaknesses were considered deficits; processes that were considered both normative and individual strengths were considered assets.

Both the WJ III COG and the KABC-II are primarily measures of cognitive processing. The WJ III COG is built on CHC theory while the KABC-II is bitheoretical, allowing interpretation from either a CHC or a Luria perspective. Given the goal of this processing assessment, the KABC-II factors are interpreted from the Luria model, with the crystallized intelligence factor (Knowledge) excluded from the MPI computation. The KABC-II Knowledge and Learning scores are also excluded from the integrated processing analysis in Table 9.8. The Comprehension-Knowledge cluster from the WJ III COG is also ex-

**Table 9.8 Processing Analysis Results**

| Name of Process | Processing Factor Score | Processing Factor Mean | Difference from Mean | Normative S or W | Ipsative S or W | Deficit or Asset |
|---|---|---|---|---|---|---|
| Auditory Processing | 97 | 86 | +11 | — | — | — |
| Fluid Reasoning | 88 | 86 | +2 | W | — | — |
| Long-Term Retrieval | 66 | 86 | −20 | W | W | D |
| Planning | 102 | 86 | +16 | — | S | — |
| Processing Speed | 80 | 86 | −6 | W | — | — |
| Short-Term Memory | 81 | 86 | −5 | W | — | — |
| Simultaneous Processing | 88 | 86 | +2 | W | — | — |
| Successive Processing | 83 | 86 | −3 | W | — | — |
| Visual Processing | 89 | 86 | +3 | W | — | — |

cluded from the processing analysis. Because there are more factors involved, the processing factor mean of 86, as well as the GIA of 87, may be more accurate estimates of Gabriel's overall cognitive processing level than his MPI of 93.

*Visual Processing.*   Visual processing is the ability to perceive, analyze, synthesize, and think with visual patterns, including the ability to store and recall visual representations. Mental manipulation and transformation of visual patterns and stimuli are usually involved, for example, constructing a design from a picture of the design. With a standard score of 89 from the WJ III COG, Gabriel's visual processing appears to be in the low average range, a mild normative weakness but not an individual weakness. If the KABC-II Simultaneous score of 88 is interpreted from a CHC perspective, it is presumed to measure visual processing, in which case it supports the visual processing score from the WJ III COG. It was hypothesized that visual processing would be a strength for Gabriel. This hypothesis appears unsupported and can be rejected.

*Auditory Processing.*   Auditory processing is the ability to perceive, analyze, synthesize, and discriminate auditory stimuli. For example, auditory processing includes the ability to discriminate speech sounds. From the score of 97 that Gabriel obtained on the WJ III COG Auditory Processing factor, it appears that his auditory processing is in the mid-average range. There does not appear to be any data to the contrary; thus, the hypothesis of a weakness in auditory processing is unsupported. It is likely that deficits in attention are accounting for the concerns that were attributed to an auditory processing weakness.

*Planning.*   Planning is a mental process that is involved in cognitive control and the use of other processes. For example, planning is often the first step in problem solving. Gabriel's KABC-II Planning score of 102 is in the mid-average range. Although, it is not a strength relative to peers, it is an individual strength for Gabriel, as it is 16 points above his processing mean of 86. Although there are few anecdotal reports regarding Gabriel's planning capacity, there is no data that clearly contradicts a relative strength in this area. For example, planning is thought to be related to math reasoning skills and his math reasoning skills are in the mid-average range (see Table 9.9). The findings are contrary to the original hypothesis. Rather than having a weakness in planning, Gabriel appears to have a strength.

*Fluid Reasoning.*   Fluid reasoning consists of using inductive and deductive reasoning to solve novel problems, such as when a learner is confronted with a new

## Table 9.9  WJ III Achievement Results

| Skill | Standard Score | Percentile | 95% Confidence Interval | Descriptive Category |
|---|---|---|---|---|
| Basic Reading Skills | 99 | 48 | 96–103 | Average |
| Reading Comprehension | 110 | 76 | 101–120 | High Average |
| Math Calculation Skills | 100 | 97 | 93–106 | Average |
| Math Reasoning | 97 | 42 | 92–102 | Average |
| Written Expression | 93 | 32 | 84–101 | Average |
| Academic Fluency | 88 | 22 | 84–92 | Low Average |
| Academic Applications | 98 | 44 | 93–103 | Average |

type of math problem for the first time. Not only is fluid reasoning related to math reasoning, but it is also related to planning. However, Gabriel's WJ III COG Fluid Reasoning score of 88 is noticeably lower, if not significantly lower than his Planning score of 102. A normative weakness in fluid reasoning is consistent with parent and teacher reports that Gabriel's reasoning and problem-solving ability is limited; for example, he has difficulty recognizing the connection between concepts. Thus, there is convergent evidence that Gabriel has a weakness in fluid reasoning. However, it is only a normative weakness and not an ipsative weakness; thus, it is not a deficit.

*Processing Speed.*    Processing speed is mental quickness, as measured by how quickly an examinee can perform simple cognitive tasks. For example, fluently and automatically completing a timed test involves processing speed. Gabriel's WJ COG Processing Speed standard score of 80 is in the low average range and a weakness compared to his peers. This low average score is corroborated by observations and reports that Gabriel seldom completes work quickly. However, a lack of motivation might also account for what appears to be slow processing speed. Thus, it appears that Gabriel has a weakness in processing speed. However, it is only a weakness compared to his peers; it is not an individual weakness and, therefore, not a deficit.

*Successive Processing.*    Successive processing is mental activity in which the individual works with stimuli that are in serial order or arranges stimuli sequentially. Basic reading decoding involves successive processing. Based on his KABC-II Sequential score of 83, Gabriel's successive processing level appears to be in the low average range, a normative weakness but not an ipsative weakness. Additional assessment data did not indicate a weakness in successive processing. Consequently, it is unclear whether a successive processing weakness hypothesis can be supported. The KABC-II subtests that measure successive processing are also tapping short-term memory, also a normative weakness. Furthermore, performance on short-term memory tasks is influenced by attention, which is known to be a weakness for Gabriel.

*Simultaneous Processing.*   Simultaneous processing involves integrating separate stimuli into groups or into a whole, for example, putting together a puzzle. From Gabriel's KABC-II Simultaneous score of 88, it appears that his simultaneous processing is in the low average range and, consequently, a normative weakness. Tutors have reported that efforts to teach mapping techniques to Gabriel have been unsuccessful, providing some evidence of at least a normative weakness in simultaneous processing. However, he does not have a deficit in simultaneous processing because it is not also an ipsative weakness.

*Short-Term Memory.*   Short-term memory is a limited-capacity processing system that involves the apprehension and holding of information in immediate awareness. For example, remembering a list of words for few seconds involves short-term memory. Gabriel's WJ III COG Short-Term Memory score of 81 was used in the processing analysis. Gabriel's short-term memory processing appears to be in the low average range, a normative weakness but not an individual weakness. If the KABC-II Sequential score of 83 is interpreted from a CHC perspective, it is presumed to measure short-term memory, in which case it supports the short-term memory score from the WJ III COG. Additional support comes from observations and teacher reports that Gabriel frequently and immediately asks to have information repeated. Thus, there is sufficient evidence for the hypothesis of a weakness in short-term memory. But it is only a weakness compared to his peers; it is not an individual weakness and, therefore, not a deficit. The influence of his attentional problems on his short-term memory also needs to be taken into account.

*Long-Term Retrieval.*   Long-term retrieval is a type of memory process that involves how effectively new information is stored and how efficiently it is retrieved. An example of long-term retrieval is the association of pairs of information, such as associating a sound with a letter. Gabriel's WJ III COG Long-Term Retrieval score of 66 was used in the analysis of processing instead of his Long-Term Retrieval (same as the Learning factor) score of 103 from the KABC-II.

The reasons for using the WJ III COG score are the KABC-II scores are being interpreted as representing Luria processes; the WJ III COG seems to more broadly sample long-term retrieval; and the lower WJ III COG score is consistent with reports from Gabriel's teachers and tutors that he does not retain new information and procedures well without frequent review. Given the significant difference between these two factors that both purport to measure long-term retrieval, it is unclear where Gabriel's true long-term retrieval processing lies. It is known that performance on long-term retrieval tasks is influenced by attention, and it is possible that he was more attentive and focused during the administration of the KABC-II. However, it is also possible that long-term retrieval is a real deficit for Gabriel. The support for a processing weakness or deficit in long-term retrieval is mixed; no conclusion can be drawn.

*Attention.* Attention is a mental process that involves focused, selective cognition, over time, as well as resistance to distraction. Instead of directly assessing Gabriel's attention with a cognitive scale, a behavior rating scale (the BASC-2) was used to assess his attention processing. Because the BASC-2 is a behavior rating scale, Gabriel's attention score was not included in the processing analysis. Gabriel's average Attention *T*-score across four raters on the BASC-2 was a 67. When this score is reversed and transformed to a mean of 100 and a standard deviation of 15, it equals approximately a 75. Thus, attention is clearly a significant normative weakness for Gabriel, but it does not appear to be an individual weakness compared to his cognitive processing mean of 86. Anecdotal reports and observations corroborate his BASC-2 score. Given how low his attention level is, it can certainly impair his performance at school, as well as influence the scores he obtains on measures of other processes, such as short-term memory. Consequently, the hypothesis of a weakness in attention accounting for some of the referral concerns is validated.

## Summary of Processing

Of the nine processes assessed, Gabriel has normative weakness in all of the areas assessed except planning and auditory processing, which are in the average range. In fact, planning appears to be an individual strength for Gabriel. It is possible that he has a deficit in long-term retrieval, but the test results are mixed. It is also unclear as to whether his short-term memory, successive processing, and processing speed are really as low as his test scores indicate, given his established difficulties with attention, which were also observed during testing.

## Achievement Assessment Summary

Whatever processing weaknesses or deficits Gabriel may have, they do not appear to be impairing his ability to acquire knowledge and academic skills. Gabriel's achievement scores in reading, math, and written language are all within the average range (see Table 9.9), commensurate with or higher than his general intellectual ability scores and most of his processing scores. It appears that tutoring and other interventions and accommodations that Gabriel receives have been effective, at least in regard to academic learning.

## Behavioral Summary

Gabriel's profile on the BASC-2 is consistent with characteristics of autism. Based on the ratings of his two teachers and two parents, all of his adaptive skills are in the at-risk or clinically significant range. On the problem behavior scales, he obtained extremely high clinically significant scores on the Atypicality, Withdrawal, and Attention Problems scales, as well as at-risk scores in Learning Problems, School Problems, and Hyperactivity.

## Diagnostic Impressions

Gabriel's processing weaknesses seem to be impairing his nonacademic functioning, such as social functioning, more than his academic learning. The two primary processing concerns that are causing impairments are his significant normative weakness in attention and his potential deficit in long-term retrieval. Given Gabriel's near average cognitive abilities and high verbal abilities, a diagnosis of Asperger's seems appropriate.

## Recommendations

1. Parents, teachers, and tutors should constantly utilize strategies that help Gabriel reduce the impact of his significant difficulties with attention. For example, make sure he is focused before given directions, provide prompts that redirect him when he is inattentive, and repeat information as necessary.
2. Gabriel's potential deficit in long-term retrieval should be investigated further. Classroom performance data should be collected, for example, data on how well he performs on classroom tests that require retrieval of information that he has studied.

**TEST YOURSELF**

1. The cross-battery processing analysis procedures should be briefly explained in the body of the psychological report. True or False?

2. The processing interpretation section of the report should be organized on a test-by-test basis. True or False?

3. Information obtained from interviews should only be reported in the Background Information section. True or False?

4. Given empirical evidence on the relationships between processes and specific areas of academic learning, Hannah's academic weaknesses are related to her processing weaknesses. True or False?

5. Ipsative strengths and weaknesses are not necessarily normative strengths and weaknesses. True or False?

*Answers:* 1. True; 2. False; 3. False; 4. True; 5. True

# Appendix A

**Selective Testing Table for Processes Measured by Cognitive Tests***

| Process | WJ III COG | WPPSI-III | WISC-IV | WAIS-III | SB5 | CAS | KABC-II |
|---|---|---|---|---|---|---|---|
| Attention | BROAD ATTENTION | | | | | ATTENTION | |
| Auditory Processing | AUDITORY PROCESSING | | | | | | |
| Executive Processing | EXECUTIVE PROCESSES | | | | | | |
| Fluid Reasoning | FLUID REASONING | Matrix Reasoning Picture Concepts Word Reasoning Similarities | Matrix Reasoning Picture Concepts Word Reasoning Similarities Arithmetic | Matrix Reasoning Similarities | FLUID REASONING | | PLANNING |
| Long-Term Retrieval | LONG-TERM RETRIEVAL DELAYED RECALL Rapid Automatic Naming | | | | | | LEARNING DELAYED RECALL |

| | | | | | | | |
|---|---|---|---|---|---|---|---|
| Phonemic Awareness | PHONEMIC AWARENESS | | | | | | |
| Planning | Planning | | | | | PLANNING | PLANNING |
| Processing Speed | PROCESSING SPEED | PROCESSING SPEED | PROCESSING SPEED | PROCESSING SPEED | | | |
| Short-Term Memory | SHORT-TERM MEMORY | | | | | | SEQUENTIAL PROCESSING |
| Simultaneous Processing | | | | | | SIMULTANEOUS PROCESSING | SIMULTANEOUS PROCESSING |
| Successive Processing | | | | | | SUCCESSIVE PROCESSING | SEQUENTIAL PROCESSING |
| Visual Processing | VISUAL-SPATIAL THINKING | Block Design<br>Object Assembly<br>Picture Completion | Block Design<br>Picture Completion | Block Design<br>Object Assembly<br>Picture Completion<br>Picture Arrangement | VISUAL-SPATIAL PROCESSING | | SIMULTANEOUS PROCESSING |
| Working Memory | WORKING MEMORY | | WORKING MEMORY | WORKING MEMORY | WORKING MEMORY | | |

*Part of this table is adapted from Essentials of WISC-IV Assessment (Flanagan & Kaufman, 2004, pp. 306–307).

Note: Capitalized items are names of factors (composites, clusters, indexes, scales). Noncapitalized items are subtest names. WJ III COG = Woodcock-Johnson III Tests of Cognitive Abilities; WPPSI-III = Wechsler Preschool and Primary Scale of Intelligence, third edition; WISC-IV = Wechsler Intelligence Scale for Children, fourth edition; WAIS-III = Wechsler Adult Intelligence Scale, third edition; SB5 = Stanford–Binet Intelligence Scales, fifth edition; CAS = Cognitive Assessment System; KABC-II = Kaufman Assessment Battery for Children, second edition.

# Appendix B

**Processing Assessment Organizer**

Student: _____ Date of Referral: _____ Form Completed By: _____ DOB: _____ Age: _____ Grade: _____ Date: _____

| Referral Concerns | Processing Hypotheses | Assessment Methods | Assessment Results | Conclusions |
|---|---|---|---|---|
| | | | | |
| | | | | |
| | | | | |
| | | | | |
| | | | | |

# Appendix C

**Processing Analysis Worksheet**

Examinee's Name: _____ DOB: _____ Age: _____

Grade: _____ Dates of Testing: _____

| Name of Process | Name of Test/ Battery | Name of Factor/ Subtests | Processing Factor Score | Processing Factor Mean | Difference from Mean | Normative S or W | Ipsative S or W | Deficit or Asset |
|---|---|---|---|---|---|---|---|---|
| | | | | | | | | |
| | | | | | | | | |
| | | | | | | | | |
| | | | | | | | | |

(continued)

|  |  |  |  |  |  |  |  |  |
|---|---|---|---|---|---|---|---|---|
|  |  |  |  |  |  |  |  |  |
|  |  |  |  |  |  |  |  |  |
|  |  |  |  |  |  |  |  |  |

<u>Directions:</u> (1) Use factor scores for analysis, not subtest scores. (2) When a factor score is not available from a test, convert subtest scores to a mean of 100 and an SD of 15. (3) For each factor, compute the mean of the subtest scores and round to the nearest whole number. Use the subtest means as clinical factor scores. (4) Compute the mean of all available factor scores (this is the processing mean). (5) Subtract the processing mean from each processing factor score and enter amount in Difference column. (6) Indicate whether the factor score is a normative weakness or strength (90–109 is average). (7) Using a criterion of 15 points, determine ipsative strengths and weaknesses. (8) Determine deficits and assets. A deficit is both a normative and ipsative weakness. When the range between the highest and lowest subtest scores exceeds 1.5 SDs, the factor is nonunitary. Nonunitary factors should be interpreted cautiously and should not be used in pairwise comparisons. (10) Compare related pairs for significant differences, using a 20-point difference as an indication of significance.

| Factor Score | Factor Score | Difference | Significant: Y/N |
|---|---|---|---|
|  |  |  |  |
|  |  |  |  |
|  |  |  |  |

# Appendix D

Conversion Table: Scaled Scores to Standard Scores

| Scaled Score<br>(M = 10; SD = 3) | Standard Score<br>(M = 100; SD = 15) |
|:---:|:---:|
| 19 | 145 |
| 18 | 140 |
| 17 | 135 |
| 16 | 130 |
| 15 | 125 |
| 14 | 120 |
| 13 | 115 |
| 12 | 110 |
| 11 | 105 |
| 10 | 100 |
| 9 | 95 |
| 8 | 90 |
| 7 | 85 |
| 6 | 80 |
| 5 | 75 |
| 4 | 70 |
| 3 | 65 |
| 2 | 60 |
| 1 | 55 |

# Appendix E

## Supplemental Processing Analysis Worksheet for All Wechsler Scales

(Also, note specific recommendations for each Wechsler scale discussed in Chapter 5.)

1. Convert the scaled scores of the available subtests that measure visual processing (VP) and fluid reasoning (FR) to a standard score that uses a mean of 100 and standard deviation of 15, using the table in Appendix D.

| Subtest | Scaled Score (M = 10; SD = 3) | | Standard Score (M = 100; SD = 15) |
|---|---|---|---|
| Matrix Reasoning (MR) | _____ | = | _____ |
| Picture Concepts (PCn) | _____ | = | _____ |
| Similarities (S) | _____ | = | _____ |
| Word Reasoning (WR) | _____ | = | _____ |
| Arithmetic (A) | _____ | = | _____ |
| Block Design (BD) | _____ | = | _____ |
| Picture Completion (PC) | _____ | = | _____ |
| Object Assembly (OA) | _____ | = | _____ |
| Picture Arrangement (PA) | _____ | = | _____ |

2. Compute the FR factor mean using standard scores.

   a. For the WAIS-III, use Matrix Reasoning and Similarities.

   $$\underset{(MR)}{\_\_\_\_} + \underset{(S)}{\_\_\_\_} = \underset{(Sum)}{\_\_\_\_} \div 2 = \underset{(FR)}{\_\_\_\_}$$

   b. For the WISC-IV, use Matrix Reasoning and Picture Concepts.

   $$\underset{(MR)}{\_\_\_\_} + \underset{(PCn)}{\_\_\_\_} = \underset{(Sum)}{\_\_\_\_} \div 2 = \underset{(FR)}{\_\_\_\_}$$

   c. For the WPPSI-III, use Word Reasoning and Similarities.

   $$\underset{(WR)}{\_\_\_\_} + \underset{(S)}{\_\_\_\_} = \underset{(Sum)}{\_\_\_\_} \div 2 = \underset{(FR)}{\_\_\_\_}$$

3. Compute the VP factor mean using standard scores.

   a. Option 1: For all three Wechsler scales, use Block Design and Picture Completion.

   $$\underset{(BD)}{\_\_\_\_} + \underset{(PC)}{\_\_\_\_} = \underset{(Sum)}{\_\_\_\_} \div 2 = \underset{(VP)}{\_\_\_\_}$$

270

b. Option 2: For WPPSI-III and WAIS-III only, use Block Design and Object Assembly.

$$\frac{\phantom{xxx}}{(BD)} + \frac{\phantom{xxx}}{(OA)} = \frac{\phantom{xxx}}{(Sum)} \div 2 = \frac{\phantom{xxx}}{(VP)}$$

c. Option 3: For WPPSI-III and WAIS-III only, use Block Design, Picture Completion, and Object Assembly.

$$\frac{\phantom{xxx}}{(BD)} + \frac{\phantom{xxx}}{(PC)} + \frac{\phantom{xxx}}{(OA)} = \frac{\phantom{xxx}}{(Sum)} \div 3 = \frac{\phantom{xxx}}{(VP)}$$

4. Compute the mean of the processing factors.

a. WISC-IV and WAIS-III mean is based on 4 factors.

$$\frac{\phantom{xxx}}{(PSI)} + \frac{\phantom{xxx}}{(WMI)} + \frac{\phantom{xxx}}{(FR)} + \frac{\phantom{xxx}}{(VP)} = \frac{\phantom{xxx}}{(Sum)} \div 4 = \frac{\phantom{xxx}}{(Mean)}$$

b. WPPSI-III mean is based on 3 factors.

$$\frac{\phantom{xxx}}{(PSI)} + \frac{\phantom{xxx}}{(FR)} + \frac{\phantom{xxx}}{(VP)} = \frac{\phantom{xxx}}{(Sum)} \div 3 = \frac{\phantom{xxx}}{(Mean)}$$

5. Determine whether each of the four factors is unitary. If the difference between the highest and lowest standard scores exceeds 22 points, then the factor is not unitary. Interpret nonunitary factors cautiously, if at all, and do not use them in pairwise comparisons.

WM: $\dfrac{\phantom{xxx}}{\text{(Highest)}} - \dfrac{\phantom{xxx}}{\text{(Lowest)}} = \dfrac{\phantom{xxx}}{\text{(Difference)}}$

PS: $\dfrac{\phantom{xxx}}{\text{(Highest)}} - \dfrac{\phantom{xxx}}{\text{(Lowest)}} = \dfrac{\phantom{xxx}}{\text{(Difference)}}$

VP: $\dfrac{\phantom{xxx}}{\text{(Highest)}} - \dfrac{\phantom{xxx}}{\text{(Lowest)}} = \dfrac{\phantom{xxx}}{\text{(Difference)}}$

FR: $\dfrac{\phantom{xxx}}{\text{(Highest)}} - \dfrac{\phantom{xxx}}{\text{(Lowest)}} = \dfrac{\phantom{xxx}}{\text{(Difference)}}$

# Appendix F

## Calculation of WISC-IV Integrated Clinical Processing Factor Scores and Pairwise Comparisons

<u>Directions:</u> (1) Clinical factor scores can only be calculated when at least two subtest scores that comprise that factor are available. (2) Begin by transforming all subtest scaled scores to standard scores with a mean of 100 and standard deviation of 15, using the table in Appendix D. (3) For each factor, add up the available subtest transformed scores and compute the mean, rounding to the nearest whole number. (4) Next, determine which clinical factors are unitary. If the difference between the highest and lowest subtest standard scores within a factor exceeds 22 points, consider the clinical cluster nonunitary. Interpret nonunitary factors cautiously, and do not use them in pairwise comparisons. (5) Then conduct pairwise comparisons of the unitary factors, using a 20-point discrepancy as an indication of significance and infrequency. (6) Transfer all clinical factors scores to the Processing Analysis Worksheet (Appendix C) for further analysis.

| **Short-Term Memory (STM)** | **Scaled Score** | **Standard Score** |
|---|---|---|
| Digit Span Forward | _____ | _____ |
| Visual Digit Span | _____ | _____ |
| Spatial Span Forward | _____ | _____ |
| Letter Span Nonrhyming | _____ | _____ |
| Letter Span Rhyming | _____ | _____ |
| Standard Score Total _____ ÷ _____ (No. of subtests) = _____ STM Factor Score | | |

| **Visual Short-Term Memory (VSTM)** | **Scaled Score** | **Standard Score** |
|---|---|---|
| Visual Digit Span | _____ | _____ |
| Spatial Span Forward | _____ | _____ |
| Standard Score Total _____ ÷ 2 = _____ VSTM Factor Score | | |

| **Auditory Short-Term Memory (ASTM)** | Scaled Score | Standard Score |
|---|---|---|
| Digit Span Forward | _____ | _____ |
| Letter Span Nonrhyming | _____ | _____ |
| Letter Span Rhyming | _____ | _____ |
| Standard Score Total _____ ÷ _____ (No. of subtests) = _____ ASTM Factor Score | | |

| **Working Memory (WM)** | Scaled Score | Standard Score |
|---|---|---|
| Digit Span Backward | _____ | _____ |
| Spatial Span Backward | _____ | _____ |
| Letter Number Sequencing PA | _____ | _____ |
| Standard Score Total _____ ÷ _____ (No. of subtests) = _____ WM Factor Score | | |

| **Visual Working Memory (VWM)** | Scaled Score | Standard Score |
|---|---|---|
| Spatial Span Backward | _____ | _____ |
| Arithmetic PA Part A | _____ | _____ |
| Standard Score Total _____ ÷ 2 = _____ VWM Factor Score | | |

| **Auditory Working Memory (AWM)** | Scaled Score | Standard Score |
|---|---|---|
| Digit Span Backward | _____ | _____ |
| Letter Number Sequencing PA | _____ | _____ |
| Standard Score Total _____ ÷ 2 = _____ AWM Factor Score | | |

| **Pairwise Clinical Comparisons** | Difference | Significant: Y/N |
|---|---|---|
| _____ Short-Term Memory versus _____ Working Memory | _____ | _____ |
| _____ Visual Short-Term Memory versus _____ Auditory Short-Term Memory | _____ | _____ |
| _____ Visual Working Memory versus _____ Auditory Working Memory | _____ | _____ |
| _____ Visual Short-Term Memory versus _____ Visual Working Memory | _____ | _____ |
| _____ Auditory Short-Term Memory versus _____ Auditory Working Memory | _____ | _____ |

# Appendix G

## Processes Measured by Standardized Tests

### Attention

Cognitive Assessment System
Comprehensive Trail-Making Test
Conners' Continuous Performance Test
Detroit Tests of Learning Aptitude, fourth
 edition
The Gordon Diagnostic System
Kaplan Baycrest Neurocognitive Assess-
 ment
Leiter International Performance Scale-
 Revised
Micro-Cog: Assessment of Cognitive
 Functioning
NEPSY: A Development Neuropsycho-
 logical Assessment
Psychological Processing Checklist
Woodcock-Johnson III Tests of Cognitive
 Abilities

### Auditory Processing

Psychological Processing Checklist
SCAN-A: A Test of Auditory Processing
 Disorders in Adolescents and Adults
SCAN-C: A Test of Auditory Processing
 Disorders in Children-Revised
Woodcock-Johnson III Tests of Cognitive
 Abilities

### Executive Processing

Behavior Rating Inventory of Executive
 Functions
Comprehensive Trail-Making Test
Delis-Kaplan Executive Function System
NEPSY: A Developmental Neuropsycho-
 logical Assessment
Wisconsin Card Sorting Test, Revised and
 Expanded
Woodcock-Johnson III Tests of Cognitive
 Abilities

### Fluid Reasoning

Detroit Tests of Learning Aptitude, fourth
 edition
Differential Ability Scales
Kaplan Baycrest Neurocognitive Assessment
Kaufman Adolescent and Adult Intelligence
 Scale
Kaufman Assessment Battery for Children,
 second edition
Leiter International Performance Scale–
 Revised
Micro-Cog: Assessment of Cognitive Func-
 tioning
Reynolds Intellectual Assessment Scales
Stanford-Binet Intelligence Scales, fifth edi-
 tion
Universal Nonverbal Intelligence Test
Wechsler Adult Intelligence Scale, third edi-
 tion
Wechsler Intelligence Scale for Children,
 fourth edition
Wechsler Preschool and Primary Scale of In-
 telligence, third edition
WISC-IV Integrated
Wisconsin Card Sorting Test, Revised and
 Expanded
Woodcock-Johnson III Tests of Cognitive
 Abilities

### Long-Term Retrieval

California Verbal Learning Test, Children's
 Version
California Verbal Learning Test, Second Edi-
 tion, Adult Version
Comprehensive Test of Phonological Pro-
 cessing
Differential Ability Scales
Kaplan Baycrest Neurocognitive Assessment
Kaufman Adolescent and Adult Intelligence
 Scale

Kaufman Assessment Battery for Children,
second edition
Kaufman Test of Educational Achievement,
second edition
Learning and Memory Battery
Leiter International Performance Scale–
Revised
Memory Assessment Scales
NEPSY: A Developmental Neuropsycho-
logical Assessment
Process Assessment of the Learner
Swanson-Cognitive Processing Test
Test of Memory and Learning
Wide Range Assessment of Memory and
Learning
WISC-IV Integrated
Woodcock-Johnson III Tests of Cognitive
Abilities

## Phonemic Awareness

Comprehensive Test of Phonological Pro-
cessing
Kaufman Test of Educational Achievement,
second edition
NEPSY: A Developmental Neuropsycho-
logical Assessment
Phonological Abilities Test
Process Assessment of the Learner
Test of Phonological Awareness
Woodcock Diagnostic Reading Battery
Woodcock-Johnson III Tests of Cognitive
Abilities

## Planning

Cognitive Assessment System
Kaufman Assessment Battery for Children,
second edition
NEPSY: A Developmental Neuropsycho-
logical Assessment
WISC-IV Integrated
Woodcock-Johnson III Tests of Cognitive
Abilities

## Processing Speed

Differential Ability Scales
Micro-Cog: Assessment of Cognitive Functioning

Wechsler Adult Intelligence Scale, third edi-
tion
Wechsler Intelligence Scale for Children,
fourth edition
Wechsler Preschool and Primary Scale of In-
telligence, third edition
Woodcock-Johnson III Tests of Cognitive
Abilities

## Short-Term Memory

California Verbal Learning Test, Children's
Version
California Verbal Learning Test, Second
Edition, Adult Version
Differential Ability Scales
Kaplan Baycrest Neurocognitive Assess-
ment
Kaufman Assessment Battery for Children,
second edition
Leiter International Performance Scale–
Revised
Memory Assessment Scales
NEPSY: A Developmental Neuropsycho-
logical Assessment
Reynolds Intellectual Assessment Scales
Universal Nonverbal Intelligence Test
Wide Range Assessment of Memory and
Learning
WISC-IV Integrated
Woodcock-Johnson III Tests of Cognitive
Abilities

## Simultaneous Processing

Cognitive Assessment System
Kaufman Assessment Battery for Children,
second edition
Detroit Tests of Learning Aptitude, fourth
edition

## Successive Processing

Cognitive Assessment System
Kaufman Assessment Battery for Children,
second edition
Detroit Tests of Learning Aptitude, fourth
edition

## Visual Processing

Differential Ability Scales

Kaplan Baycrest Neurocognitive Assessment

Kaufman Assessment Battery for Children, second edition

Leiter International Performance Scale–Revised

Micro-Cog: Assessment of Cognitive Functioning

NEPSY: A Developmental Neuropsychological Assessment

Psychological Processing Checklist

Stanford-Binet Intelligence Scales, fifth edition

Wechsler Adult Intelligence Scale, third edition

Wechsler Intelligence Scale for Children, fourth edition

Wechsler Preschool and Primary Scale of Intelligence, third edition

WISC-IV Integrated

Woodcock-Johnson III Tests of Cognitive Abilities

## Working Memory

Stanford-Binet Intelligence Scales, fifth edition

Wechsler Adult Intelligence Scale, third edition

Wechsler Intelligence Scale for Children, fourth edition

WISC-IV Integrated

Woodcock-Johnson III Tests of Cognitive Abilities

Working Memory Test Battery for Children

*Note:* The tests listed for each process may measure additional processes or even contain nonprocessing factors. It is only necessary to administer the factors and subtests that measure the selected processes. Only tests with evidence of adequate reliability and tests published since 1990 are included.

# References

Anderson, J. R. (1990). *Cognitive psychology and its implications* (3rd ed.). New York: W. H. Freeman & Company.

Bannatyne, A. (1974). Diagnosis: A note on recategorization of the WISC scaled scores. *Journal of Learning Disabilities, 7*, 272–274.

Barkley, R. A. (1997). *ADHD and the nature of self-control.* New York: Guilford Press.

Berninger, V. W., & Richards, T. L. (2002). *Brain literacy for educators and psychologists.* San Diego: Academic Press.

Bracken, B. A., & McCallum, R. S. (1998). *Universal Nonverbal Intelligence Test.* Itasca, IL: Riverside.

Carroll, J. B. (1993). *Human cognitive abilities: A survey of factor-analytic studies.* Cambridge: Cambridge University Press.

Cohen, J. (1997a). *Children's Memory Scale.* San Antonio, TX: The Psychological Corporation.

Cohen, J. (1997b). *Children's Memory Scale manual.* San Antonio, TX: The Psychological Corporation.

Cruickshank, W. M. (1977). Myths and realities in learning disabilities. *Journal of Learning Disabilities, 10,* 51–58.

Das, J. P., Naglieri, J. A., & Kirby, J. R. (1994). *Assessment of cognitive processes: The PASS theory of intelligence.* Needham Heights, MA: Allyn & Bacon.

Dawson, P., & Guare, R. (2004). *Executive skills in children and adolescents.* New York: Guilford Press.

Dehn, M. J. (1997). *The effects of informed strategy training and computer mediated text on comprehension monitoring and reading comprehension.* (ERIC Document Reproduction Service No. ED402545)

Dehn, M. J. (2004, December). A comparison of learning disabled students' WISC-III and WISC-IV scores. *Communique, 33*(4), 16.

Delis, D. C., Kaplan, E., & Kramer, J. H. (2001). *Delis-Kaplan Executive Function System.* San Antonio, TX: The Psychological Corporation.

Delis, D. C., Kramer, J. H., Kaplan, E., & Ober, B. A. (1994). *California Verbal Learning Test— Children's Version.* San Antonio, TX: The Psychological Corporation.

Elliot, C. D. (1990). *Differential Ability Scales.* San Antonio, TX: The Psychological Corporation.

Evans, J. J., Floyd, R. G., McGrew, K. S., & Leforgee, M. H. (2002). The relations between measures of Cattell-Horn-Carroll (CHC) cognitive abilities and reading achievement during childhood and adolescence. *School Psychology Review, 31*(2), 246–262.

Federal Register. (December 29, 1977). 42:250. Washington, DC: U.S. Government Printing Office.

Flanagan, D. P., & Harrison, P. L. (Eds.). (2005). *Contemporary intellectual assessment: Theories, tests, and issues* (2nd ed.). New York: Guilford Press.

Flanagan, D. P., & Kaufman, A. S. (2004). *Essentials of WISC-IV assessment.* Hoboken: Wiley.

Flanagan, D. P., McGrew, K. S., & Ortiz, S. O. (2000). *The Wechsler intelligence scales and CHC theory: A contemporary approach to interpretation.* Boston: Allyn & Bacon.

Flanagan, D. P., & Ortiz, S. (2001). *Essentials of cross-battery assessment.* New York: Wiley.

Floyd, R. G. (2005). Information-processing approaches to interpretation of contemporary intellectual assessment instruments. In D. P. Flanagan & P. L. Harrison (Eds.), *Contemporary intellectual assessment: Theories, tests, and issues* (2nd ed., pp. 203–233). New York: Guilford Press.

Flynn, J. R. (1999). Searching for justice: The discovery of IQ gains over time. *American Psychologist, 54,* 5–20.

Gagne, E. D. (1993). *The cognitive psychology of school learning* (2nd ed.). New York: HarperCollins College.

Galton, F. (1883). *Inquiries into human faculty and development.* London: Macmillan.

Gillon, G. T. (2004). *Phonological awareness.* New York: Guilford Press.

Gioia, G. A., Isquith, P. K., Guy, S. C., & Kenworthy, L. (2000). *Behavior Rating Inventory of Executive Function.* Odessa, FL: Psychological Assessment Resources.

Glutting, J. J., McDermott, P. A., & Konold, T. R. (1997). Ontology, structure, and diagnostic benefits of a normative subtest taxonomy from the WISC-III standardization sample. In D. P. Flanagan, J. L. Genshaft, & P. L. Harrison (Eds.), *Contemporary intellectual assessment: Theories, tests, and issues* (pp. 340–372). New York: Guilford Press.

Glutting, J. J., & Oakland, T. D. (1993). *Guide to the assessment of test session behavior for the WISC-III and WIAT.* San Antonio, TX: The Psychological Corporation.

Hale, J. B., & Fiorello, C. A. (2004). *School neuropsychology: A practitioner's handbook.* New York: Guilford Press.

Hammill, D. D., & Bryant, B. R. (1998). *Learning Disabilities Diagnostic Inventory.* Austin, TX: Pro Ed.

Hammill, D. D., Leigh, J. E., McNutt, G., & Larsen, S. C. (1981). A new definition of learning disabilities. *Learning Disability Quarterly, 4,* 336–342.

Heaton, R. K., Chelune, G. J., Talley, J. L., Kay, G. G., & Curtiss, G. (1993). *Wisconsin Card Sorting Test, Revised and Expanded.* Lutz, FL: Psychological Assessment Resources.

Hebben, N., & Milberg, W. (2002). *Essentials of neuropsychological assessment.* New York: Wiley.

Horn, J. L., & Blankson, N. (2005). Foundations for better understanding of cognitive abilities. In D. P. Flanagan & P. L. Harrison (Eds.), *Contemporary intellectual assessment: Theories, tests, and issues* (2nd ed., pp. 41–68). New York: Guilford Press.

Horn, J. L., & Noll, J. (1997). Human cognitive capabilities: *Gf-Gc* theory. In D. P. Flanagan, J. L. Genshaft, & P. L. Harrison (Eds.), *Contemporary intellectual assessment: Theories, tests, and issues* (pp. 53–91). New York: Guilford Press.

Hoskyn, M., & Swanson, H. L. (2000). Cognitive processing of low achievers and children with reading disabilities: A selective meta-analytic review of the published literature. *School Psychology Review, 29,* 102–119.

Individuals with Disabilities Education Act, Pub. L. 108-446 (2004).

Kaplan, E., Fein, D., Kramer, J., Delis, D., & Morris, R. (1999). *Wechsler Intelligence Scale for Children—third edition as a process instrument.* San Antonio, TX: The Psychological Corporation.

Kaplan, E., Fein, D., Morris, R., & Delis, D. C. (1991). *WAIS-R as a neuropsychological instrument.* San Antonio, TX: The Psychological Corporation.

Kaufman, A. S. (1979). *Intelligent testing with the WISC-R.* New York: Wiley.

Kaufman, A. S. (1994). *Intelligent testing with the WISC-III.* New York: Wiley.

Kaufman, A. S., & Kaufman, N. L. (1983). *Kaufman Assessment Battery for Children.* Circle Pines, MN: American Guidance Service.

Kaufman, A. S., & Kaufman, N. L. (2004a). *Kaufman Assessment Battery for Children, second edition.* Circle Pines, MN: AGS Publishing.

Kaufman, A. S., & Kaufman, N. L. (2004b). *Kaufman Assessment Battery for Children, second edition manual.* Circle Pines, MN: AGS Publishing.

Kaufman, A. S., & Kaufman, N. L. (2004c). *Kaufman Test of Educational Achievement, second edition.* Circle Pines, MN: AGS Publishing.

Kaufman, A. S., & Lichtenberger, E. O. (1999). *Essentials of WAIS-III assessment.* New York: Wiley.

Kaufman, A. S., Lichtenberger, E. O., Fletcher-Janzen, E., & Kaufman, N. L. (2005). *Essentials of KABC-II assessment.* Hoboken: Wiley.

Keith, T. Z., Fine, J. G., Taub, G. E., Reynolds, M. R., & Kranzler, J. H. (2004). *Hierarchical multi-sample, confirmatory factor analysis of the Wechsler Intelligence Scale for Children—Fourth Edition: What does it measure?* Manuscript submitted for publication.

Keith, T. Z., Kranzler, J. H., & Flanagan, D. P. (2001). Joint CFA of the CAS and WJ III. *School Psychology Review, 29,* 203–307.

Kemp, S. L., Kirk, U., & Korkman, M. (2001). *Essentials of NEPSY assessment.* New York: Wiley.

Korkman, M., Kirk, U., & Kemp, S. (1998). *NEPSY: A Developmental Neuropsychological Assessment.* San Antonio, TX: The Psychological Corporation.

Levine, M. D. (1997). *The ANSER System—Aggregate Neurobehavioral Student Health and Educational Review-Revised.* Cambridge, MA: Educators Publishing Service.

Lichtenberger, E. O., & Kaufman, A. S. (2004). *Essentials of WPPSI-III assessment.* Hoboken: Wiley.

Lichtenberger, E. O., Kaufman, A. S., & Lai, Z. C. (2002). *Essentials of WMS-III assessment.* New York: Wiley.

Lichtenberger, E. O., Mather, N., Kaufman, N. L., & Kaufman, A. S. (2004). *Essentials of assessment report writing.* Hoboken: Wiley.

Livingston, J. A. (2003). *Metacognition: An overview.* (ERIC Document Reproduction Service No. ED474273)

Luria, A. R. (1970). The functional organization of the brain. *Scientific American, 222,* 66–78.

Manis, F. R., Seidenber, M. S., & Doi, L. M. (1999). See Dick RAN: Rapid naming and the longitudinal prediction of reading subskills in first and second graders. *Scientific Studies of Reading, 3,* 129–157.

Mather, N., & Wendling, B. J. (2005). Linking cognitive assessment results to academic interventions for students with learning disabilities. In D. P. Flanagan & P. L. Harrison (Eds.), *Contemporary intellectual assessment: Theories, tests, and issues* (2nd ed., pp. 269–298). New York: Guilford Press.

Mather, N., & Woodcock, R. W. (2001). *Woodcock-Johnson III Tests of Cognitive Abilities examiner's manual.* Itasca, IL: Riverside Publishing.

McCarney, S. B. (1983). *Learning Disability Evaluation Scale.* Columbia, MO: Hawthorne Educational Services.

McGrew, K. S. (2005). The Cattell-Horn-Carroll theory of cognitive abilities. In D. P. Flanagan & P. L. Harrison (Eds.), *Contemporary intellectual assessment: Theories, tests, and issues* (2nd ed., pp. 136–182). New York: Guilford Press.

McGrew, K. S., & Flanagan, D. P. (1998). *The intelligence test desk reference (ITDR): Gf-Gc cross-battery assessment.* Boston: Allyn & Bacon.

McGrew, K. S., & Woodcock, R. W. (2001). *Woodcock-Johnson III technical manual.* Itasca, IL: Riverside Publishing.

Metsala, J. L. (1999). The development of phonemic awareness in reading-disabled children. *Applied Psycholinguistics, 20,* 149–158.

Miller, L. T. (1999). Psychometric and information processing approaches to measuring cognitive abilities: Paradigms in military testing. *Canadian Psychology, 40,* 241–254.

Mueller, H. H., Dennis, S. S., & Short, R. H. (1986). A meta-exploration of WISC-R factor score profiles as a function of diagnosis and intellectual level. *Canadian Journal of School Psychology, 2,* 21–43.

Naglieri, J. A. (1997). Planning, attention, simultaneous, and successive theory and the Cognitive Assessment System: A new theory-based measure of intelligence. In D. P. Flanagan, J. L. Genshaft, & P. L. Harrison (Eds.), *Contemporary intellectual assessment: Theories, tests, and issues* (pp. 53–91). New York: Guilford Press.

Naglieri, J. A. (1999). *Essentials of CAS assessment.* New York: Wiley.

Naglieri, J. A., & Das, J. P. (1997a). *Cognitive Assessment System.* Itasca, IL: Riverside Publishing.

Naglieri, J. A., & Das, J. P. (1997b). *Cognitive Assessment System administration and scoring manual.* Itasca, IL: Riverside Publishing.

Naglieri, J. A., & Das, J. P. (1997c). *Cognitive Assessment System interpretative handbook.* Itasca, IL: Riverside Publishing.

National Reading Panel (2000). *Teaching children to read: An evidence-based assessment of the scientific research literature on reading and its applications for reading instruction.* Washington, DC: National Institute of Child Health and Human Development (NICHD).

Neisser, U. (1967). *Cognitive psychology.* New York: Appleton-Century-Crofts.

Prifitera, A., Saklofske, D. H., Weiss, L. G., & Rolfhus, E. (Eds.). (2004). *WISC-IV clinical use and interpretation: Scientist-practitioner perspectives.* San Diego: Academic Press.

Raiford, S. E., Rolfus, E., Weiss, L. G., & Coalson, D. (2005). *WISC-IV technical report #4: General ability index.* San Antonio, TX: Harcourt Assessment.

Reynolds, C. R. (2002). *Comprehensive Trail-Making Test.* Point Roberts, WA: M. D. Angus & Associates.

Reynolds, C. R., & Kamphaus, R. W. (2003). *Reynolds Intellectual Assessment Scales.* Lutz, FL: Psychological Assessment Resources.

Roid, G. H. (2003a). *Stanford-Binet Intelligence Scales, fifth edition.* Itasca, IL: Riverside Publishing.

Roid, G. H. (2003b). *Stanford-Binet Intelligence Scales, fifth edition examiner's manual.* Itasca, IL: Riverside Publishing.

Roid, G. H. (2003c). *Stanford-Binet Intelligence Scales, fifth edition technical manual.* Itasca, IL: Riverside Publishing.

Roid, G. H., & Barram, R. A. (2004). *Essentials of Stanford-Binet Intelligence Scales (SB5) assessment.* Hoboken: Wiley.

Roid, G. H., & Miller, L. J. (1997). *Leiter International Performance Scale* (rev. ed.). Wood Dale, IL: Stoelting.

Sattler, J. M. (2001). *Assessment of children: Cognitive applications* (4th ed.). La Mesa, CA: Author.

Sattler, J. M. (2002). *Assessment of children: Behavioral and clinical applications* (4th ed.). La Mesa, CA: Author.

Sattler, J. M., & Dumont, R. (2004). *Assessment of children WISC-IV and WPPSI-III supplement.* La Mesa, CA: Author.

Schrank, F. A., Flanagan, D. P., Woodcock, R. W., & Mascolo, J. T. (2002). *Essentials of WJ III Cognitive Abilities assessment.* New York: Wiley.

Seigneuric, A., Ehrlich, M., Oakhill, J. V., & Nicola, M. (2000). Working memory resources and children's reading comprehension. *Reading and Writing: An Interdisciplinary Journal, 12,* 81–103.

Sheslow, D., & Adams, W. (1990). *Wide Range Assessment of Memory and Learning.* Wilmington, DE: Jastak Associates.

Singer, B. D., & Bashir, A. S. (1999). What are executive functions and self-regulation and what do they have to do with language-learning disorders? *Language, Speech, and Hearing Services in Schools, 30,* 265–273.

Smith, C. B., & Watkins, M. W. (2004). Diagnostic utility of the Bannatyne WISC-III pattern. *Learning Disabilities Research and Practice, 19*(1), 49–56.

Steele, A., & Dehn, M. J. (2003). The Cognitive Assessment System and the Differential Ability Scales with referred students. *The Wisconsin School Psychologist, 03*(01), 17–22.

Sternberg, R. J. (1977). *Intelligence, information processing, and analogical reasoning: The componential analysis of human abilities.* Hillsdale, NJ: Erlbaum.

Sternberg, R. J., & Detterman, D. K. (Eds.). (1986). *What is intelligence?* Norwood, NJ: Ablex.

Swanson, H. L. (1999). What develops in working memory? A life span perspective. *Developmental Psychology, 35,* 986–1000.

Swanson, H. L. (2000). Are working memory deficits in readers with learning disabilities hard to change? *Journal of Learning Disabilities, 33,* 551–566.

Swanson, H. L., & Berninger, V. W. (1996). Individual differences in children's working memory and writing skill. *Journal of Experimental Child Psychology, 63,* 358–385.

Swerdlik, M. E., Swerdlik, P., Kahn, J. H., & Thomas, T. (2003a). *Psychological Processing Checklist.* North Tonawanda, NY: Multi-Health Systems.

Swerdlik, M. E., Swerdlik, P., & Kahn, J. H. (2003b). *Psychological Processing Checklist technical manual.* North Tonawanda, NY: Multi-Health Systems.

Torgesen, J., Wagner, R., & Rashotte, C. (1994). Longitudinal studies of phonological processing and reading. *Journal of Reading Disabilities, 27,* 276–286.

Volpiansky, P., Chiang, B., Dehn, M., Frankenburger, W., & Griffin, M. (2003). *Specific learning disability assessment and decision-making: Technical assistance guide.* Madison, WI: Wisconsin Department of Public Instruction.

Watson, T. S., & Steege, M. W. (2003). *Conducting school-based functional behavioral assessments.* New York: Guilford Press.

Wechsler, D. (1991). *Wechsler Intelligence Scale for Children—third edition.* San Antonio, TX: The Psychological Corporation.

Wechsler, D. (1997a). *WAIS-III WMS-III technical manual.* San Antonio, TX: The Psychological Corporation.

Wechsler, D. (1997b). *Wechsler Adult Intelligence Scale—third edition.* San Antonio, TX: The Psychological Corporation.

Wechsler, D. (1997c). *Wechsler Memory Scale—third edition.* San Antonio, TX: The Psychological Corporation.

Wechsler, D. (1997d). *Wechsler Memory Scale—third edition administration and scoring manual.* San Antonio, TX: The Psychological Corporation.

Wechsler, D. (2002a). *Wechsler Preschool and Primary Scale of Intelligence—third edition.* San Antonio, TX: The Psychological Corporation.

Wechsler, D. (2002b). *WPPSI-III technical and interpretative manual.* San Antonio, TX: The Psychological Corporation.

Wechsler, D. (2003a). *Wechsler Intelligence Scale for Children—fourth edition.* San Antonio, TX: The Psychological Corporation.

Wechsler, D. (2003b). *WISC-IV technical and interpretative manual.* San Antonio, TX: The Psychological Corporation.

Wechsler, D., Kaplan, E., Fein, D., Kramer, J., Morris, R., Delis, D., & Maerlender, A. (2004a). *Wechsler Intelligence Scale for Children Fourth Edition—Integrated.* San Antonio, TX: PsychCorp.

Wechsler, D., Kaplan, E., Fein, D., Kramer, J., Morris, R., Delis, D., & Maerlender, A. (2004b). *Wechsler Intelligence Scale for Children Fourth Edition—Integrated: Administration and scoring manual.* San Antonio, TX: PsychCorp.

Wechsler, D., Kaplan, E., Fein, D., Kramer, J., Morris, R., Delis, D., & Maerlender, A. (2004c). *Wechsler Intelligence Scale for Children Fourth Edition—Integrated: Technical and interpretative manual.* San Antonio, TX: PsychCorp.

Wilson, K. M., & Swanson, H. L. (2001). Are mathematics disabilities due to a domain-general or a domain-specific working memory deficit? *Journal of Learning Disabilities, 34,* 237–248.

Wilson, S. (1998). *Phonemic awareness: A review of the literature.* (ERIC Document Reproduction Service No. ED416462)

Woodcock, R. W. (1998) Extending Gf-Gc theory into practice. In J. J. McArdle & R. W. Woodcock (Eds.), *Human cognitive abilities in theory and practice* (pp. 137–156). Mahwah, NJ: Erlbaum.

Woodcock, R. W., & Johnson, M. B. (1977). *Woodcock-Johnson Psycho-Educational Battery.* Itasca, IL: Riverside Publishing.

Woodcock, R. W., McGrew, K. S., & Mather, N. (2001a). *Woodcock-Johnson III Tests of Achievement.* Itasca, IL: Riverside Publishing.

Woodcock, R. W., McGrew, K. S., & Mather, N. (2001b). *Woodcock-Johnson III Tests of Cognitive Abilities.* Itasca, IL: Riverside Publishing.

Zurcher, R. (1995). Memory and learning assessment: Missing from the learning disabilities identification process for too long. *LD Forum, 21,* 27–30.

# Annotated Bibliography

Berninger, V. W., & Richards, T. L. (2002). *Brain literacy for educators and psychologists.* San Diego: Academic Press.

> *The primary objective of this book is to link neuroscience research with literacy research. The structure of the brain and how it functions during learning reading, math, and writing is explained in terms that educators can understand. Recommendations for applying this knowledge to specific academic instruction and the educational environment in general are developed in detail.*

Carroll, J. B. (1993). *Human cognitive abilities: A survey of factor-analytic studies.* Cambridge: Cambridge University Press.

> *This meta-analytic study of human cognitive abilities resulted in a hierarchical, trilevel model that supported Cattell-Horn theory and was later used as the basis for CHC theory. All of the broad and narrow abilities are discussed in detail, along with the empirical evidence for each.*

Dawson, P., & Guare, R. (2004). *Executive skills in children and adolescents.* New York: Guilford Press.

> *This practical guide to assessment and intervention is based on Barkley's inhibition model. After a review of assessment methods, the text provides detailed strategies for teaching executive skills.*

Flanagan, D. P., & Harrison, P. L. (Eds.). (2005). *Contemporary intellectual assessment: Theories, tests, and issues* (2nd ed.). New York: Guilford Press.

> *This edited volume includes chapters on all of the major intellectual and cognitive scales, as well as chapters on contemporary intellectual and cognitive theories. Several chapters address interpretative approaches, including a chapter that discusses an information-processing approach.*

Flanagan, D. P., & Kaufman, A. S. (2004). *Essentials of WISC-IV assessment.* Hoboken: Wiley.

> *This book includes the administration, scoring, interpretation, and clinical applications of the WISC-IV. The clinical applications chapter discusses the assessment of gifted, learning disabled, and culturally and linguistically diverse populations. In addition to analyzing the structure of the WISC-IV from a CHC perspective, the book introduces new clinical factors, such as Verbal Fluid Reasoning.*

Flanagan, D. P., & Ortiz, S. (2001). *Essentials of cross-battery assessment.* New York: Wiley.

> *This volume describes the CHC (Cattell-Horn-Carroll)-based cross-battery assessment method, which systematically integrates tests from the major intellectual and cognitive batteries. The text discusses the rationale for and methodology of the cross-battery approach, as well providing practical interpretation worksheets and summary sheets for those who conduct cross-battery assessments. The text also discusses the relative strengths and weaknesses of cognitive test batteries, gives advice on clinical applications, and provides illustrative case reports.*

Gagne, E. D. (1993). *The cognitive psychology of school learning* (2nd ed.). New York: HarperCollins College.

> *This work provides an in-depth analysis of processing and learning from the perspective of the human information-processing model. The suggested teaching strategies for several academic subjects address the learner's information processing limitations.*

Gillon, G. T. (2004). *Phonological awareness*. New York: Guilford Press.

*This work reviews the current knowledge about phonological awareness, along with practical guidance for teaching children the needed skills. The text also includes a discussion of the phonological awareness deficits found in children with dyslexia.*

Hale, J. B., & Fiorello, C. A. (2004). *School neuropsychology: A practitioner's handbook*. New York: Guilford Press.

*Based on a cognitive hypothesis-testing model, this volume brings neuropsychology into the classroom by linking neuropsychological assessment with intervention. After explaining basic brain processes, such as visual and auditory, the text discusses the neuropsychology of reading, math, and written language disorders.*

Kaufman, A. S., Lichtenberger, E. O., Fletcher-Janzen, E., & Kaufman, N. L. (2005). *Essentials of KABC-II assessment*. Hoboken: Wiley.

*This book emphasizes the step-by-step interpretation of the KABC-II from both a CHC and a Luria perspective, as well as the clinical applications of the KABC-II. The text also includes a case illustration of how to integrate the WISC-IV with the KABC-II in a cross-battery fashion.*

Naglieri, J. A. (1999). *Essentials of CAS assessment*. New York: Wiley.

*After a review of the PASS theory, this text provides details on administration, scoring, and interpretation of the CAS. The empirical evidence for the suggested clinical applications and interventions is also reviewed.*

National Reading Panel (2000). *Teaching children to read: An evidence-based assessment of the scientific research literature on reading and its applications for reading instruction*. Washington, DC: National Institute of Child Health and Human Development (NICHD).

*This report assesses the status of research-based knowledge regarding the effectiveness of various approaches to teaching children to read. The report contains sections on phonemic awareness, reading fluency, reading comprehension, and reading instruction. The report also includes recommendations for instructional strategies for each area of reading.*

# Index

# Acknowledgments

I wish to acknowledge Dale Farland from the University of South Dakota for introducing me to information processing and encouraging my dissertation on metacognition. I am grateful to Paula Volpiansky from the Wisconsin Department of Public Instruction for allowing me to write my first chapter on assessment of processing. I would like to thank Don Foy and Heidi Horton for their feedback on manuscript chapters. I am also appreciative of the numerous children and their parents who volunteered their time so that I could learn more about the assessment of processing.

## About the Author

Milton J. Dehn is an Associate Professor in the Department of Psychology at the University of Wisconsin-La Crosse, where he has taught psychoeducational assessment courses for 15 years and formerly directed the School Psychology training program. He is also the program director for Schoolhouse Educational Services, an agency that provides continuing education for mental health professionals, as well as instruction and tutoring for K–12 students with learning problems. Dr. Dehn holds a doctorate in educational psychology from the University of South Dakota.

9269

# DATE DUE

MeLCat  APR 1 3 2009
COMPLETED MAY 1 8 2009